SUCCESS SIMPLIFIED

SIMPLE
SOLUTIONS
MEASURABLE
RESULTS

Published in the United States by
Insight Publishing Company
707 West Main Street, Suite 5
Sevierville, TN 37862
800-987-7771
www.insightpublishing.com

ISBN-978-1-60013-597-2

10 9 8 7 6 5 4 3 2 1

The interviews found in this book are conducted by David Wright, President of ISN Works and Insight Publishing.

Achieving success is serious business, or so it would seem. So many people are striving for this nebulous concept known as "success." I've asked many people what their definition of success is and I've heard different answers from just about all of them. Some people appear successful and on the surface it seems that they should be very happy about what they've accomplished. But often they are not. Their lives have become so complicated that they feel harried and on a treadmill of endless things to do to keep their hard-won success.

Can't success be simple? I wondered if anyone else had ever thought about this, so I searched for speakers and authors who would give me some answers.

In this book, *Success Simplified,* the successful businesspeople I found gave several different answers to my question. The answers were very insightful, in my opinion. I think they will give you a new perspective on success and how to make it simple.

DAVID E. WRIGHT, PRESIDENT
INTERNATIONAL SPEAKERS NETWORK
& INSIGHT PUBLISHING

TABLE OF CONTENTS

CHAPTER ONE

BUILDING LEADERSHIP CAPACITY: INDIVIDUALS, TEAMS, AND ORGANIZATIONS

BY DR. RONALD P. DAVIS

DAVID WRIGHT (WRIGHT)

Today we're talking with Dr. Ronald P. Davis. Dr. Davis is committed to building leadership skills in others for the twenty-first century. He understands this need in order for organizations to be successful as we continue to move deeper into a competitive global society. Focusing on developing leadership qualities in the individual is vital to building high performing teams. In addition to leadership development, Dr. Davis emphasizes that organizations understand how to manage complex change for continuous improvement. Complimenting the change process is the role of data—quality leaders make data driven decisions. Dr. Davis believes, however, that vision-driven decisions are the new paradigm with data gauging the progress! Dr. Davis couches the development of individuals, teams, and organizations in the framework GREAT, an acronym that stands for Goals, Roles, Expectations, Attitudes, and Tools.

Dr. Davis welcome to *Success Simplified.*

RONALD P. DAVIS (DAVIS)

Thank you.

WRIGHT

So what are the key ingredients in a great success story?

DAVIS

As you said in the introduction, GREAT is an acronym I use that stands for Goals, Roles, Expectations, Attitude, and Tools. I believe that when you put those five elements together in a systemic approach for continuous improvement, not only can an individual develop but so can a team or organization. I'll elaborate a little more on each of the categories before discussing them in detail.

I'll start with G, which stands for goals. In my estimation, goals are the vision that a person, team, or organization has for its improvement plan. These goals are the foundation for success. Clear goals provide focus, direction, and inspiration to improve. Unfortunately, if a person or a team or an organization doesn't have clear goals, I think they're like a sailboat out in the middle of the pond that would move in changing directions with the wind. In this analogy, the course toward continuous improvement is uncertain, making it difficult to see positive results.

WRIGHT

So how does understanding a person's R or role in an organization attribute to his or her success?

DAVIS

I think that the element of roles represents the skills an individual brings to a position, allowing him or her to function in various capacities. Ultimately, I want to position people for success by having them perform with skills they've already developed, while at the same time challenging them to increase or develop leadership skills. Through people developing or enhancing communication skills, task management skills, collaboration skills, delegation skills (to name a few examples), I really think that you can set these individuals up for success in the role(s) you are asking them to assume on the team or in the organization. By building competence, one can increase confidence; with confidence comes increased competence.

WRIGHT

Can clear expectations (the E in your acronym) increase a person's performance?

DAVIS

Most certainly! Understanding the expectations being placed on the person allows him or her to make the necessary commitment or investment so that the team or organization will be able to achieve success.

WRIGHT

I know you're a principal and have been for years. In the school system, do you think by and large expectations are laid out for students?

DAVIS

Very clearly, when you think about standards or standards-based education, which is very common in many states today, the standards set the expectations for students—at least the academic expectations. In the classroom, teachers set the performance expectations and the cultural expectations for an organization. With the effective delivery of these performance and cultural expectations, I truly believe that students understand what is required of them when they walk in the schoolhouse door, whether it's in kindergarten or in the eleventh grade.

WRIGHT

There has been more talk about attitude having to do with success than anything, I've heard or read in the last thirty or forty years. Does attitude really shape success?

DAVIS

Attitude is the driver to success. You can have the greatest skill set, you can have goals for yourself, you can know what expectations are placed upon you, but if you don't have the appropriate attitude, you will not find your desired success. So in my estimation, I believe that attitude is the driver.

WRIGHT

In your acronym the T stands for tools. Would you tell our readers what are some of the essential tools a person needs to have to find success?

DAVIS

Certainly. Tools are a person's ability to develop capacity, whether it's leadership capacity, employment capacity, or some other form of capacity.

One of the tools I think successful people have includes relational talents. Often, the information I have shared with individuals is based on how a person interact with others—a person's interpersonal skills. Relational talents are huge, not only with students, staff, and community members (in my case as a high school principal). When you look at what the Fortune 500 companies may be looking for in employability skills, they are looking for that employee who can work effectively as part of a collaborative team, capitalizing on his or her relational talents.

As I continue to think through the tools that are expected of successful people, I think communications skills are essential. I know communication skills have been talked about in a number of venues. To me, the most essential element of the communication process is one that is often overlooked—the skill of listening. I think that when people listen to each other—truly listen to each other—they have the ability to decipher the sometimes hidden, clouded, or unspoken meaning in a message. They have the ability to sort through some of the "noise" that may occur in the communication process and truly get at the heart of the message. So, effective listening for the intended message is probably the most critical component in terms of a communication tool for a successful individual.

Relational talents and communication skills are being more commonly referred to as twenty-first century skills. Given this frame of reference, technological skills, then, would have to play into conversation as well. The person's ability to effectively utilize technology in some aspect, I think, is a precursor for success. Along those same lines, in addition to technology, another essential employability skill is problem-solving. Many organizations look for individuals who have the ability to assess the situation, identify what potential solutions that may exist, and then take the initiative to move through to a solution for a particular problem. I think that's a skill set that is appreciated—a tool that a successful person will have.

Let me give you another example of a tool that is important in order to build capacity for success—the ability for others to praise the work of the people who are performing admirably in the attainment of their goals. These are people who understand their role(s) in an organization, people who clearly understand and meet the expectations placed on them, and people who have the right attitude. But for praise to be meaningful, it needs to be very specific. For example, it must identify the role the person has taken in the success initiative and his or her contribution. I believe that praise also has to be authentic—it has to come from the heart and be sincere. It needs to be timely. You have to capture the moment or the opportunity to use praise in a timely manner.

Then, the final piece of what I'll share with you in terms of tools is just basic information. Information is knowledge, and as mentioned previously in the tool segment in this conversation, I believe tools build capacity or develop capacity. If information is viewed as knowledge, knowledge is the capacity to take action. So, having a knowledge base or the ability to be a lifelong learner and build your knowledge base, gives a person the capacity to take action and bring about organization improvements.

WRIGHT

You have said that focusing on developing the leadership qualities in the individual is vital to building high performing teams. So can the GREAT acronym individual success story be applied to a team's development and performance?

DAVIS

Most certainly. Let me expand upon the G in GREAT—goals. Goals are the vision of the team for improvement. Goals are the foundational building blocks for a team that describe the dynamic purpose(s) for the individual(s) within the team. So, goals set the stage so that everybody can invest in and be excited about the outcomes that are to be attained.

Then I think you divide goals into two components as they relate to a team, performance, and improvement. There should be a performance goal.

Here are some examples: The team wants to perform at a certain level in terms of winning percentage. The team has defined situations or games where it wants to perform exceptionally well and the team wants to execute certain plays or strategies or the team wants to achieve the playoffs/championships. Whatever the case may be, there needs to be an established performance goal toward which the team strives.

Then, there needs to be another component of an improvement goal, and these goals are where the individuals who are members of a team identify how they can improve for the betterment of the team. Individual goals allow for team goals to be achieved. Performance goals inspire individuals to achieve their goals.

Both types of goals are interrelated. It is important to note, though, that the individual is not more important than the team. When an individual is not committed to the team's concepts/goals, the ability for the team to realize its fullest potential is limited.

When a leader thinks about establishing goals for team success, the goals need to be *Specific* so the team understands, specifically, what they're striving for. Goals also need to be *Measurable*. Measurable goals help the team members. Just as vision and using data can gauge progress, measurable goals allow individuals to realize where they are in that journey for improvement, how much further they need to go, or what adjustments need to be made in order to advance their efforts for success.

As a leader, an individual needs to be realistic in goal-setting so the goals are *Attainable*. For example, if the leader inherits a team that is a state champion, it would be realistic to expect much success. If a leader inherits a team that has not won a game in three years, it might not be realistic that they're going to win the state championship in the next year. I give coaches a lot of credit for their optimism and motivation because in this situation they will approach their team as if they will be competing for the state championship. So being *Realistic* in goal-setting, based on the skill set of the players, is important.

Of course, there needs to be a *Time* element involved in this process. A time component allows the team to understand the parameters that are being set for performance and improvement goals. The time aspect should be open ended. Members of a team should not be left out there to guess as to when progress is going to be measured. The time factor establishes a sense of urgency to improve, so I think that's important as well.

The final piece that I'd share with you in terms of goals and the relationship to GREAT is there needs to be, by the leadership, an analysis of team members' behaviors regarding their capacity or ability to achieve the goals. In this analysis, the leader needs to determine what behaviors need to be institutionalized or continued in order for the team to achieve its goals and find success. I also think it's important for the leader to do an analysis to which behaviors need to cease in order for the organization or the team to achieve its goals. Along those same lines of stopping some behaviors, a team may need to start some new behaviors.

Wright

So how does a leader build up a high performing GREAT team?

Davis

Leaders need to make people feel uncomfortable with this notion of status quo. There needs to be a mantra or an attitude of continuous improvement. I think that's where data comes in, as we talked a little bit about how data can help illustrate the need for change. Also, there needs to be a process for the leader to use in order to bring about a high performing or GREAT team, and the process is about managing change.

Take vision, for example. I talked early on about goals being the vision for organizational improvement. I think in the change process of building a high performing team, visions are important. Without vision (as I used in the sailboat analogy), a leader brings about ambiguity or uncertainty within the team. I talked about having an appropriate skill set to be able to implement the goals of the team. I think that without that skill set you're going to create anxiety for people by asking them to take on a specific role for which they don't have the skills to perform in that role. So role development, or skill development, is important.

I talked about a person's investment in relation to expectations. Being on a high performing team is demanding. A person needs to have the investment or commitment to perform at the necessary level and find success on a high performing team. If a person is not invested or committed to the challenge(s) before him or her, I think you will have resistance from or the resentment of others who are invested and trying to develop a high performing team. Of course, the individual needs to have the appropriate attitude, as we talked about earlier with this being the driver to individual development. Also, there needs to be resources that are available for that team to be able to move forward in its development. If you're asking people to perform at a higher level and you're not giving them the appropriate resources, you're creating a system where you're going to have frustration. Then finally, of course, you need to have plan of action that gives you that clear direction to obtain those goals.

Vision, skills, investment, resources, and a plan of action are the needed elements to manage the change process.

Wright

So how does one successfully collaborate in a GREAT organization?

Davis

It is important to realize that collaboration is a process and involves a focus on what is in the best interest of the organization, analysis of data, prioritization of efforts, negotiation, shared decision-making and at times, compromise.

Along the lines of compromise, it is important to recognize and understand that the amount of control or authority a person is willing to relinquish in a situation will be a factor with which to deal. Also, collaboration means empowering others to do their best in their position. So as a leader, a person needs to be comfortable with relinquishing control in a process so as to responsibly empower others to fully utilize their knowledge base and skill set. It's an element of distributive leadership.

As a leader, I often say that if I have five people on my leadership team saying the same things to me, what do I need five people for? There is power in diversity of thought. Granted, the process at drawing a conclusion or making a finding may take a little longer, but the decisional product at the end of the process is so much richer. With better information, and the notion of information being knowledge, the capacity for action is enhanced.

WRIGHT

Would you share with our readers what are successful strategies to build followership in a GREAT organization?

DAVIS

Delegating to a person's strengths as you're forming a team, I think, is the way that you can build a followership. Everybody likes to feel successful in what they're doing, and if you build a team where you are putting people in a position to achieve success, they will follow that leader more quickly.

Another component of building followership is availability by the leader. Leadership means mentoring. To build followership—people who are going to subscribe to your vision and help you to achieve that vision—a leader needs to be available to help mentor them, to help foster them, and to help coach them through this process. If a leader does not have the luxury to match people's skill sets to the tasks at hand, then he or she should be growing the skill set of others through the mentoring process. Understand, too, there needs to be a sense of support when people are struggling because there may be instances when the people who are subscribing to your vision may not have all the resources to bring the vision to fruition, or they may not have the exact skill set as we already mentioned. There may be moments of frustration that occur, and as a result the leader needs to demonstrate empathy and support.

Delegating to a person's strengths, capitalizing on moments of success, being available to others to serve as a mentor, and being empathetic and supportive all result in increased followership.

WRIGHT

What degree does risk-taking play in the GREAT individual or team?

DAVIS

I think risk-taking needs to be calculated. In order for any vision to become a reality, you're talking about changing the status quo in a manner in which the likelihood of success is great. When working to improve conditions, consideration of how the process to bring about change is utilized. A leader does an analysis of the situation (we already talked about data). Options can be identified and considered, given the data or information available, and then moving forward can be predicated on the best case scenario.

The other component relative to risk-taking is the importance of being resolute or steadfast to the vision. Sometimes a leader takes risks that may be unpopular or unfavorable because it is not the most subscribed to philosophy or the most endorsed perspective. So, there may be some instances where you meet resistance. In cases like this, it's important to be resolute or steadfast to that vision, which is where a person's comfort level with risk-taking plays a role.

WRIGHT

What communication strategies do you think are essential to achieve GREATness?

DAVIS

I talked about the importance of listening earlier on. Other components that are often overlooked when considering the communication process are noise and interference. External noise is when you're trying to conduct a conversation in competition with environmental noises. Interference is any personal, mental distractions, from either party in the conversation that may distract attention from the communication process. Clarity of the intended message can be compromised due to these factors, and the individuals involved in the communication process need to understand these component when making an effort to achieve GREATness.

It's important as part of the process, too, to be effective in providing feedback. If you think about communication as a cyclical process, you're in essence sharing a message and then waiting for your recipient to provide you with some feedback that the message was received as intended. This feedback may be verbal or it may be nonverbal, for example, body language. Again, the feedback allows you to determine whether or not your message was received as intended, or whether or not you need to do some clarification and then communicate in a different fashion.

A final piece that is often overlooked, which needs to be considered in order to communicate with GREATness is the notion of emotions and how emotions influence the communication process. Oftentimes emotion contributes positively to the communication process. Emotion is a driver in that it excites people; they're inspired through emotion, which places the needed connotation on the message. In the same respect, a communicator has to be careful that emotion doesn't become a detractor in the communication process. If people are paying more attention to the emotional state of the communicator instead of the message, then I think emotion is a detractor instead of being an enhancer.

Wright

Are we solving problems correctly in our efforts to improve organizations and achieve GREATness?

Davis

Oftentimes, we may be trying to correctly solve problems, but this is where the notion of doing some sort of an analysis to identify what the true cause(s) of the problem are. Without the proper analysis of the problem at hand, a person may not uncover what the underlying issues are that need to be addressed. Again, I believe effective communication, particularly listening, is a critical skill in this process. Listening allows a person to sift through the vast amounts of information surrounding an issue, determine what questions need to be asked to get at the underlying causes, and collect the information that will allow for efficiency and effectiveness when solving a problem.

Once the problem is defined properly, solving it becomes the next task. Reflecting back on the process of managing complex change that I talked about earlier, resources are a factor to solving a problem, and recognizing that resources are often limited, a person wants to be judicious in his or her use.

In addition to managing resources to effectively solve a problem, a person should be strategic in the calculated risks that are employed to address the problem at hand. Being strategic in our approach to achieving a solution will result in investment from the members of the organization to overcome challenges in a productive manner and bring about positive outcomes.

So, it is critical to properly define the problem that an organization is facing so that resources can be effectively allocated to bring about positive change.

Wright

So how does one deal with the challenges and setbacks in the GREAT model?

Davis

Let's refer back to the "A" in GREAT—Attitude. Through a positive mindset, I think the way to do that is to view challenges or setbacks as an opportunity for growth and improvement. I think that dealing with challenges or setbacks goes back to the notion of attitude. I think the people who view challenges or setbacks as opportunities are opportunistic and optimistic. Here's a hint to remain an eternal optimist: You often hear the analogy of the glass being half full or half empty. Quite frankly, I subscribe to the theory that you should get the appropriately sized glass so that it is always full. Taking the notion of an appropriately sized glass, realistic goals are critical when striving to prevent setbacks from occurring. In addition to the attitudes of being opportunistic and optimistic, a person who is motivated and takes initiative to work through challenges will encounter fewer setbacks.

When I talked about the communication process, I talked a little about the role that emotion can play. Along the lines of emotions, people effective in dealing with challenges are also passionate, dedicated, and committed. This fire in the human spirit, so to speak, allows the person to work through the setback when faced with overwhelming circumstances. Integrity, also, is important. There will be times when dealing with challenges that you will not find the success you are hoping for. In the face of adversity, integrity is important because it provides the ability to be resolute or steadfast. It is important to understand that doing the right thing isn't always easy, and when adversity arises, people with integrity will do the right thing. GREAT teams and organizations need leaders with integrity.

I talked about opportunity, attitude being the driver, and being resolute. I think a person's confidence plays a factor in dealing with challenges or setbacks. If you have a skill set and you are able to execute that skill set successfully, which is competence, you are going to find confidence. Realizing that success begets success, competence fosters confidence. Then, the greater your confidence becomes, the more willing are to take risks with your skill set and develop new skills. As you find success with taking risks, confidence continues to grow. This interplay between confidence and competence is a growth process resulting in those who are better equipped to handled challenges and setbacks.

I'd just like to share one or two other ideas about attitude. One of the ideas is the notion of trust. In respect to people you would interact with in an organization or on a team, whenever confronted with setbacks or challenges, the character of the organization or the team could be tested. How the organization as a whole or how a team responds to adversity will attest to the trust they have in one another. Also, in terms of relational talents, empathy is an important topic because understanding what others are going through in an adverse situation and helping them through that process will only strengthen a team. Trust and support one another!

WRIGHT

Well, what a great conversation! The acronym GREAT is not as simple as it sounds. Apparently, you've got something that really might work.

DAVIS

If I may I'll take a minute or two to elaborate on the "R" and "E" of GREAT—roles and expectations.

WRIGHT

Absolutely.

DAVIS

I'll start with "R," roles. Remember, roles are skills you have that allow you to perform in certain situations. It's important to recognize, using this framework, that your role on a team, or potentially in an organization, can be situational dependent.

For example, I'll use baseball as an analogy. A player may be asked to be the first baseman, the starting pitcher, a relief pitcher, or the player may be asked to be a utility player who is on the bench and only comes into the game during critical situations. In this utility player concept, the player's skill set has to be tuned and ready to go when called upon.

Understanding and recognizing what a person's role is on a team or in an organization speaks to that notion of followership. Also, understanding that roles are dynamic is important. Roles can change based on the situation at hand. An individual who recognizes what his or her role will be on a team or in an organization will have expectations that are realistic.

If you don't clearly understand expectations being placed on you, you could easily become frustrated. A clearly defined role, even if it is dynamic in nature, will mitigate frustration. A leader (a coach in this analogy) would not want a person to believe that he or she is going to be the starting second base player when the role is really that of a utility player coming off of the bench. Effectively communicating clear roles in relation to the team's needs is necessary to advance a team's cohesion and success. If the person does not perceive his or her role to be as defined, feedback and data are necessary components to help the individual realize the capacity of his or her current skill set and the steps necessary to improve.

Character traits such as self-improvement, initiative, and leadership require taking on a role that has a level of independence.

To explain the evolution of independence, an analogy that I often use is that of a glider. When a glider leaves the ground, it needs a fully functioning airplane in front of it that will pull it into the air; each plane has a specific role in that process. The lead plane is, in essence, the mentor. At some point, the glider is going to be flying at the same altitude as the fully functioning airplane in front of it. Again, each plane has a specific role in that process. At some point, the glider will be able to break away and chart its own course. It will be independent and be able to make its own journey. So, understanding roles in the journey or in the process speaks to the relationship between the leader and the follower.

Developing your capacity to function independently builds your competence and confidence in your skill set, not only allowing you to chart your own course, but to advance the goals of the team/organization.

The last idea I'd share with you in terms of roles is relative to the building of a team. It's important as a leader to minimize your weaknesses by surrounding yourself with individuals who have your weaknesses as strengths. For example, as a school leader, I do not have the skill set that will enable me to do every specific task expected within the organization. Understanding my role in the organization, the expectations being placed upon me, and surrounding myself with people who can minimize my weaknesses to help our organization meet its goals and grow will contribute to my success as a school leader.

I framed expectations as commitment or investment in the vision. Commitment, of course, suggests a level of time commitment. Often, I hear people talk about time management and their inability to manage their time. Because people today are very busy, they're very committed to a number of organizations or a number of initiatives and managing time is important. In talking to people about the notion of time management, I often introduce the notion of *task* management. In the analogy I share with them, when thinking about the term "management" it denotes some sort of control. I often tell people, jokingly, that you cannot manage or control time; it continues to pass. The real paradigm shift is managing one's tasks in available time which requires the person to do some analysis and some priority setting in order to be able to achieve the goals that the person have set for him/herself. So task management is a practice people should employ to meet the expectations placed upon them.

People need to have a clear understanding of the desired outcomes from the team or organization relative to the expectations that are placed upon them. Referring back to the baseball analogy used earlier, if the desired outcome for a player is a .300 batting average, the player needs to know it. It's unfair to not set clear performance or improvement goals for an individual while expecting him or her to perform at a particular level. A leader will not set others up for failure if the person does not clearly communicate or define expectations.

Clear expectations, then, allow you to attend to the details necessary to achieve the desired outcomes. One of the separating characteristics in people that allows them to achieve GREATness is that they attend to the details. Successful people do not listen to the advice of "don't sweat the small stuff." Successful people sweat the big stuff *and* the small stuff; this is what makes them successful. They attend to details because they want things to be right, they want the expectations that were placed upon them to be met, and they want those desired outcomes to be attained.

The final two ideas to consider relative to expectations are accountability and celebration. Expectations establish a sense of accountability to the vision. They informally hold people accountable to the goals, the successes, and setbacks. Given that a followership will work hard, using the skill set that they have to achieve the vision, celebrating or recognizing the efforts and successes of the followership is an ingredient that cannot be overlooked. Earlier on, we talked about relational talents. Leaders will have strong relations with the followership when they celebrate those who are working alongside them in pursuit of the team or organization's vision(s).

WRIGHT

Well, I really appreciate all this time you've taken with me, Dr. Davis. This has been a great conversation on a very important topic. I just really appreciate your answering all these questions for me.

DAVIS

My pleasure.

WRIGHT

Today we've been talking with Dr. Ronald P. Davis who is committed to building leadership skills in others for the twenty-first century. Dr. Davis believes that vision driven decision-making using data to gauge an organization's progress is the new paradigm rather than quality leaders making decisions strictly on data without considering the vision.

Dr. Davis, thank you so much for being with us today on *Success Simplified*.

DAVIS

Again, my pleasure and thank you!

About the Author

Ronald P. Davis, EdD, is an author and accomplished professional in the field of education, having served as a classroom teacher and Athletic Director. He continues to lead public schools and has been doing so for more than ten years as a school principal. Leadership for the twenty-first century is the theme that Dr. Davis has delivered at national, state, and regional presentations. In addition to sharing his topics of leadership, the change process, process/data analysis, building high performing teams, strategic planning, and communication in presentation forums, he is a university professor striving to prepare future educators and administrators for the challenges that exist as we continue to live in global society in the twenty-first century.

Ronald P. Davis, EdD

Inspiring Leaders, Inc.

812 Bethany Drive

Pittsburgh, PA 15243

412-276-3091

RDavis2061@Aol.com

Chapter Two

Set People-Centered Values

By Dr. Stephen R. Covey

David Wright (Wright)

We're talking today with Dr. Stephen R. Covey, cofounder and vice-chairman of Franklin Covey Company, the largest management company and leadership development organization in the world. Dr. Covey is perhaps best known as author of The 7 Habits of Highly Effective People, which is ranked as a number one best-seller by the New York Times, having sold more than fourteen million copies in thirty-eight languages throughout the world. Dr. Covey is an internationally respected leadership authority, family expert, teacher, and organizational consultant. He has made teaching principle-centered living and principle-centered leadership his life's work. Dr. Covey is the recipient of the Thomas More College Medallion for Continuing Service to Humanity and has been awarded four honorary doctorate degrees. Other awards given Dr. Covey include the Sikh's 1989 International Man of Peace award, the 1994 International Entrepreneur of the Year award, *Inc.* magazine's Services Entrepreneur of the Year award, and in 1996 the National Entrepreneur of the Year Lifetime Achievement award for Entrepreneurial leadership. He has also been recognized as one of *Time* magazine's twenty-five most influential Americans and one of Sales and Marketing Management's top twenty-five power brokers. As the father of nine and grandfather of forty-four, Dr. Covey received the 2003 National Fatherhood Award, which he says is the most meaningful award he has ever received. Dr. Covey earned his undergraduate degree from the University of Utah, his MBA from

Harvard, and completed his doctorate at Brigham Young University. While at Brigham Young, he served as assistant to the President and was also a professor of Business Management and Organizational Behavior.

Dr. Covey, welcome to *Success Simplified.*

DR. STEPHEN R. COVEY (COVEY)

Thank you.

WRIGHT

Dr. Covey, most companies make decisions and filter them down through their organization. You, however, state that no company can succeed until individuals within it succeed. Are the goals of the company the result of the combined goals of the individuals?

COVEY

Absolutely—if people aren't on the same page, they're going to be pulling in different directions. To teach this concept, I frequently ask large audiences to close their eyes and point north, and then to keep pointing and open their eyes. They find themselves pointing all over the place. I say to them, "Tomorrow morning if you want a similar experience, ask the first ten people you meet in your organization what the purpose of your organization is and you'll find it's a very similar experience. They'll point all over the place." When people have a different sense of purpose and values, every decision that is made from then on is governed by those. There's no question that this is one of the fundamental causes of misalignment, low trust, interpersonal conflict, interdepartmental rivalry, people operating on personal agendas, and so forth.

WRIGHT

Is that primarily a result of an inability to communicate from the top?

COVEY

That's one aspect, but I think it's more fundamental. There's an inability to involve people—an unwillingness. Leaders may communicate what their mission and their strategy is, but that doesn't mean there's any emotional connection to it. Mission statements that are rushed and then announced are soon forgotten. They become nothing more than just a bunch of platitudes on the wall that mean essentially nothing and even create a source of cynicism and a sense of hypocrisy inside the culture of an organization.

WRIGHT

How do companies ensure survival and prosperity in these tumultuous times of technological advances, mergers, downsizing, and change?

COVEY

I think that it takes a lot of high trust in a culture that has something that doesn't change—principles—at its core. There are principles that people agree upon that are valued. It gives a sense of stability. Then you have the power to adapt and be flexible when you experience these kinds of disruptive new economic models or technologies that come in and sideswipe you. You don't know how to handle them unless you have something you can depend upon.

If people have not agreed to a common set of principles that guide them and a common purpose, then they get their security from the outside. They tend to freeze the structure, systems, and processes inside and they cease becoming adaptable. They don't change with the changing realities of the new marketplace out there; gradually they become obsolete.

WRIGHT

I was interested in one portion of your book, *The 7 Habits of Highly Effective People,* where you talk about behaviors. How does an individual go about the process of replacing ineffective behaviors with effective ones?

COVEY

I think that for most people it usually requires a crisis that humbles them to become aware of their ineffective behaviors. If there's not a crisis, the tendency is to perpetuate those behaviors and not change.

You don't have to wait until the marketplace creates the crisis for you. Have everyone accountable on a 360 degree basis to everyone else they interact with—with feedback either formal or informal—where they are getting data as to what's happening. They will then start to realize that the consequences of their ineffective behavior require them to be humble enough to look at that behavior and to adopt new, more effective ways of doing things.

Sometimes people can be stirred up to this if you just appeal to their conscience—to their inward sense of what is right and wrong. A lot of people sometimes know inwardly that they're doing wrong, but the culture doesn't necessarily discourage them from continuing. They either need feedback from people or they need feedback from the marketplace or they need feedback from their conscience. Then they can begin to develop a step-by-step process of replacing old habits with new, better habits.

Wright

It's almost like saying, "Let's make all the mistakes in the laboratory before we put this thing in the air."

Covey

Right. And I also think what is necessary is a paradigm shift, which is analogous to having a correct map, like the map of a city or of a country. If people have an inaccurate paradigm of life, of other people, and of themselves, it really doesn't make much difference what their behavior or habits or attitudes are. What they need is a correct paradigm—a correct map—that describes what's going on.

For instance, in the Middle Ages they used to heal people through bloodletting. It wasn't until Samuel Weiss and Pasteur and other empirical scientists discovered the germ theory that they realized for the first time they weren't dealing with the real issue. They realized why women preferred to use midwives who washed rather than doctors who didn't wash. They gradually got a new paradigm.

Once you have a new paradigm, then your behavior and your attitude flows directly from it. If you have a bad paradigm or a bad map, there's no way, no matter what your behavior or your habits or your attitudes are—how positive they are—you'll never be able to find the location you're looking for. This is why I believe that to change paradigms is far more fundamental than to work on attitude and behavior.

WRIGHT

One of your seven habits of highly effective people is to "begin with the end in mind." If circumstances change and hardships or miscalculation occur, how does one view the end with clarity?

COVEY

Many people think that to begin with the end in mind means you have some fixed definition of a goal that's accomplished and if changes come about you're not going to adapt to them. Instead, the "end in mind" you begin with is that you are going to create a flexible culture of high trust so that no matter what comes along you are going to do whatever it takes to accommodate that new change or that new reality and maintain a culture of high performance and high trust. You're talking more in terms of values and overall purposes that don't change, rather than specific strategies or programs that will have to change to accommodate the changing realities in the marketplace.

WRIGHT

In this time of mistrust between people, corporations, and nations, for that matter, how do we create high levels of trust?

COVEY

That's a great question and it's complicated because there are so many elements that go into the creating of a culture of trust. Obviously, the most fundamental one is just to have trustworthy people. But that is not sufficient because what if the organization itself is misaligned? For instance, what if you say you value cooperation but you really reward people for internal competition? Then you have a systemic or a structure problem that creates low trust inside the culture, even though the people themselves are trustworthy.

This is one of the insights of Edward Deming and the work he did. That's why he said that most problems are not personal—they're systemic. That's why you have to work on structure, systems, and processes to make sure that they institutionalize principle-centered values. Otherwise, you could have good people with bad systems and you'll get bad results.

When it comes to developing interpersonal trust between people, it is made up of many, many elements such as taking the time to listen to other people, to understand them, and to see what is important to them. What we think is important to another may only be important to us, not to another. It takes empathy. You have to make and keep promises to them. You have to treat people with kindness and courtesy. You have to be completely .honest and open. You have to live up to your commitments. You can't betray people behind their back. You can't badmouth them behind their back and sweet-talk them to their face. That will send out vibes of hypocrisy and it will be detected.

You have to learn to apologize when you make mistakes, to admit mistakes, and to also get feedback going in every direction as much as possible. It doesn't necessarily require formal forums—it requires trust between people who will be open with each other and give each other feedback.

Wright

My mother told me to do a lot of what you're saying now, but it seems that when I got in business I simply forgot.

Covey

Sometimes we forget, but sometimes culture doesn't nurture it. That's why I say unless you work with the institutionalizing—that means formalizing into structure, systems, and processes the values—you will not have a nurturing culture. You have to constantly work on that.

This is one of the big mistakes organizations make. They think trust is simply a function of being honest. That's only one small aspect. It's an important aspect, obviously, but there are so many other elements that go into the creation of a high trust culture.

Wright

"Seek first to understand then to be understood" is another of your seven habits. Do you find that people try to communicate without really understanding what other people want?

COVEY

Absolutely. The tendency is to project out of our own autobiography—our own life, our own value system—onto other people, thinking we know what they want. So we don't really listen to them. We pretend to listen, but we really don't listen from within *their* frame of reference. We listen from within our own frame of reference and we're really preparing our reply rather than seeking to understand. This is a very common thing. In fact, very few people have had any training in seriously listening. They're trained in how to read, write, and speak, but not to listen.

Reading, writing, speaking, and listening are the four modes of communication and they represent about two-thirds to three-fourths of our waking hours. About half of that time is spent listening, but it's the one skill people have not been trained in. People have had all this training in the other forms of communication. In a large audience of 1,000 people, you wouldn't have more than twenty people who have had more than two weeks of training in listening. Listening is more than a skill or a technique so that you're listening within another frame of reference. It takes tremendous courage to listen because you're at risk when you listen. You don't know what's going to happen; you're vulnerable.

WRIGHT

Sales gurus always tell me that the number one skill in selling is listening.

COVEY

Yes—listening from within the customer's frame of reference. That is so true. You can see that it takes some security to do that because you don't know what's going to happen.

WRIGHT

With this book, we're trying to encourage people to be better, to live better, and be more fulfilled by listening to the examples of our guest authors. Is there anything or anyone in your life that has made a difference for you and helped you to become a better person?

Covey

I think the most influential people in my life have been my parents. I think that what they modeled was not to make comparisons and harbor jealousy or to seek recognition. They were humble people.

I remember one time when my mother and I were going up in an elevator and the most prominent person in the state was also in the elevator. She knew him, but she spent her time talking to the elevator operator. I was just a little kid and I was so awed by the famous person. I said to her, "Why didn't you talk to the important person?" She said, "I was. I had never met him."

My parents were really humble, modest people who were focused on service and other people rather than on themselves. I think they were very inspiring models to me.

Wright

In almost every research paper I've ever read, those who write about people who have influenced their lives, among the top five people include three teachers. My seventh grade English teacher was the greatest teacher I ever had and she influenced me a great deal.

Covey

Would it be correct to say that she saw in you probably some qualities of greatness you didn't even see in yourself?

Wright

Absolutely.

Covey

That's been my general experience—the key aspect of a mentor or a teacher is someone who sees in you potential that you don't even see in yourself. Those teachers/mentors treat you accordingly and eventually you come to see it in yourself. That's my definition of leadership or influence—communicating people's worth and potential so clearly that they are inspired to see it in themselves.

WRIGHT

Most of my teachers treated me as a student, but she treated me with much more respect than that. As a matter of fact, she called me Mr. Wright. I was in the seventh grade at the time and I'd never been addressed by anything but a nickname. I stood a little taller; she just made a tremendous difference.

Do you think there are other characteristics that mentors seem to have in common?

COVEY

I think they are, first of all, good examples in their own personal lives. Their personal lives and their family lives are not all messed up—they come from a base of good character. They are also usually very confident and they take the time to do what your teacher did to you—to treat you with uncommon respect and courtesy.

They also, I think, explicitly teach principles rather than practices so that rules don't take the place of human judgment. You gradually come to have faith in your own judgment in making decisions because of the affirmation of such a mentor. Good mentors care about you—you can feel the sincerity of their caring. It's like the expression, "I don't care how much you know until I know how much you care."

WRIGHT

Most people are fascinated with television shows about being a survivor. What has been the greatest comeback that you've made from adversity in your career or your life?

COVEY

When I was in grade school, I experienced a disease in my legs. It caused me to use crutches for a while. I tried to get off them fast and get back. The disease wasn't corrected yet so I went back on crutches for another year. The disease went to the other leg and I went on for another year. It essentially took me out of my favorite thing—athletics—and it took me more into being a student. So that was a life-defining experience, which at the time seemed very negative, but has proven to be the basis on which I've focused my life—being more of a learner.

WRIGHT

What you teach that's different from anybody I've read or listened to is principle-based learning.

COVEY

The concept is embodied in the Far East expression, "Give a man a fish, you feed him for the day; teach him how to fish, you feed him for a lifetime." When you teach principles that are universal and timeless, they don't belong to just any one person's religion or to a particular culture or geography. They seem to be timeless and universal like the ones we've been talking about here: trustworthiness, honesty, caring, service, growth, and development. These are universal principles. If you focus on these things, then little by little people become independent of you, and then they start to believe in themselves and their own judgment becomes better. You don't need as many rules. You don't need as much bureaucracy and as many controls, and you can empower people.

The problem in most business operations today—and not just business but outside of the business world—is that they're using the industrial model in an information age. Arnold Toynbee, the great historian, said, "You can pretty well summarize all of history in four words: nothing fails like success." The industrial model was based on the asset of the machine. The information model is based on the asset of the person—the knowledge worker. It's an altogether different model.

The machine model was the main asset of the twentieth century. It enabled productivity to increase fifty times. The new asset is intellectual and social capital—the qualities of people and the quality of the relationship they have with each other. As Toynbee said, "Nothing fails like success." The industrial model does not work in an information age. It requires a focus on the new wealth, not capital and material things.

A good illustration that demonstrates how much we were into the industrial model, and still are, is to notice where people are on the balance sheet. They're not found there. Machines are found there. Machines become investments. People are on the profit and loss statement and people are expenses. Think of that—if that isn't bloodletting.

WRIGHT

It sure is.

When you consider the choices you've made down through the years, has faith played an important role in your life?

COVEY

It has played an extremely important role. I believe deeply that we should put principles at the center of our lives, but I believe that God is the source of those principles. I did not invent them. I get credit sometimes for some of the Seven Habits material and some of the other things I've done, but it's really all based on principles that have been given by God to all of His children from the beginning of time. You'll find that you can teach these same principles from the sacred texts and the wisdom literature of almost any tradition. I think the ultimate source of that is God and that is one thing you can absolutely depend upon—"in God we trust."

WRIGHT

If you could have a platform and tell our audience something you feel would help them or encourage them, what would you say?

COVEY

I think I would say to put God at the center of your life and then prioritize your family. No one on their deathbed ever wished they had spent more time at the office.

WRIGHT

That's right. We have come down to the end of our program and I know you're a busy person. I could talk with you all day, Dr. Covey.

COVEY

It's good to talk with you as well and to be a part of this program. It looks like an excellent one that you've got going on here.

WRIGHT

Thank you.

We have been talking today with Dr. Stephen R. Covey, cofounder and vice chairman of Franklin Covey Company. He's also the author of *The 7 Habits of Highly Effective People,* which has been ranked as a number one bestseller by the *New York Times*, selling more than fourteen million copies in thirty-eight languages.

Dr. Covey, thank you so much for being with us today.

Covey

Thank you for the honor of participating.

About the Author

Dr. Stephen R. Covey was recognized in 1996 as one of *Time* magazine's twenty-five most influential Americans and one of *Sales and Marketing Management* magazine's top twenty-five power brokers. Dr. Covey is the author of several acclaimed books, including the international bestseller, *The 7 Habits of Highly Effective People*, named the number one Most Influential Business Book of the Twentieth Century, and other bestsellers that include *First Things First*, *Principle-Centered Leadership,* (with sales exceeding one million) and *The 7 Habits of Highly Effective Families.*

Dr. Covey's book, *The 8th Habit: From Effectiveness to Greatness*, which was released in November 2004, rose to the top of several bestseller lists, including *New York Times, Wall Street Journal, USA Today, Money, Business Week,* Amazon.com, and Barnes & Noble.

Dr. Covey earned his undergraduate degree from the University of Utah, his MBA from Harvard, and completed his doctorate at Brigham Young University. While at Brigham Young University, he served as assistant to the President and was also a professor of Business Management and Organizational Behavior. He received the National Fatherhood Award in 2003, which, as the father of nine and grandfather of forty-four, he says is the most meaningful award he has ever received.

Dr. Covey currently serves on the board of directors for the Points of Light Foundation. Based in Washington, D.C., the Foundation, through its partnership with the Volunteer Center National Network, engages and mobilizes millions of volunteers from all walks of life—businesses, nonprofits, faith-based organizations, low-income communities, families, youth, and older adults—to help solve serious social problems in thousands of communities.

Dr. Stephen R. Covey

www.stephencovey.com

CHAPTER THREE

EVERYBODY NEEDS A COACH IN LIFE

BY MICHEAL BURT

DAVID WRIGHT (WRIGHT)

Today we're talking with Micheal Burt. Coach Micheal Burt speaks, trains, coaches, and leads some of the top performing organizations in the Southeast including Ole South Properties, the number one home builder in Tennessee, the John Jones Real Estate Team, Kendra Cooke and Associates, Reeves Sain, State Farm, and First Bank. This former championship women's basketball coach partners with companies to drive initiatives with a systems approach, high intensity energy, accountability, score boards, and a new mindset. Known as having the ability to take the best and make them better, Coach Burt brings a message that has resonated with more than 120,000 people all across the country around four core values: voice, leadership, execution, and culture.

Featured as a leadership expert every morning on Super Talk 99.7 WTN, Nashville's largest talk radio station, Micheal is also the host of *The Coach Micheal Burt Radio Show* with Dr. Colby Jubenville, around the theme of Change your Life Radio on WLAC. Micheal has appeared on numerous television and radio shows and is the author of four books; the most popular being *This Ain't No Practice Life: Seven Decisions to Play at a Different Level in Life*. Look for his forthcoming book, *Zebras and Cheetahs: There is a Different, Faster Leader in You.* For all things Micheal Burt, visit him on the Web at www.coachburt.com.

Micheal welcome to *Success Simplified.*

MICHEAL BURT (BURT)

Thank you, thanks for having me. I'm delighted to be included in this book.

WRIGHT

You spent a decade of your life as a top high school women's basketball coach in the Southeastern United States, what were the most important lessons you learned about building teams that win?

BURT

One of the most important lessons that I learned is that everybody needs a coach in life. Understanding "potential" as kinetic energy that is stored until utilized allows for a great coach to take raw natural ability and harness it so that team members can realize their potential. This idea of embryonic growth—realizing that people can be better today than they were yesterday and better tomorrow than today—is what I focused on throughout each season. I learned that a great coach could take raw talent and materialize or manifest that potential. Each one of my teams hit ceilings of success, and with the help of others broke through those ceilings by focusing on their own special skill sets that they currently did not possess.

WRIGHT

When you wrote your first book and corporate America began to call upon you to motivate and inspire their employees, why did you think they were ready to listen?

BURT

I wrote my first book when I was twenty-five. This is a simple book, titled *Changing Lives through Coaching*. It captured the imagination of corporate America just as leaders were beginning to understand the value of personal and professional coaches in the workplace. It began with the idea that a manager, a supervisor, or a boss is actually a person who should be viewed as a coach who affirms and validates the worth and potential of people and helps them move from point A to point B, adding value to their life.

In the twenty-first century, management began moving away from command and control structures to a mindset that is less strict and controlled and focused on the concept of releasing human talent and potential. At that time when I wrote that book, many large companies approached me saying "Coach, will you speak to our group and motivate our people?" I believe the word "motivate" means to move and inspire people on certain key principles.

At that time, it was strictly about motivation for me and trying to maximize the potential of every person just as I was attempting to do with the very teams I was coaching in sports. This message has further been refined, focusing on systems development, driving initiatives, and building cultures that give birth to the potential of people. The methodology I used to build a championship culture in sports is obviously relevant to what was needed in corporate America, specifically regarding outcomes like focus, execution, energy, and accountability.

Wright

Your four core values are voice, leadership, execution, and culture. Why are core values so important to you and how do they help tell your story?

Burt

I look at core values a little bit differently than most people. I think there are certain values that people typically try to practice—trust, honesty, and integrity. I look at core values as the framework that gives meaning and purpose to answer why people do what they do.

I started to cultivate my four core values of voice focusing on how to help people to find their voice and connect to a unique ability that they have, what some people refer to as their calling in life. I saw this as a source of much of the frustration in corporate America. When people are not doing what they were supposed to be doing with their life, their time and talents are being drastically wasted. This necessitates external motivation—hovering over, checking up on, psyching up. I began to see this once I found my unique calling in life, which was coaching; my life's work was to unlock the potential in others. Until I found my unique calling, I could not help others find theirs.

I start with voice with people I work with to help them understand that the average person spends thirty-five to fifty years of his or her life working and the need to move away from an occupational mindset to a vocational mindset. It is important to get people to acknowledge their voice or calling in life and that they're contributing their talents and passions with real needs in the world that only they can fulfill.

Once people get to a level of understanding their voice and they are on the right team and in the right positions, the focus is shifted to leadership. The central question around leadership is how do you define it in a way that affirms and validates it in others? Asking how to become a coach who can see the good in people versus the bad and build people up versus tear people down is important. What is your true definition of leadership and are you executing that definition of leadership that you espouse? In many situations, there is a disconnect between how we want to lead versus how we actually lead based on all the stimuli we get daily. In some instances, we wouldn't be excited about working for ourselves; when this is the case, it's time to address your leadership philosophy in a new way.

Once there is an understanding of the different roles of leadership, different types of leadership, and different models of leadership, then we shift the focus to execution. This is where there is a real gap in corporate America. It's the gap between thinking and doing; it's between what we know we should be doing and what we actually do every day.

This is often where I focus on the sales structures of the company and how to build systems that can be automated and monetized. The question becomes, "How can we put people in a system that closes the gap between thinking and doing that makes it easy and automatic to do every day?" Sales is about systems of prospecting, systems of touches, and systems to drive clients to be promoters for life. I build these systems for companies in such a way that the only way to fail is by not executing the system.

Understanding execution and the role it plays within each of our lives allows us to move into understanding culture. I define "culture" as how we do business when nobody has told us what to do. John Kotter said that "culture will eat strategy any day of the week," and I believe that is true. I focus on the seven components of a winning culture—a culture that is high energy, positive, uplifting, open, and receptive. I avoid a cancerous culture that is being restricted, filled with the emotional cancer of scarcity, complaining, criticism, and those type actions that tear people and teams apart. With my model, I take people through that cycle around those four core values: voice, leadership, execution, and culture. I discuss each of these seven components of a winning culture in my fourth book, *From Here to Anywhere: Unique Habits of Successful Teams*.

Wright

Specific outcomes of your brand include speaking, training, coaching, and leading. How are each of these outcomes different and how do the outcomes connect to your core values?

Burt

There are inputs, throughputs, and outputs to every model and mine is no different. Around the four core values, or four core drivers, we manifest four different ways that I help companies achieve the level of success they want to achieve. It began by just speaking on a regular basis to these companies on the four core values: voice, leadership, execution, and culture.

I have found that when I speak, people will approach me and ask if I would come back and train their people on a consistent basis. Once I start training their people, they start to see measurable results in productivity and sales numbers and an increase in morale and culture. They ask if I can stay and coach their people on a consistent basis or work with certain departments and coach those people. I call this "Coaching up corporate America." I define training as engaging people in a set of consistent behaviors with structured support so that they can do something tomorrow they cannot do today.

Companies now ask me to stay and drive a major initiative and help connect the initiative with leadership. Some of the companies will simply say, "Will you help us lead this company?" So I go in and serve in a capacity similar to a chief leadership officer. I take the initiative and drive whatever number of people they want to drive toward that initiative. Whether it is the number of accounts in banking, the number of homes sold in real estate development, the number of transactions with individual and groups of Real Estate agents, or the number of new clients with new customer acquisition strategies, I create the plan and execute the plan. That's where my coaching background and a decade of coaching really gives me a unique advantage with focus, intensity, and urgency to take a dominant aspiration through to its logical conclusion.

I have found that these attributes, along with strong, critical thinking skills, play a major role in moving groups of people toward a dominant focus. With this progress and continuing to try to be one of the top motivators in this country I have come to the conclusion that far too few leaders create a constancy of purpose toward a destination and discuss that vision daily and weekly with their people. This taps into the spirit of legacy inside people; more than anything, people want to be counted. They want to be known for the influence they have.

Wright

You have driven initiatives in a variety of disciplines including most recently Real Estate, banking, and financial services. So what is your core methodology and how have you been able to create results that some thought were impossible?

Burt

Manifesting anything in life begins with the basic belief that it can be done and with an abundant mindset that we can create anything we want to create. So the first place I start with the companies is to recharge the base. I normally do this through a companywide motivational rally that speaks to the four core values of voice, leadership, execution, and culture. I then create a dominant focus, or a dominant aspiration.

I very seldom use the word "goals" because I think it's an overused, underdone word in America. People set goals and they don't reach them so they lower them, and they continue along until eventually the goals they set create no real value. So I start with a dominant aspiration. This dominant focus keeps you up at night, wakes you up in the morning, and drives your energy toward a singleness of purpose.

From the dominant aspiration we create a theme that has an emotional pull; it could be reflect, refine, remarkable. It could be a concept I created called *Rock and Roll Management* where we incentivize people in the company to become "rock stars" of the industry. We treat them like rock stars and use terminology around the universal touch point of music. The concept is to create an emotional pull that ties into the hearts and minds of the people. It creates a common language that everyone is constantly talking about.

Once we have that dominant focus, we create scoreboards that measure the daily activity toward the dominant focus of every person in the organization. Creating a laser-like focus around where we want to go and how we're going to get there is key to the success of any initiative. Then we create a system around what I call "high value activities," or what Mark LeBlanc taught me about high value activities. You place your time and energy that will yield the most return on investment of that time and energy. We measure those activities each week and make a really big deal out of the scoreboard. We add heavy coaching to the equation for everybody focused on heavy training, heavy leadership, and we look at incentives based on autonomy, progress, purpose, and mastery of what they are trying to do.

Inevitably, as we go through this cycle, there is a need to implant "thunderbolts"—jolts of energy. These could be in the form of a quarterly motivational rally, totally unexpected, to keep everyone from becoming complacent.

Thunderbolts have helped us increase sales as much as 43 percent in one year with the First Bank initiative. In a bad economy, those are tremendous numbers that could result in millions of dollars of new revenue just through a systematic approach with a coach leading the way with a new methodology, new focus, and new energy.

Wright

Motivation continues to be a critical factor facing organizations. How do you use your high value activity concept to build high performance cultures that consistently win?

Burt

The high value activity system was something that was taught to me many years ago by a business coach I had, Mark LeBlanc. Mark taught me that every day we make a bet with our time and our energy and we always want a return on investment on that time and energy toward where we want to ultimately be. The question then becomes, "What if every day that you go to work you either work in your business or on your business, you're either getting new business or you're tending to your current business and improving your business?" From that you create certain activities that are the highest value of your time, not the lowest value of your time.

One of the things I do for these companies is create a bucket of High Value Activities (HVAs) so that they have the autonomy to choose but they have to do a certain number per day. For example, if they did three high value activities per day, every day to get new business, that would be three a day, five days a week, which would be fifteen a week, and sixty a month. Every person in every organization is asked to do just three things a day to bring new customers to the table. This is part of their customer acquisition strategy. Then they would have no problem, for the most part, achieving their financial numbers.

This system creates a laser-like focus. If you're not getting new customers, you need to either be tending to your current customers so they become a referral base, which is a good growth concept, or you're getting better yourself in activities such as coaching, learning, studying, reading, and ongoing training. These are activities that work on your business. Every day I put people on that system, we track and measure and we ensure that the entire culture is involved in these activities every single day. The number one rule of any business is to get and keep customers. As Covey says, "The main thing is to keep the main thing the main thing."

WRIGHT

So throughout the past two years, many of the top companies in the state of Tennessee have turned to you because they needed to achieve a specific outcome. You call this, *"coaching them up."* What is your methodology and can it work for all companies?

BURT

First of all, I do believe it can work for all companies. We've done this in Real Estate, banking, pharmaceuticals, financial services, and retail. It really doesn't matter what the industry is, it's a basic concept of specific methodology I have found that works consistently. Then we can take current people, assuming they're the right people, and we can give them additional training, coaching, and leadership and they can perform better than they did before I got there.

The problem as I see it in most corporate America situations is only about 10 to 15 percent of companies invest in their people. They want them to get better but they want them to do it on their dime and during their own time. They expect their people to get better after work. If you make an assumption that your people will get better after work, it's the wrong assumption. In most cases, you can make the assumption that they will not get better because they don't spend their time and energy reading, studying, learning how to be a better salesperson or how to be a better leader. Some will but most won't. You simply have to build it into the very fabric of the organization and give your people a reach chance to grow all parts of their nature.

The really great companies build this into the fabric—into the DNA—of the company where they get ongoing training, development, leadership, new methodologies, and consistency of purpose with a coach who holds them accountable and pushes them forward. Whatever resistance you see on the front end, you don't on the back end because the cultures are better, the working environments are better, the results are better, and everybody is happier. So the key component of this is companies have got to make a gut level decision. They don't need new people necessarily, they just need to make the ones they have better and that only happens through some ongoing coaching or leadership. Great coaches pull the potential out of their people.

Wright

Each of your books tie into different themes about personal growth, leadership, and building high performance teams. Is that intentional and why?

Burt

I believe that the first place to start with any company is to be intentional; I think that leadership is intentional. I think that when you start with trying to build a great team—a remarkable team, a world-class team—you first start by becoming highly effective at the personal level, which is where you begin. You can't give great customer service with a disengaged person in his or her own life. Whatever problems people bring to the table or issues or challenges, they'll bring to work with them. I always start with personal growth and development. This is where voice or calling comes into play. This is marrying their special gifts with a need in the company.

Then we move through a natural cycle of leadership and how you define it, and how you implement it, and how you teach it. What I've seen in most companies is there is not real leadership but rather a lot of commanding and control. There is a lot of management, but there is very little real leadership, which is the unlocking of human potential not straightjacketing human potential.

This concept that people are motivated today by autonomy and progress is vital. There are no meetings where leaders are actually transferring their knowledge, skills, desires, and beliefs into their people, there are just meetings about what we need to do today. There is really no coaching or leadership going on, so therefore there is a constant gap between the top leaders and the entire team. The person at the top is there because he or she did have the knowledge, skill, desire, and belief to get there but how do you grow a world-class team if you don't transfer that knowledge to your people? There is no mechanism for that, there is no accountability—it's just business as usual and people become automated, scripted, impersonal, and it becomes transactional in nature, which usually doesn't lead to a remarkable business, but rather a stagnant one.

As it relates to high performance teams, it's so much easier to build a bad team than it is a good team. It's like when you look at sports, there are only a few champions—the people who consistently win. There are so many bad teams out there that have these common dysfunctions that come into the equation. They are not managed properly because of uneven levels of commitment because their coach or leader is not harnessing the energy of that team. They're going nowhere and everybody knows it; this feeds directly into the culture. The culture is the big piece of this puzzle because if the culture doesn't support the growth, the leadership, the new methodologies, then people will be stuck in hold ways of thinking and they'll either leave or become part of the very fabric of what they do not want to become.

WRIGHT

Does your coaching background give your clients a competitive advantage of choosing you over other corporate coaches?

BURT

I think one of the common themes in business today is for people who work with corporate clients to call themselves coaches and there is nothing wrong with this. I spent a decade of my life actually building a championship culture with the high intensity of eighty-hour work weeks, the driving of players who were on my team whom I didn't pick and whom I had to get the most out of. This helped me to develop a very special acumen and skill set that I utilize today. I think there's a difference between this skill set and somebody who wakes up one day and says he or she has some business knowledge so therefore he or she is a business coach. Real coaches understand the dynamics of building world-class teams. There is a lot to that when people start looking at what separates them from other people.

One of the things that is a real niche for me is this intensity, focus, and systems thinking I learned directly from coaching. I see how parts affect the whole and how can I move a group of people from here to there or from here to anywhere they would like to go, for that matter. By marrying my focus from coaching with my business acumen, I create a solid differential advantage in the marketplace.

WRIGHT

Coach, how do you define training and why is it so important that individuals and organizations engage in systematic behaviors to improve?

BURT

One of the things I see that is a top motivator for people is progress toward a destination—it's not just work for work's sake. I define training as engaging in consistent and systematic behaviors that allow you to do something tomorrow that you simply cannot do today. If you think about a coach in any area of your life, he or she engages you in a set of new behaviors. Over a period of time, those behaviors become habits; you then start doing things in the future that you couldn't do in the past. This is why people hire trainers and it's why some of the weight loss programs are highly effective—there is accountability and they have someone pushing them.

Training is so important that it is delivered in a systematic way by a skilled professional. For years, companies and organizations had very weak strategies to grow their people, including sending all of their people to a one-day motivational rally. There is no way that motivation given in one day will stay in their company or in their life if it's not consistent. What's being imbedded into the mind, heart, and spirit every day is what becomes consistent in your life. I try to encourage companies to realize that they need someone who will tend the growth and development of every person in the company based on the premise that if you want new results tomorrow, you've got to have new behavior today. That's what training and coaches can do for people as they begin to see the big picture, how can they move people from point to point, and tap into kinetic energy. If you truly want to play "at a different level in life," then you need someone who can challenge you and coach you to that level.

Wright

The book that really introduced you to the world and illustrated that you were a seasoned leadership and personal development coach was *This Ain't No Practice Life; How to Live and Work with Purpose, Passion, and Intention Daily*. What did you say in that book that connected with so many people?

Burt

The greatest leadership influence in my life has been Dr. Stephen Covey. I read *The 7 Habits of Highly Effective People* in 1994 at the suggestion of another coach. I was only eighteen at the time. I began to understand that we can create certain mental models and frameworks that we can teach our organization—our people—that will give them a framework to operate in a common language. I also began to understand that we can teach people how to be highly effective. I began to think at that time that when I became a head coach I would teach my organization those principles and I began to teach that to all of my players. Every single year I would teach the principles of *Good to Great*,

The Five Dysfunctions of Teams, and all of the principles people really don't understand. From that I think the natural process of a leader is to look out at people they admire. For many years that was Dr. Covey for me.

Then there came a point when I wanted to be introspective. I asked myself, "What is Micheal Burt really about? What do I believe in? What are my core values?" When I began to figure out what I wanted to say to the world I said it in that third book, *This Ain't No Practice Life: 7 Core Decisions that a Person Can Make, that manifests itself in seven seasons in your life*.

The first season is a season of awakening. It's that sudden intuitive breakthrough that usually happens as a result of a breakdown or pain or potential that tells you, "This is who I used to be, and this is how I am going to be." It's a line of demarcation in the sand, the new future. It's the ability to confront the facts about your life; you wake up in that period.

Then it moves into a dreaming period—a season of imagining a future that has not yet manifested, believing that you can manifest that future and specifically designing that future. It's the ability to break with the past and not let your past hold your future hostage—the ability to believe that you can manifest what you want to in your life.

That leads to a cleansing period—the third season. This is the season when you rid yourself of the emotional cancers that are prohibiting your future success and start to "play up" with who you associate with. You begin to create an intentional congruence between who you said you were versus who you actually are. You begin to walk your talk and live based on your conscious versus your ego.

Then you move into a period of learning, of making a decision of constant ongoing growth to create a curiosity quotient where you continually learn from other people and you see every day as a learning opportunity. You have made a decision to become a lifelong learner, which puts you into a season of creation. This is what I call "pay up"—the law of the harvest—where you add value to people's life versus subtract from it.

I have always liked what Dr. Charles Stanley said, "We always reap what we sow, more than we sowed it, for longer than it was sown." The real principle of creation here in life is that we can add value to people's lives, sometimes through how we handle adversity and struggle. If there is one constant thing in our lives it's opportunity and struggle. Sometimes it seems there is more opportunity and less struggle, sometimes more struggle and less opportunity, but those are two consistent variables. The question is how do you handle those variables?

The sixth season of life is a leading season—a season of building people to make a decision to see abundance versus scarcity. With this mindset, I believe in the good of people versus the bad. I don't sit around and confess the weaknesses or sins of everybody else; every day I make a decision to believe in a new way. I want to be a new era leader who believes in tapping into every part of a person's nature.

This leads to the seventh season. The seventh season is a season of responding—a season between stimulus and response, closing the gap and actually creating the life that you want by not making a "grand canyon" of excuses that many people make. It is a season of response in life so that when life is over we don't have more regret about what we could have done, should have done. We will have a feeling of accomplishment about what we actually did and we will realize that we have so much capacity and so much more ability to do the things that we want to do with our life.

Those are the seven seasons I wrote about in the book. I'm fortunate that this book has been wildly popular with the people I've spoken to across the country and has been a very universal touch point.

Wright

So what's the next step for you and your company as you continue to evolve? What is CoachBurt.com and where do you see training and development going in the future?

Burt

The natural evolution of my company revolves around building a global training and development company that touches people around the world. My personal vision is to become the next Covey, the next Maxwell, the next big thought leader in this country with a mindset scripted in coaching and the principle that everybody needs a coach in life. That's really where we're going with CoachBurt.com. It's my signature brand series that has various divisions from training, speaking, coaching, and leading. We're in the process now of growing a bigger team and more people who are excited about these opportunities.

I see training and development going to new levels in the future. People are coming to the realization that we can't always go out and get more people—we just need to make the ones we've got better. The only way to make those people better is engage them in a consistent structure and in systematic ways today so that they can do something tomorrow they can't do today. Training and development of people is going to be one of the single most important decisions that leaders and companies around this world are going to make. They're going to be forced to make it as competition increases and leaders are looking for ways to improve their current people with new insights and wisdom.

Marshall Goldsmith said, "What got us here won't get us there." The remnant of today's economy based on poor decisions in 2004 and 2005 is that there was bad growth with poor customer service mindsets. Everybody thought they could win, when in essence one could sell used chewing gum and make money in those eras. Those days are gone. The competitive environments are forcing us to learn how can we make the people we have better—better in every dimension: knowledge, skills, desire, and confidence. How can we grow those people in a holistic way that touches every person in the company? That is the wave of the future and that's where training and development are going from my perspective.

WRIGHT

Well, what a great conversation here. I have really learned a lot here today, especially about coaching. I really appreciate all this time you've taken with me to answer these questions. I think our readers are really going to get a lot out of this chapter.

BURT

Thank you, it's been my pleasure.

WRIGHT

Today we've been talking with Micheal Burt. Coach Micheal Burt speaks, trains, coaches, and leads some of the top performing organizations in and around the Southeast. Known as having the ability to take the best and make them better, he brings a message that has resonated with more than 120,000 people across the country on four leadership principles and key drivers: voice, leadership, execution, and culture.

Micheal, thank you so much for being with us today on *Success Simplified.*

BURT

Thank you.

Coach Micheal Burt speaks, trains, coaches, and leads some of the top performing organizations in the Southeast including Ole South Properties, the number one home builder in Tennessee, the John Jones Real Estate Team, Kendra Cooke and Associates, Reeves Sain, State Farm, and First Bank, the largest independently owned bank in TN. This former championship women's basketball coach now helps companies drive initiatives with a systems approach, high intensity energy, accountability, score boards, and a new mindset. Known as having the ability to take the best and make them better, Coach Burt brings a message that has resonated with more than 120,000 people across the country around four key drivers: voice, leadership, execution and culture.

Featured as a leadership expert every morning on Super Talk 99.7 WTN, Nashville's largest talk radio station, Micheal is also the host of *The Coach Micheal Burt Radio Show* with Dr. Colby Jubenville, around the theme of Change your Life Radio on WLAC. Micheal has appeared on numerous television and radio shows and is the author of four books; the most popular being *This Ain't No Practice Life: Seven Decisions to Play at a Different Level in Life*. Look for his forthcoming book, *Zebras and Cheetahs: There is a Different, Faster Leader in You*. For all things Micheal Burt, visit him on the Web at www.coachburt.com.

Micheal Burt

Coachburt.com, Maximum Success
P.O. Box 332963
Murfreesboro, TN 37133
615-225-8380
coach@coachburt.com
www.hearcoachburtspeak.com
www.maximumsuccess.org

CHAPTER FOUR

THE ATTITUDE OF THE EMPLOYEE IS CONTAGIOUS TO THE CUSTOMER

BY DAVID K. AAKER, IOM

DAVID WRIGHT (WRIGHT)

Today we're talking with David K. Aaker. David is a nationally recognized motivational speaker and trainer on customer service, leadership, and communication.

His keynote presentations have successfully ignited national conferences and banquets for corporations, associations, and organizations in the United States and Canada.

After twenty years as a chamber of commerce CEO, David was invited to join the faculty of the U.S. Chamber Institute of Organization Management. He is an instructor at five universities, teaching organizational management courses.

David has received two Hall of Fame Awards, one from Palmdale High School for Community and Economic Development, and the second from the City of Palm Springs Bureau of Tourism.

Aaker & Associates customer service training programs have been presented to many clients, including: FTD Florist, SuperCuts, Tenet Healthcare Hospital Corporation, hotels, casinos, state departments of tourism, private sector corporations, and municipal governments in North America.

David also serves as Vice-Chairman of the Indian Planning Commission for the Sovereign Nation of the Agua Caliente Band of Cahuilla Indians in Palm Springs, California.

David was recently named "Among America's Best Speakers" by Sky Radio on American Airlines, and was featured on forty-two thousand world-wide flights in May of 2009.

David, welcome to *Success Simplified.*

How did twenty years as a chamber of commerce CEO prepare you for public speaking?

David K. Aaker (Aaker)

Serving the Palmdale, California, Chamber for ten years, and then the Palm Springs, California Chamber of Commerce as their CEO/President for ten years was the best on-the-job training for a speaker one can imagine.

Chamber of commerce management was a great base to build on as the point of business promotion in the community. I was often asked to speak on the local economy, local legislative issues, and community promotion events. This also included writing press releases and participating in interviews with radio, television, newspapers, and press conferences.

One does not wake up in the morning being a professional speaker. Just like any other profession, it is built one presentation, speech, outline, article, interview at a time. What you learn is what to say, when to say it, and when to listen. The learned skill of listening more than you talk, when you are a professional speaker, is one of the fundamental foundations of being not just a professional speaker, but a profitable professional speaker.

The twenty years when I was a CEO brought dozens of opportunities a week to participate in the communication avenues to get our message out. Quite often, I realized that if the topic, content, or validity of the presentation was not in my realm of knowledge or responsibility, I would delegate it to the person who could best present our organization's point of view and position. This accomplished two major things: The first was to give accurate, current, and precise information to those who needed to hear it and secondly, it gave the opportunity to another person to be part of the success of the organization by being the spokesperson for the organization.

One of the best lessons as CEO of two large business development organizations like the Palmdale and Palm Springs Chambers was that even when one's message is not good news, one must speak with honesty, sincerity, and "face the music" of the issue.

Large employers moving out of town, union strikes, local elections that invited the organization's support, and candidates who assumed the Chamber of Commerce would back their position, viewpoints, and personal contribution and support were all issues that needed to be addressed through speaking.

Often the chief elected official was not comfortable "making the announcement" or doing the interview with the media on a hot topic. This is where lessons are learned in speaking. The good times as well as the challenging times both offered lessons on public speaking that formed the foundation for my speaking.

In summary, my speaking skills, listening skills, and communication skills, had a twenty-year learning curve. No better training can be bought, taught, or inherited than living the adventure firsthand. I would not trade that twenty-year lesson, with homework assigned to me each day, for anything. My speaking style, message, passion, and enthusiasm are all part of that twenty-year journey.

Wright

Your focus is customer service on most of your keynote and training programs. What other topics do you share with your clients?

Aaker

I agree, "Customer Service" is my most requested topic for a keynote or training programs for small to large companies.

Being a faculty member for the United States Chamber of Commerce for their Institute for Organizational Management, I have been invited to create and build several courses in management, leadership, communication, delegation, phone skills, board of directors orientation, and ethics. I have taken a bit from each topic and created a presentation that has value, information, and worth to a specific client.

One valuable tool I use is to call a client before each presentation, and get a few of the hot points, issues, and challenges that they and their employees are currently dealing with. I take these three to five points and weave them into their presentation. I can actually see someone in the audience make the non-verbal expression as if to say "That just happened to me last week!" That simple addition is of great value to each client and his or her commitment to better serve others.

A great example of that is one of my largest clients, Tenet Healthcare Corporation. I was invited to participate regularly in its "General Orientation" for new employees each month."

I invite them to consider how many patients, family members, fellow medical staff, hospital employees, etc. that they will contact each day. An example I give is I had a hernia surgery scheduled for July 2009 (this was before my monthly programs started). I kept a total of how many employees I had contact with before my out-patient surgery was completed and I was rolled out after surgery for my wife to pick me up. Starting with the insurance paperwork at the hospital, all the pre-testing (e.g., blood, heart, etc.) and checkups needed, interactions with the accounting department, the scheduling departments, the surgery, and all the people I remember speaking to, all were "points of contact" to me. My paperwork and tests took only two hours. The next morning was my surgery, and counting the young man who wheeled me out for my waiting ride and my wife, forty-two team members had a chance to impress me, make me welcome, and make me comfortable. When I ask the question to the new hospital employees each month as to how many employees I had contact with the usual guess is from five to fifteen employees. For them, when they realize how many chances were taken or lost to make a positive impression, it is a real eye-opener.

The topic of leadership is always highly requested. I have worked with companies like FTD Florist and Super Cuts, both different industries, but both involve leadership, communication, and customer service. For a keynote, it is also of worth to the spouse of the conference attendee because so many examples I use are also applicable to life, work, leisure, and family dynamics.

Keeping these topics simple or complex is not the issue. What one takes away from a presentation is the bottom line. I like to offer those in an audience an invitation to take several points, ideas, thoughts, or actions with them and put a few to work within the first two hours of returning to their workplace, company, organization, or association.

Offerings from Aaker & Associates include:

- Keynote presentations for conferences, banquets, and dinners
- Breakout sessions for conferences
- Facilitation for annual strategic planning sessions and annual board retreats
- Customer service workshops as a fundraiser for chambers, organizations, and associations.

WRIGHT

Where did your passion for customer service come from?

AAKER

Living my life and paying attention to how we treat each other has been the foundation of my understanding and passion. I believe we have become a bit numb about how we treat each other. In business, life, or on vacation, we all want to be treated with respect, honor, and sincerity.

Watching others use their customer skills or lack of skills has always fascinated me. I was in the retail business prior to my twenty-year chamber management career, and both were a hands-on learning session of how humans treat humans.

I have a theme and title of my customer service programs. The title of my presentation is "The Attitude of the Employee is Contagious to the Customer." The theme I weave into each program is "Serving Others is a Privilege, Not an Obligation." Both create expectations; both are a commitment from each employee on a company's payroll.

My passion for customer service is also driven by the reaction of those who attend my programs. They are invited to become a "Warrior of Service" for their team. The old thought that "when one gets there, we all get there" is the best example of serving others.

Quite often we assume that if most of the employees are doing a good job, that is enough, but when one employee, either through his or her actions disappoints one customer, client, patient, or guest, the person feeling disappointed tends to paint all of the team with a broad brush of disappointment. Paying attention to our actions is not an easy task, which is why we must be constantly reminded of our level of service.

A great example of my passion for customer service is when I was a CEO. Every employee I hired in a twenty-year span was invited to the same personal invitation from me on his or her first day. Being in the chamber of commerce business, one must deal with hundreds of phone calls and walk-in visitors each day. To that end, our customer service, listening skills, and attitude toward every person had to be the best every day.

I reminded each new employee that for any reason if they could not bring a great attitude to work each day, I would offer them a day off with pay to not come in to work that day. I then gave each new employee my home phone number to stress how serious I was with the value of a great attitude. I reminded them I would never ask them why they were not coming in to work on that day, just that they respect the value of serving others, which includes a great attitude every day. In twenty years, I only had two employees call me at home in the morning that they would not be part of the team that day because of their attitude. I consider this to be a great return on investment in my employees, and their value of attitude in the workplace.

Customer service is something you cannot see, feel, or touch, but you also know what customer service is when you do not receive it or are disappointed with it. I often ask audiences a question I refer to as my "five-alarm fire question." When I ask it, I can just hear the screams in the minds of those I'm talking with when they answer the question internally. The question I ask is, "What would be the value to your company or business if each of you created and built a 'Customer for Life' every day?" My answer is priceless! I have never had a client admit that he or she invited employees to build a customer for life. When I give my clients the green light to ask that question, a new level of customer service is born.

Passion for customer service is a full-time 24/7 responsibility. It never stops, never sleeps, and it takes constant effort from everyone on your payroll. It can start with you, but will not end with you. Invite your team members to be "Warriors for Customer Service;" it is a battle just waiting for you to win.

WRIGHT

Describe what one would expect from your full two-hour customer service training program.

Aaker

Expectations are focused with each client. A private sector client with twenty-three hundred employees will have as much success as a small employer with twenty-five employees. The main two ingredients of every program are that it is participatory and enthusiastic. I am often told that the program was the fastest two hours of information the audience member has experienced in a long time.

True, specific examples of customer service are brought to the forefront with shared experiences I have had or those that have been shared with me. This includes newspaper articles of service, or lack of it. Every time we open our wallet or purses and pull out our credit card or cash or checkbook to purchase goods or services, part of the fee paid is the expectation that there is also an experience of service included in the transaction.

A good example is a restaurant. You expect good food and good service. When one overpowers the other, it is the diminished element you recall and will share with others. No matter how good the food, if the service is lacking or disappointing, that is what we remember. Now the balancing act comes in to play. We often focus our training on the product, not the delivery of the product. When you give balanced attention to both, you deliver balanced food and service.

During these examples of service, and during the program, I conduct a "Hot Idea Contest" during most programs. At any time, audience members can suggest a hot idea for service. The audience votes at the end of the program, and I provide an award to the top voted idea. What the employer/client gets out of this is more than ten great ideas from his or her employees. Staff will often suggest an idea at a training program much easier than they can at a structured staff meeting. I have also suggested that the clients use these ideas in their monthly employee meetings or company newsletter. Ask for one or two ideas a month, and give the person who shared the best idea credit for it.

At the close of the two-hour program, I hand out a Commitment Card to each in attendance (this is with the approval of the client) and each person makes a written commitment of something he or she will do to improve customer service in the business or company.

The last item on my program is a summary of what this program is all about. With a larger audience, I may only use the front two or three rows, but if there are a hundred or more in the audience, we can include everyone. I ask each person to share one idea he or she received from the program that can be taken back to the company and put to use within the first hour of the next workday. This contributes amazing points of service. Some ideas were discussed during the program and some others were thought of but not mentioned. This is the richest benefit of each program, and I learn one or more great ideas each time I have done this. There are no limits on their thinking and no limits on the benefit that these shared ideas bring to each audience, each time, in each program. I have found that the feedback from this two-hour program is almost overwhelming.

When you provide a program that ignites and engages the experience, and they can take away one or several great ideas that will bring them more customers, more profits, and more success, it is worth all the effort and energy.

It is a pleasure to learn from each program. I start each program with the quote: "Everyone I meet knows something I don't." This reminds me that I learn or am taught a new lesson about service from each audience. I am thankful for each lesson.

Wright

Is there any specific industry or company that invites you to share your programs and message?

Aaker

The smallest group I have ever had for a two-hour program consisted of seven CEOs for the two hours. The largest attendance in a two-hour program was twenty-one hundred.

What it boils down to is to get the entire team to participate in the program. Quite often I hear from the clients, "I just want my managers and vice presidents to attend your program." I have always suggested that if time, location, and logistics can be worked out, it is best for everyone on the payroll to be invited to attend. Quite often, a message with specific ideas and concepts can be diluted or overly condensed when the information is passed through the ranks.

A new concept bringing great response from my clients is to consider inviting their top customers of their companies. This number can be from ten to one hundred. Even the vendors who cannot attend this "Customer Appreciation" event will remember that your company made the invitation. I suspect their competitors have not extended the same invitation. Vendors and suppliers will always remember this invitation, especially when you might need a rush order, special design, or product for a more expedient delivery.

I have received feedback from clients who have shared that their vendors were very appreciative of the invitation, even more so when they attended. A restaurant, for instance, would include all the employees on the payroll and all of the vendors found in their accounts payable department. Examples would include: laundry (tablecloths, napkins, etc.), food providers, beverage suppliers, landscapers for the outside/inside of the building, valet, security, and insurance carriers. Do not let this idea slip by. One client held two programs a day for his employees only, and a special "Vendor Appreciation Luncheon." The owner had a personal, uninterrupted opportunity to thank those who contributed to his success and the success of the restaurant over the years. Wow, what a win-win that was. I condensed the program to about an hour for the luncheon only.

When we do not take the time, effort, or initiative to go out of our way to thank those who contribute to our success, we lose that moment forever. You can make it up one at a time when you have their attention, but to do it in a relaxed luncheon, the sincerity can be amplified by all, and creates a larger "family atmosphere" for the company.

So if clients have only a few employees, they can partner with their peers, vendors, and their guests. Clients can often inform me that it is for their staff only. It is at this point where personalization of each program comes in. I have had several municipal governments hire me to conduct my programs for all city employees. I offer to call several of their department heads with a quick three-minute survey about the success of customer service in their department. Often they will share with me a few issues that they are having—issues that they may not share with their city manager. I then share those surveys with the city manager, and I weave into that specific client's program most of the issues they are dealing with and potential solutions for each. Often the solutions come from the audience.

As I said, all my programs are participatory and attendees are enthusiastic in contributing. Every employee is a valuable asset to every company; every employee can be a cheerleader and warrior for your company. I also invite employees to add more equity to their position. There is no specific industry or occupation that inquires about customer service training more than others. It is about the employees' ongoing offerings of communication, leadership, ethics, listening skills, phone skills, etc. than a particular industry. I am often surprised when I ask a client when is the last time he or she had a customer service training program for all the employees. The usual answer is, "David, yours will be the first; we always just gave each new hire a few tips on being nice to the customers."

WRIGHT

What are some of the "nuggets" that your audience members will take with them after your program?

AAKER

I have mentioned the "Hot Idea Contest" that is included in most programs. That alone is a "gold mine" of ideas straight from their employees. At the end of the program, a vote is taken and a winner is declared by the vote. After the award is presented and the program is over, each client gets a written list of all the ideas shared. These can often be included in their employee or company newsletter, and believe me, there are some fabulous ideas that are revealed with each audience.

Additional nuggets are best described by the section I include on the "Top Ten Golden Nuggets of Customer Service." This is also the name of my CD, which is an audible ten-minute bonus clients are given. I suggest that they pick one of the Ten Nuggets and make it the theme of the week for their company. Drawn at the next staff meeting, that specific nugget can be applied by all employees all week long. The staff person who picks that week's "nugget" is the "cheerleader" for that nugget.

The Top Ten Golden Nuggets of Customer Service are:

1. Know your customer by his or her first name.
2. Listen twice as much as you talk.

3. Always tell the truth.
4. Never argue with the customer, client, patient, or guest.
5. Under-promise, over-perform.
6. Follow-up, Follow-up, Follow-up.
7. Be thankful for your customers who complain, for you still have the opportunity to make them happy.
8. Enthusiasm.
9. Be thankful for each and every customer, every time.
10. The Golden Rule—do to others what you would have them do to you.

These are just a few of the "nuggets" that will be taken away from each presentation.

Every session produces new thoughts, ideas, concepts, opportunities, and challenges to build a better toolbox of ideas to better serve our existing customers and future customers, most of which will be referred to your company as a result of how you treated your existing customers.

WRIGHT

Is there a theme to your programs?

AAKER

The answer is yes. The title of my customer service program is "The Attitude of the Employee is Contagious to the Customer."This title is a direct result of how I have observed employees when they interact with the next customer who comes within their sphere of influence or department in their business.

I have witnessed customers start the conversation with a raised and aggressive voice, and the employee steps right up to that level with his or her first response. Now, where do you think that conversation is going?

When one raises his or her voice, that person loses control of the communication. It is difficult at the time, but keep your voice lower and listen—really listen—to what others are saying more than how you are saying it. This will give you a more clear understanding of what they are asking or what they are concerned about. I have often found that in conversation, customers will include in their communication the outcome that they desire. When you listen more than you talk, this offers the opportunity to hear what they are really asking for and perhaps, if it is best and equitable and ethical for both parties, you can usually find a middle-of-the-road solution to their concern or question.

This tool is an additional nugget they can take away from the program. I always ask myself after a program, "What is the take-away I have learned from the audience in this last session that I can include in the theme of my next programs?"

I also start and finish each program with sharing the thought of "Serving Others is a Privilege, not an Obligation." So many times we are in the zone of helping one customer after another. A good example of this is a return department in a large retail store. The employee is assisting one customer after another, after another. What can that employee do to personalize his or her interaction with each customer that would be a positive impression on each? It could be no more than a sincere smile and a few words of thanks for their patience while they waited for you to help them. I would always rather offer this brief "touch point" than pass it up. The customer can immediately form a positive opinion of his or her experience as a result of what the employee has just done.

So in summary, there are two themes to my customer service programs. The title of the program is "The Attitude of the Employee is Contagious to the Customer" and the theme that is woven throughout the program is "Serving Others is a Privilege, Not an Obligation." From the first mention, to the last closing comments, both are repeated and audience members are reminded of the value this will have as they create the opportunity to build a customer for life each day.

Wright

How has customer service changed in the last ten years?

Aaker

With the huge advancements in technology in the last decade, customer service was also caught up in the tsunami of change. Let's look back ten years ago. When you returned to a certain store, you were greeted with your name, and were perhaps asked a question about your family or your work. That was almost an assumption when you returned to your regular grocery store, gas station, and shoe store. There was also less competition in most product lines, which also contributed to the expectations of the retailers for their customers' return next time they needed a similar product or service.

Fast forward ten years. The Internet has provided additional shopping opportunities. Television sales programs provide a different shopping experience for some from the comfort of their homes.

Customer service and its concept of the value and the foundation of each company or business must be re-evaluated almost every few months to keep up with the additional offerings to find your next new customer and lead them to your front door or phone number or Web site.

I have often said to those who are in business—whether in an organization, association, municipal government, hospital, school district, shopping mall—that the unique offerings of their company are an integral part of their customer service success. Consider the offerings your company has access to, and see if they are included in your customer service by your staff and employees and everyone on your payroll. Next time you have a staff meeting, lay out the "buffet" of items that could be considered in your customer service buffet line: Your ingredients could include:

Hard Work
Integrity
Fairness
Compassion
Loyalty
Respect
Communication
Listening Skills
Understanding
Respectful Humor
Ethics
Follow-up

There are several more that could be added, but if you just took one of those ingredients, made that the theme of the week for your company, and let all departments know the value of that ingredient to the customer, it would make a very positive and profitable impact on your team and their reaction to customers. This is where the titles of my programs are best explained by the theme, "The Attitude of the Employee is Contagious to the Customer."

So when you digest the history of service to your customers, you must look at your company and service and products. Ask yourself if you have changed your offerings of service to your customers or are you in a comfort zone with receiving what you are sending in the way of customer service.

Yes, customer service has changed in the last ten years, and I look at it as a huge opportunity to take what wisdom we have had and the opportunity to learn from the present, add to both, and plan for the future.

I sincerely believe that people will pay more for a product if service is implied. This is perhaps more true today, as we interact less with a salesperson, or his or her voice when doing business with each other.

What can you do to meet this challenge? Gather your employees and ask those who have been on your team the longest what has worked for them in the past. Ask the newer employees what they think will take the company or business to new levels of success in the area of customer service offerings. Here is where you listen—really listen—to both their explanations of their history and expectations of service. Again, this is an example of the saying, "when one of us gets there, we all get there."

Customer service is no different. When we accept the fact that we drive the level of service in our companies, we also drive our products or services in the same positive direction. It is not our competitors, new products, new locations, new marketing ideas that drive the service we offer as a team, it is us—one of us, all of us.

When we each take the equity of the value of our product and the value of service as seriously as the customer does when he or she contacts us, this is where business is built, one customer at a time.

When Retail Fair Trade was applicable, many years ago, I remember paying the same price for a pair of Levi's blue jeans where ever you found them. The difference of the experience was the service that went with the purchase. Retailers knew they would sell this product because everyone had the same price. A little extra comment, question, attention, or offerings of a matching shirt or shoes to go with the new jeans often had a benefit on several levels, including more sales and a positive customer service experience.

Be thankful for the change in customer service in the last ten years. This gives us all a wake-up call on polishing and adding our offerings to our valuable customers. We need to be constantly aware of improving our service; our customers expect it and deserve it.

Wright

Would a small company with twenty-five employees benefit from your programs as much as a company with twenty-five hundred employees?

Aaker

The answer is yes. Every medium and large company started as a small company. With this thought in mind, the foundation of the level of service you offer is the tone that is set for the growth of your company. As your success in business builds, so do your employees. To set an example of your level of customer service with each new employee means to follow up and build on that foundation. This is a huge reason businesses grow or fail to grow.

One of my largest clients has a total of fifty-two thousand employees. On a monthly basis, I am invited to join the general orientation of forty to fifty new employees every month. A brief overview of the level of service they have offered for fifty-eight years has grown each year and now they are part of a very successful industry that others have built during the six decades of its existence. Quarterly, I offer my full two-hour programs, usually two a day for a few days each quarter. All attendees are offered the up-to-date goals, expectations, and opportunities that they have to offer to be recognized as one of the best healthcare institutions in the nation.

So when small retailers give me a call and ask how their employees would benefit from my programs, I ask them what they would like employees to take away from the program that would be a direct, immediate value to their specific business. This is the key to the success of each program.

Often smaller companies have a bigger advantage to make a positive impression on each customer every day; the results often appear sooner than expected. Take that thought and apply it to a larger employer, say one hundred employees or more. The more employees, the more responsibility there is for establishing and maintaining a positive experience in serving others.

Often one employee will miss a great chance to serve a customer, either by communication, not calling back in a timely manner, or not paying attention to their conversation, and it reflects on us all. Take a very large retailer, for instance. There are twenty check-out counters, hundreds of parking spaces outside their store, twenty thousand square feet of retail products. It only takes one employee to disappoint a customer in some interaction with that retailer. When that happens, customers tend to form a broad opinion of the entire franchise or brand of store with that experience. This is where the power of serving others comes in. Take a leadership role in sharing, informing, giving examples of what good or great service is. Share these examples with everyone on your payroll; the impact will show up in your day's gross sales, or lack of sales.

What a pleasure to get a "thank you" from a customer when one of your team members receives a verbal or written thank you from someone who chose to come to your business.

Never miss a chance to acknowledge a compliment from a customer. This is a great form of what I call "Psychic Income." It is the "paycheck" we get from doing our work in a manner that is beneficial to the customer and the employer at the same time.

I frequently ask the following question to an audience during a program, and I invite you to consider it for your next staff meeting. "In your mind, evaluate the level of customer service that you offered to the last three customers you had the privilege to work and communicate with. As a result of how you treated those three customers, would you hire you?"

That is how important this ingredient of your business success is. Each of us needs to understand and value how we treat each other. This includes those we work with and those we work for. Both groups need our personal, sincere attention to service.

So if you have twenty-five employees or twenty-five hundred employees, everyone needs to be reminded and encouraged to remember that the customer came to you, and not to your competitors, so let's use all the tools in our toolbox to make that customer a customer for life because of how we treat them.

Wright

Human resource directors have often referred to your programs as "an *hors d'œuvre* or appetizer to their existing training program." What do they mean by that statement?

Aaker

Human resource directors are such a valuable asset to any company, and their responsibilities are numerous, including offering all the employees a level of training that will be consistent with the company's vision and standards, expectations, and mission statement.

My programs have a solid foundation of information, offered in an enthusiastic and participatory way that can be applicable to most clients with few adjustments. After several conversations with industry specific clients, we establish what issues they choose to include in my programs, and we weave them in to match their expectations.

By offering my two-hour program on customer service, human resource directors have one more tool to offer their employees that can be added to, included with, and available to them to service their customer base.

My programs are not in competition with HR directors' established training schedules, but they have shared that my programs, in partnership with their existing programs, are a treat or special or an additional offering for their company.

A few years ago, a large newspaper publishing company hired me to give a presentation to their sixteen hundred employees. They let me know that the two-hour programs would have to be convenient to their work schedules, not mine. I learned that the circulation department had a different time frame for their work than the accounting department or the printing press operators. This resulted in classes at 6 AM, and even a few at midnight to match their work shifts.

My point is that when a client included me in the success of their employees' training program, it is my privilege to participate. It reminded me of how flexible we all need to be in business. A plumber works when clients need them, a Realtor shows property when he or she gets a request. All these examples go back to the HR directors. We can all learn from them. When you think you have the ordering, display, marketing, training, merchandising, shipping, and advertising all down to a science, you probably do. This is where you add the customer service ingredient to make it all work toward your success and advantage and to that of your company and your customer.

To add my program to an existing training program has often led to a keynote presentation at a national conference to share the benefit it has brought to a company as a result of the director of human resources knowing what to offer to their employees that will contribute to the growth of their company.

Wright

What makes your programs stand out from other training programs or keynote presentations?

Aaker

Comments that have been often shared with me from post-client conversations include: enthusiasm in the presentation and ideas and offerings that can be used within an hour of the presentation back in the office.

Participation from each audience is my trademark. Giving an audience the invitation and freedom to contribute what works for them creates a conversational atmosphere with the audience than a straightforward presentation or workshop. I remind each audience member at the beginning of the program that "Everyone here today knows something I don't. If I do not hear from you, I might miss some new idea or thought." This is often a new path for those who have sat through other training programs or speeches. Wow, does this work. I have been sharing my customer service programs with thousands of people in hundreds of programs, and I always walk away with one more great idea, new thought, or tool to add to my next program. When a speaker concludes a program, and someone comes up after the program to share that he or she thought I was talking directly to him or her and not the other three hundred in the room, it is a sincere privilege to thank that person for his or her comment and acknowledge the person's great listening skills.

As a twenty-year chamber executive, I sat on the board of directors for multi-state organizations and associations, and have enjoyed and endured hundreds of presentations and speeches. I can recall with vivid memory what held my attention, kept my head tilted to hear every word, and made me take a few notes that I found would build my inventory of tools as I returned to build a better chamber of commerce.

This has been a great learning path for me, so now that I am doing this full time in the training world, I remember pivot points in my appreciation of investing my time and money in those conferences. Payday does often not come to us in the short term, but rather a planting of ideas for a future harvest.

I try to plant several seeds of interest and ideas in serving others in each program and I also realize that some will harvest the ideas in the short term, and others a little later, just as I did. I keep fun in my programs and I keep them informative. I keep the audience engaged, which keeps everyone on the same page; we all get to the finish line at the same time. I have heard, perhaps too often, that I speak too fast. I am quick to say that I have a lot to share, and I also have a lot to learn from each audience.

Every speaker is different and every presentation of customer service has its own personality. Blending those two major ingredients together with sincere enthusiasm and welcomed participation with the audience has been a formula that has worked for me for more than twenty years.

Wright

What are your clients looking for when they first contact you for your training programs?

Aaker

Each client is asked what they would like their employees to experience during the two-hour programs, and what would they expect to take away from the program.

Small, medium and large businesses are amplified with tasks with marketing, advertising, promotions etc. and often training programs for the team are often not the priority in a busy business environment. I understand that, and am also frequently surprised when it has been a year or more since a training program was offered. What seems to have the largest impact is that when everyone on the payroll gets the opportunity to attend the program, all advance on the same plateau. Often I have clients invite only their managers and supervisors. I understand this, but quite often, the message is transferred without the experience of being with all the employees who form the team in order to build a better business.

Clients are also looking for the team effort from their employees to the customers. Internal customers, those we work with, and the external customers, those we work for.

Clients are also looking for new, exciting, out-of-the-box, fresh, crisp new ideas that they can add to their "toolbox" of ideas in serving the customer.

Often great ideas come from each audience through the hot idea contest that most of my programs provide. I find it easier for an employee to share what may be a wild idea with the group setting in a two-hour program that retains the flavor of "respectful fun." These ideas are mostly very realistic in being part of a new program, policy, and/or service that comes right from the employees and staff. I have even had past clients mail me a copy of their latest newsletter where they highlighted the hot idea, and the employee who contributed the idea with an article, a photo of the employee, and recognition of the contribution of the employee as being part of the success of the company.

Clients often comment after a program that they did not expect the participation aspect and the celebration of success from the audience. This is the "paycheck" for the company—to have the opportunity to share what could work, what could make a difference, and what would take the client's business to the next level. This is just what the client is looking for. They're not sure how to call for action, but they discover that the reaction of their employees is a frequent victory for the client.

Recent feedback from a leader in a large client company included a comment from a registered nurse who had attended one of my training programs offered by her hospital. It went like this:

"David, I thought you should see this. One of the attendees at one of your six classes this week called to thank us for running this training program. She said it was the 'best class she has ever attended.' She said she 'picked up pearls of wisdom that will help here on the job and off.' She came in on her day off to attend your class. She thinks we should make it mandatory. . . no one will mind that they have to attend after they see what the course offers."

The above feedback letter best answers the question of what clients are looking for. It reminds me what my customers are looking for. It also reminds me of the question: what are your customers looking for?

Wright

What do you see in the future for customer service?

Aaker

Spending more time looking through the windshield of life, instead of the rear-view mirror of life, provides a much broader view of the path—your journey, your mission.

I clearly understand the value of inviting your staff—and I mean *all* of your staff—to be more proactive in their interaction with each customer, client, patient, vendor, guest, etc. It will provide the opportunity to build a customer for life. When we do not take advantage of this golden opportunity each time, it has faded from our grasp; it sails away like a ship that has left the harbor. We have to then wait for the next opportunity or the next "ship" to come into our "harbor."

I see the resurgence of more face-to-face, voice-to-voice communication with the customer. I understand the value and opportunity this provides, and long-time retailers and businessmen and businesswomen will validate my thoughts on this tried and true tool.

E-mail, Internet, texting, U.S. mail will always be a bridge from you and your products or services to your potential customers. When we choose to communicate on a personal level, we have the opportunity to make them feel special, well taken care of, and will give them a reason to choose your company before all the competition. That is the success you have earned by the efforts you have invested in your staff, management, and your customers. This is easy to say, but challenging to implement and follow up on, but it is among the major ingredients of success that has built the businesses of the world to their current levels of success.

Remember that each large corporation, business, or company was a start-up company at one time. It takes years and years to build a reputation of sincere, value-added, and personal attention to your customers. Your company constantly needs new ideas, tools, and techniques to maintain your level of service, and then take it to the next level. You set the benchmark of your service; your customers will have expectations of service before they call, e-mail, or walk in your front door.

The theme of "Serving Others is a Privilege, Not an Obligation" is more than a theme, it can be the slogan of a company, the implied brand of expected service, or the established level the company has built over the years that customers and potential customers look forward to and expect when they return to your business.

Every employee on your payroll has the potential to be a warrior of customer service, if they are provided a sincere invitation from the owners, CEOs, managers, and presidents of companies. It starts with the invitation, training, and follow-through. When the victories occur, celebrate them, share them, and it will ignite other team members to make a difference in their department, division, or region. The victor in all this effort is the customer who chooses to do business with you. That decision, made by the customer, to return to your business, before all the competition in your industry, is the golden ticket, the lottery win.

I invite you to invite your employees to the challenge of creating a "Customer for Life" each day.

If customer service is your sharpest arrow in your quiver and the main ingredient in the success of your business, the other ingredients will also blend when the opportunity comes along. Leadership, ethics, communications, marketing, advertising, production, and distribution are all ingredients of a successful business. Customer service, added to each of the above ingredients, can only be a benefit for you, your business, and your customers.

Consider the suggestions listed above and add your own fingerprint and ingredients to how you choose to create a customer for life.

To your continued success!

About the Author

David Aaker, IOM, is a nationally recognized motivational speaker and trainer on customer service, leadership, and communication.

His keynote presentations have successfully ignited national conferences and banquets for corporations, associations and organizations in the United States and Canada.

After twenty years as a chamber of commerce CEO, David was invited to join the faculty of the U.S. Chamber, and is an instructor at five universities, teaching organizational management courses.

David has been given two Hall of Fame Awards, one from Palmdale High School for Community and Economic Development, and the second from the City of Palm Springs Bureau of Tourism.

Aaker & Associates customer service training programs have been presented to many clients including: FTD Florist, SuperCuts, Tenet Healthcare Hospital Corporation, hotels, casinos, state departments of tourism, private sector corporations, and municipal governments in North America.

David also serves as Vice-Chairman of the Indian Planning Commission for the Sovereign Nation of the Agua Caliente Band of Cahuilla Indians in Palm Springs, California.

David was recently named "Among America's Best Speakers" by Sky Radio on American Airlines, and was featured on forty-two thousand world-wide flights in May of 2009.

David K. Aaker, IOM

760-323-4600

david@davidkaaker.com

www.davidkaaker.com

CHAPTER FIVE

MOOD IS EVERYTHING

BY PAUL TEMPLER

DAVID WRIGHT (WRIGHT)

We're pleased to include Paul Templer in our group of contributors for *Success Simplified*. When it comes to overcoming obstacles and turning them into new opportunities, Mr. Templer is a true authority.

Mr. Templer grew up in war-torn Rhodesia (now known as Zimbabwe) living an exotic life surrounded by the wildlife most children read about in storybooks. He spent his youth dreaming of the day when he'd be able to run safaris on Africa's mighty Zambezi River and share his love of the crocodiles, elephants, and hippopotamuses with tourists from around the world. And at the age of twenty-four, he saw that dream come true. Every sun-filled morning, his team of river guides would ease their canoes into the water, feeling confident that the day ahead would be filled with adventure and that they would once again avert any dangers that the river might hold.

A student of the great Zambezi, Mr. Templer knew the rhythms of the animals that lived beneath the river and had become a master of predicting their every move. But as anyone who has lived in the jungles of Africa will attest, danger lurks where you least expect it.

On a crystal blue Saturday morning in March of 1996, as Mr. Templer joked with an eager group of tourists and warned them to keep their hands inside the boat, what he didn't know was that a deadly monster was waiting, silently below. Without warning, an enraged hippopotamus plucked him from his canoe, dragged him into the river, and then went about its deadly attack.

With his body torn in shreds and his crewmates attempting to rescue him—even amid the chaos—Mr. Templer's thoughts were already rising to the surface. His dreams had just been shattered and the life he had envisioned since childhood would never be the same.

Mr. Templer, I'll start by asking what everyone is probably wondering—how do you maintain such a positive outlook after experiencing such a traumatic event?

Paul Templer (Templer)

Well, it wasn't always easy. There were quite a few weeks after the attack when I was feeling pretty low. At one point, I was lying in a hospital bed, feeling terribly sorry for myself, when the surgeon, Dr. Ncube, dropped by and gave me a mini pep talk. He said, "Paul, you are the sum of your choices—you're exactly who, what, and where you choose to be in life."

Conceptually, I understood what he was talking about, but I couldn't get out of my own way. I was just so angry and frustrated, and I wasn't ready yet to be accountable for what had happened to me and whatever might happen next. While I'd survived the attack, I'd lost my left arm and any hope of continuing the business I'd worked so hard to build. I guess you could say I was caught up in an unproductive mood.

Wright

What do you mean by "unproductive mood"?

Templer

I'm referring specifically to those times when things aren't working out quite the way we'd like them to and we allow ourselves to get caught up in degenerative moods like distrust, resentment, resignation, complacency, arrogance, and cynicism. When we're caught up in these moods, we often procrastinate, become quite grumpy, and find that most people don't seem to want to play with us.

I used to think I had no choice but to give in to the grumpiness. I actually felt entitled to sink into these unproductive moods. It was almost as if I'd earned the right to play a part, to fall into the "victim role." And it worked, for a while—until I realized that when I allowed myself to get caught up in those moods, I was miserable and that being miserable was a choice.

Let me be clear that when I use the word "mood," I'm describing the stories we make up—the thoughts, feelings, sensations we're experiencing—those are what determine the actions we take. They're the stories we choose to believe. So given the choice, why not see things in a more productive light.

If I believe things are going well, it's easy to make the assumption that they'll continue that way. That creates more of a positive, generative mood, which often shows up as ambition, confidence, trust and acceptance. With all those things going for you, you can't help but feel like the world is full of possibilities!

Wright

When did it start to change for you?

Templer

I'd say that Dr. Ncube challenging me to consider that I was the sum of my choices; that I was who, what, and where I chose to be in life, began a change process that continues today. One day does stand out though. I can give you the exact date—March 9, 2004. It was eight years to the day after my run-in with that angry hippo, and my wife, Carrie, and I were sitting in the waiting room of Children's Hospital of Michigan waiting for our four-month-old daughter, Erin, to come out of surgery. She was having a brain tumor removed. Unfortunately, the procedure didn't accomplish everything the doctors had hoped. It was a very long, difficult, and emotional day.

At first I felt many of those same emotions I'd experienced in the weeks after the hippo attack—anger, fear, sadness, self-pity. There were moments when I blamed God, my wife, myself, Erin's inoculations, the doctors—everyone and everything I could think of.

And then I remembered what Dr. Ncube had said to me eight years before: "Paul, you are the sum of your choices; you're who, what, and where you choose to be in life." Back then, I wasn't ready to fully grasp those words and apply them to my situation, but this time, they really resonated with me and kick-started a gradual shift in my outlook. Suddenly, I was able to interpret his message to mean "whatever happens next is entirely up to you." I realized he hadn't been just placating me with a cliché, he was trying to alert me to the possibilities and opportunities surrounding me.

During the next month, I spent a lot of time surrounded by gravely ill children—many of them with terminal diseases—and their families. I could see that the families were angry, frustrated, and scared, and most of them fell into the victim role. This resulted in lost possibilities and opportunities for both themselves and their dying children, adding even more sadness and stress to an already sad and stressful situation. The compassionate side of me could justify their behavior, but the pragmatic side was appalled at the cost.

I understood that I now had the capability to manage my mood, to banish the dark thoughts, and to embrace each new day—each passing moment—with gratitude. The most miraculous discovery of all was that positivity is contagious. I learned how my newfound optimism had the power to influence the moods of those around me.

Wright

Would you say this was a decision to reject the "victim role" you mentioned?

Templer

Absolutely. Sitting there in Children's Hospital of Michigan, I knew I had a choice to make. I could play the victim role; I could wallow in self-pity again, but I knew from experience that no good would come of that. As long as I was in that grumpy, grief-stricken mentality, I wouldn't be of much support to Carrie or Erin or our older daughter, two-year-old Kate. Instead, I decided I wanted to be the kind of person who takes care of the people he loves.

And this can be applied to anyone—not just those who have been violently attacked or experienced the heartbreak of a sick child. Everyone plays the victim role at some time or another. There's always an opportunity to feel sorry for yourself about something, whether it's a late report, a delayed flight, an out-of-stock item at the grocery store, or a car that won't start. The key is rising above that knee-jerk "woe is me" reaction.

WRIGHT

And how do you rise above that?

TEMPLER

Easier said than done, right? For me, the first step is acceptance. You have to just face the situation head-on and come to terms with it. I know that's easier said than done, but until you accept where you are, you simply can't move forward. Next, you have to understand that while you might not have the power to change your situation, you *do* have control over how you respond to it. Whatever happens next is entirely up to you.

This doesn't necessarily mean that you're going to like or that you'll be happy about the choices you're faced with, but it does mean that you'll enjoy a happier and more productive outcome if you take action rather than wallowing in stagnant self-pity. Life is always richer when you feel empowered by your options, rather than just letting the chips fall around you.

Even when faced with an emotionally challenging ordeal, like seeing your child struggling with a serious illness, you've got an opportunity to manage your mood and serve as an example for others who are struggling with a similar situation.

WRIGHT

How does all of this translate to a corporate setting?

TEMPLER

After I began working in corporate development, coaching high-performing leaders and their teams, I quickly realized that effectively managing moods and emotions is fundamental to success in the business world as well. It also became apparent that most people—even some of the most influential executives in the world—lack the capacity to effectively manage them.

If leaders can't or won't effectively manage their own and their organization's mood, then nothing else they do is going to matter and optimal performance becomes a fantasy.

In most cases, bad managers aren't lacking in knowledge or skill—they're mired in and evoke unproductive moods that impair their ability to inspire, motivate, and lead others. So essentially, one person's unproductive mood can limit the performance of an entire team.

With my corporate coaching practice, I set out to help managers and teams effectively manage their moods and emotions. In my experience, the most effective leaders are those who master the art of responding effectively to stressful and challenging situations.

WRIGHT

You've talked a lot about unproductive moods. What about the opposite? What does a productive mood look like?

TEMPLER

I want to be clear—a productive mood isn't necessarily going to look or feel good. During particularly stressful and challenging situations like our daughter's illness, I didn't experience moods of ambition, confidence, or wonder. My productive mood showed up in my acceptance of what was going on and my resolve and commitment to do everything in my power to maximize the possibilities for Erin and the rest of my family.

WRIGHT

Are some people more easily taught than others? Do some have a better ability to manage their moods?

TEMPLER

I used to think so. For years, I'd gone through life thinking some people were better at managing their moods than others. I almost believed there was some genetic lottery—either you were born with the ability to manage chaos or you were destined to unravel in stressful situations. So I would often make excuses for myself and others, assuming I had no choice but to react with grumpiness or anger or self-pity.

But while working with Chris Majer and his team at the Human Potential Project, I learned a great deal about optimal human performance. Specifically, I learned how, through practice, anyone can learn to effectively manage his or her mood. I started to understand how tolerating unproductive moods—in both myself and others—wasn't doing anyone any favors. Only by gaining awareness of ourselves and what is going on around us can we function and interact at an optimal level.

Wright

The term "self-fulfilling prophecy" springs to mind.

Templer

Absolutely! With 20/20 hindsight, I can see that where my attention went, my energy followed. When I looked for the things that were wrong in my life, I found them. And then later, when I looked for the good things—opportunities and possibilities—I found those, too.

I knew without a doubt that I never wanted to fall back into the victim role if things didn't go my way. So when I realized that proper management of my moods was the key to responding in a healthy and constructive way, I knew I had my solution.

Wright

How did the people you learned from inspire you?

Templer

What really intrigued me and paved the way to learning was that the people sharing their stories with me had been "in the trenches," so to speak—they'd faced adversity, hardship, and heartbreak and emerged with newfound strength and capabilities.

The people I was learning from had success stories to back up their teachings. They'd worked with professional and amateur athletes, members of the military (including special forces like Green Berets and Navy SEALs) and corporate organizations around the world, using a simple and straightforward approach based on hard science.

Wright

Some scientists assert that our reactions to stress are largely biological. Do you agree?

Templer

Yes, to an extent I do agree with that. When we experience stress or danger—whether it's real or imagined—our "fight-or-flight" response is activated.

This causes some dramatic physical reactions. The respiratory rate increases. Blood is diverted from the digestive tract to the muscles and limbs, which require extra energy for running or fighting. At the same time, the pupils dilate, sight becomes more focused, awareness intensifies, impulses quicken, and pain threshold heightens. Our perception of time seems to slow down and we prepare ourselves—physically and psychologically—to fight or flee.

This heightened state of fear and awareness causes us to think irrationally, perceiving almost everything around us as a possible threat or enemy. In this fight or flight mentality, it's almost impossible to adopt a productive mood, explore possibilities, trust others, or make sound and coherent choices. In this state, our ability to be creative and to come up with options or alternatives is diminished; we're more rigid, less resilient, and focused on short-term survival, not long-term consequences.

Wright

There are times though, that the fight-or-flight response is necessary—actually, a good thing—right?

Templer

Absolutely! After all, our fight-or-flight response was designed to protect us from the wild animals and unfriendly people that lurked in the jungles our forefathers inhabited. In situations when our actual physical survival is threatened, this is a very good protective measure. I can vouch for that personally. During the attack, as the hippopotamus was tearing me apart, the surging adrenaline and other stress hormones pumping through my body, in no small part, enabled me to survive.

That said, it's pretty unlikely that most people will experience a threat to their physical survival on a daily basis. Most of us are more likely to stress out from being caught in traffic, missing a deadline, having a flight delayed, or arguing with our boss or spouse. Nonetheless, these mini-crises still trigger our fight-or-flight response, just as if our well-being was threatened. On a daily basis, toxic stress hormones flow into our bodies as a result of events that pose no real threat to our physical survival.

The tricky thing is that in most cases, once our fight-or-flight response is activated, we can't run away and we can't fight. When faced with our "hippos"—whether they include a cranky co-worker, a stalled car, or a missed commitment—we have no choice but to face and accept them.

Wright

When does stress become unhealthy?

Templer

When we have a string of stressful or overwhelming situations, life becomes a series of fire drills or short-term emergencies. We lose the capacity to be present, to be open, and to connect with the things and the people important to us.

Living from one crisis to another, with no relief in sight, is a surefire way to fall into the victim role and slip into a grumpy, aggressive, and unproductive mood. For those who lack the competence to manage their mood amid chaos, this can turn into a toxic and vicious cycle of "heroic suffering." They may act or respond in ways that are actually counterproductive to their survival.

Wright

How did you learn to deal with the fight-or-flight reaction?

Templer

In the case of Erin's surgery and hospitalization, sitting in the doctor's office being hammered with scary information that threatened someone I loved, my fight-or-flight process was running in overdrive. But because of my prior experience with the hippo attack, I was able to recognize my knee-jerk reaction, divert it, and respond in a healthier way.

You see, I'd learned a thing or two about managing my moods. Sitting in that hospital, I knew I wasn't in any immediate physical danger, and that my body was responding to perceived psychological threats. I looked and listened for the signals of fight-or-flight mode such as tension in my muscles, headache, upset stomach, racing heartbeat, deep sighing, or shallow breathing. I paid attention to whether I had butterflies in my belly or if my tongue was pasted to the roof of my mouth, if my jaw was clenched, or if there was pressure at my temples and behind my eyes. I was also cognizant of the more emotional symptoms of an unproductive mood such as anxiety, hopelessness, frustration, anger, sadness, fear, resignation, resentment, or arrogance.

In times of emotional strain, our fight-or-flight response can sharpen our mental acuity, help us deal more decisively with issues, and move us to action. But it can also make us hyper-vigilant and over-reactive, instead of being calm and open to possibilities. The key is to utilize the beneficial effects, like heightened awareness and mental acuity, to manage our own moods and influence the moods of others.

Instead of fighting with or running away from people who weren't really to blame—such as the doctors, nurses, and my wife—I was able to curb my counterproductive behavior, recognize new possibilities, and provide a higher level of emotional support to my family.

Wright

But you're not suggesting that it's healthy to ignore stress, are you?

Templer

Not at all. A buildup of stress hormones can lead to a host of unpleasant symptoms including headaches, high blood pressure, immunity weaknesses, chronic fatigue, depression, and autoimmune diseases like rheumatoid arthritis, lupus, and allergies. The key isn't disregarding stressful or overwhelming situations—it's being aware of the signs and dealing with them in a healthy and constructive way.

Wright

What actual steps do you follow to get out of fight-or-flight mode?

Templer

As I've studied practical ways of detecting and shifting my moods, I've had a number of intriguing conversations with a friend and colleague, Peter Yaholkovsky, MD. He's given me great insight to the physiology of moods and mood management, including all the neurology, psychology, and endocrinology involved. And while there's nothing simple about how the brain and body work, the take-away always seems to be the same—I need to ask myself two questions:

1. What am I paying attention to?
2. What is important to me about that?

This enables me to see the story I'm in and to determine whether or not it's a story I want to commit to. The biochemistry and physiology is amazingly complex and can be quite interesting, but in simple terms, this how it works:

- First, when I find myself in a situation that my body interprets as stressful—I usually have an emotional response that includes something along the lines of "Oh crikey!"
- The next thing that might normally happen would be my fight-or-flight response kicks in and I get engaged in the drama and the unproductive mood that often goes with that.
- So once I become aware of all this, that's the point where I have the opportunity to change things. I take a few deep breaths and feel myself becoming more relaxed and present and remind myself about what's really important here.
- At this point the adrenaline and all the other crazy neurochemicals coursing around my brain begin to settle down. The urgency that I was feeling begins to dissipate and I remind myself that I have a choice as to how I respond to this situation.
- The new story I come up with enables me to move out of the stressful narrative I was caught up in and into a more productive place where I have an expanded set of choices. For example, in that hospital setting, as a nurse was struggling to insert my daughter's IV and I was watching Erin crying hysterically, I could have lashed out at the nurse and grumbled to myself and anyone who would have listened about how incompetent she was or I could have simply asked how I could help. Which do you think would work better for everyone concerned?

- Having left fight-or-flight mode, I'll often acknowledge the negative emotions I'm experiencing and recognize their futility. I can now choose the mood I want to adopt.

This doesn't mean it's always easy or that I automatically shift into a productive mood. I've been practicing this for a long time and sometimes I'll even choose to remain grumpy or angry for a period of time! The important thing to note is that I'm in a place where I'm aware of what's going on in and around me and the neurochemicals aren't controlling my reactions, I am.

WRIGHT

You have something you call the "Five-Step Approach" to mood management. What are the steps?

TEMPLER

I first put the five steps into effect during our time in the hospital with Erin. I knew it was extremely important for me to effectively manage my mood as that, more than anything, would open or close possibilities for me and for the people I loved. I also knew that I had to influence the moods of the others around us. Unproductive moods are toxic and contagious and during those trying times, I needed everyone who came into contact with us to be on their A Game. I was determined not to let anyone contaminate me or my family.

This is what helped me and what I recommend to others:

1. Center yourself. Other people's moods and emotions can trigger yours. If you lose your center and get caught up in an unproductive mood, you'll also lose the opportunity to make a difference.
2. Remember that you can't really afford to be in an unproductive mood, in a high-pressure situation, as it probably won't take you where you want to go.
3. Given that moods are often contagious, ask yourself, "What mood am I evoking in others? Do people want to play with me? Is the way I'm showing up, opening or closing possibilities?"

4. Ask yourself if the story you're caught up in is taking you where you want to go.
    a. If it is, great! (Reminder: Ensure that there is some substance to your story. Naively telling yourself that "these things always seem to work themselves out and everything is going to be okay" may or may not work so well for you in the long run.)
    b. If it isn't, find a story that will. Remember, you don't have to get it 100 percent right—the future is and always will be unknown. Useful questions to ask yourself as you put together your new narrative include:
        i. Why am I caught up in my current story? (Usual suspects include, heroic suffering, feeling out of my depth, feeling superior, needing to be right and someone/something else to be wrong, covering my backside.)
        ii. What are the facts?
        iii. Just how much drama am I adding to the situation, and how's that working for me?
5. Now that you've removed the drama and can clearly just look at the facts, adjust the story you've been telling yourself accordingly and begin moving forward.

Wright

This is easy enough to understand and it makes sense. That said, it seems to me that during stressful situations, there is a big difference between knowing what to do and being able to do it.

Templer

There sure is, and therein lies the difference between understanding and learning. The mind understands and the body learns. When I get caught up in an unproductive mood, understanding what is going on and what to do about it isn't enough. Being able to take action, shift my mood, and influence the mood of others is what's really important.

Before I can utilize the Five-Step Approach, I first need to be able to catch myself getting stressed and knocked off center so that I don't get caught up for too long in an unproductive mood. I need to be able to bring my attention to what is going on in and around me.

That's where "Attention Training" comes in. Through regular, rigorous practice I've been able to:

- Build my capacity to catch myself before I get too caught up in the drama that I'm creating,
- Develop my capacity to be calmer and in turn more present, open, and connected.

Attention training is the most important component of this—it builds the muscles you're going to need when you're in a critical situation and there's real heavy lifting to be done.

But for the record, it helps when you're stuck in traffic, too.

Wright

Let's talk more about this concept of attention training. What do we need to do?

Templer

Well first of all, you need to practice, practice, practice and then practice some more. I do this at least five days per week, for a minimum of four minutes per day. I usually do it first thing in the morning. Here's the routine that works best for me:

- Find somewhere where you can sit quietly and comfortably, feet squarely planted on the ground, back straight, neck comfortably supporting your head. Close your eyes.
- Pay close attention to your breathing. Take four deep breaths, each breath a little deeper than the last.
- Bring your attention to the top of your head and then behind your eyes, to your jaw and to your teeth. Check to see if your tongue is pasted to the roof of your mouth. Relax your neck, rolling your head once to the right and then once to the left. Transfer your attention to your shoulders, arms, and hands. Feel the

air between your fingers and then take your attention back up to your arms and shoulders, making sure that they're completely relaxed. Connect with your heartbeat. Go down your back, bottom, thighs, knees, calves, ankles, and feet. Wiggle your toes around and then briefly press your feet down into the ground to engage your thighs before releasing them.

- Return your attention to your breath. Take four more deep breaths, each breath a little deeper than the last
- After four minutes (yes, you can set an alarm), listen to your body and it will tell you when it's time to stand up (I know that sounds crazy, but once you try it, you'll understand it completely.) Then just get on with your day.

The breathing aspect is most important, especially when feeling for the air between your fingers and connecting with your heartbeat. If your attention strays, acknowledge it, and then bring it back to your body and your breath. If you catch yourself getting annoyed or impatient, ask yourself, "How's that working for ya?" and then get out of your own way and continue with the practice.

If you skip your practice for a day (or a few), don't beat yourself up for it. Instead, take the opportunity to evaluate the difference in how your day unfolded when you didn't start it with attention training. For the first two months of performing this practice, it may be useful to make brief notes about your discoveries.

Within a month you'll notice an amazing difference in the way you see and react to the world.

Wright

Anything else we need to keep in mind?

Templer

Yes, I think it's important to recognize that managing our mood is obviously not going to change a lot of the events we experience. There are still going to be traffic jams, cranky co-workers, colleagues who miss critical deadlines, and loved ones who will still, unfortunately, become ill. What it can change is how we experience those moments when life doesn't go the way we'd like it to, and that's what it's all about. If we can manage our moods, everything in life just becomes a little simpler.

Paul Templer began his career in Africa, guiding tourists through the dangerous waters of the Zambezi River, until "a bad day at the office"—a deadly hippo attack—forced him to rebuild his life and career.

Today, Mr. Templer is the Chief Executive Officer of Templer Consulting, a global consulting practice that specializes in leadership development, conflict resolution, and guiding organizations so that they can better navigate the turbulent waters of the ever-changing business world. He is also a sought-after keynote speaker, inspiring audiences from all walks of life on how to create the lives they want—one decision at a time.

A dedicated husband and father, Mr. Templer and his family live in Michigan where they have established the Templer Foundation, a non-profit organization dedicated to supporting disabled and terminally ill children.

Paul Templer

www.paultempler.com
www.templerconsulting.com
www.templerfoundation.org
paul@paultempler.com

CHAPTER SIX

ROAD MAP FOR YOUR JOURNEY

BY AL DAMPIER

DAVID WRIGHT (WRIGHT)

Today we're talking with Al Dampier who is the Chief Executive Officer of Dampier Your HR Partner. Career strategist and workplace authority, Al is an energetic, engaging, and entertaining speaker. Drawing on his more than twenty-five years in HR, talent acquisition, and management consulting, he injects every event he leaves with useful knowledge and workable insights that propel audience members to make positive changes in their career goals. His dynamic personality commands audiences to listen to him and his vast knowledge warrants attention.

Al began his career in the competitive health care industry. In this arena, he honed his management consulting and HR skills crafting unique executive search models developing platforms for workplace excellence and gaining material for his hiring and recruiting seminars. He can share his unique perspectives with your team.

Al, welcome to *Success Simplified.*

AL DAMPIER (DAMPIER)

Thanks, David; happy to be here.

WRIGHT

So I'm interested in your story. Please tell me about your background and how you got to where you are today.

Dampier

Well thanks David, I'm glad to share my story. I'm the oldest of six. I came from humble beginnings like many people but went to college and became a pharmacist, thanks to the great mentoring of my grandfather. Along the way, I entered the corporate world. There I got a lot of training in management and began to progress within the organization. Eventually, I was being asked to relocate around the world for a major corporation and came to a decision point that this wasn't what I wanted to do. I was told, "Well then, you don't have a job anymore." I said, "Thank you; now what?"

I went through a process where I learned that there were other things I was interested in. Eventually, that led me to open an executive search company and an HR company. Now we've grown and have a positive influence on people and companies around the world.

Wright

So let's talk about stories and key moments and how they apply to your roadmap and several things that have to do with your success.

Dampier

Well, David, I think one of the things I've learned in interviewing literally thousands of people is that there are common threads to all stories. While market conditions continue to change, if we listen to our lives we can learn from each other. We go through similar processes and similar challenges. We find that, remarkably, we are resilient, and if we pay attention really closely to our lives along the way we find that there are key answers and opportunities there that can help us choose work that is more meaningful to us.

I'm a big fan of "The Journey," a poem by Mary Oliver. Paraphrased, it says one day you'll finally know what you need to do despite the voices around you shouting bad advice. I think for many people in career transition or in unfulfilling jobs, sometimes they find meaningful work if they're forced, and other times they take or keep a job just because they need a paycheck. But if they can listen to their own lives—if they can identify their passion, their purpose—they will have the ability to find meaningful work and make a greater contribution to society, and therefore be rewarded doing something they enjoy.

Wright

So there are key moments that are common to a lot of the people you interviewed?

Dampier

When I'm interviewing people, one of the things I ask them is to tell their stories. If they begin to talk about their stories, they begin to talk about challenges they've faced along the way. They talk about when times were good and bad. In between those extremes, there are many things that have happened, and if we can find those key moments—whatever they are—it becomes a process of identifying how they faced situations and what they did to turn things around.

In this economy right now we've seen so many stories of tragedy, but we also have seen many stories where people have turned negative circumstances into positive opportunities, where they've risen above the challenges. In every person's story you find those key moments that really become a roadmap for the journey. And everybody's journey is different—unlike anybody else's. Now we can all learn from each other's journeys, and apply those lessons to our own individual passions and roadmaps. As we learn to listen to our own stories and rely on those key moments, we can move forward.

Certainly, it's sometimes helpful to listen to other people around us, to hear how they view us, how they perceive us, and understand how they've seen us make a difference in someone else's life.

Wright

I'm really interested in some of your methods. I know that you "ask better questions." What does that mean?

Dampier

When you want to know something from someone else, what do you do? You ask a question. So often, we're really good at asking other people questions and listening to what they're saying. It's often much harder to ask ourselves questions and listen to that small voice inside of us—that deepest knowing if you will. That little voice inside keeps shouting out, and by asking questions of ourselves, we eventually learn to ask better questions. These questions might be: "What am I going to do today?" or "How do I want to influence others?" or "How do I want to change the world?"

I ask that last question of groups at times. Their response is to say I must be smoking crack to think that merely asking the question and trying to answer it honestly could bring about world-changing ideas or actions. But the truth is, little ideas can make big differences. We can cite numerous examples of people like Mother Teresa or the guys who started Twitter, for example, who did little things but made a big difference. So, there are a lot of different questions that we can ask ourselves about our own personal journeys.

And we can even begin to write down our answers to those questions. As we write those down, we begin to let the subconscious ponder the questions, and it all works together to propel us forward, directing us on our roadmap of where we want to go.

Wright

I would think that everyone reading this book—and almost everyone on Earth—has at some point in time been in some kind of transition, and we know how difficult that is. So what do you say to someone who is career transition?

Dampier

Well, I really resonate with those who are in transition because I went through it myself. The first thing that anyone in career transition wants to do is polish the resume and send it to thousands of people because they want to get a job—immediately. But perhaps that's not the best thing to do. It's really a blessing to be able to sit back, sit down, take stock, take a step back, and first look at the situation. Look at what happened and take a little bit of a breather so that you can think more clearly about where you're headed.

It's important to take the opportunity to look deep inside and identify your passions. Ask yourself if the job you're transitioning from was really meaningful and if it was the type of work you've always wanted to do. Ask if you were able to truly serve your community, your associates, and your friends while in that job. Perhaps there's something from childhood that you've always wanted to do but haven't yet. If you take a moment to take stock and look back, there are numerous examples where you can find a way to have a better path.

I'll give you an example. It wasn't too long ago that my wife and I traveled to Mexico. We got off the plane, so excited to be there. I don't speak Spanish, so I didn't really understand what anyone was saying as we navigated through customs, baggage claim, and on to figure out our shuttle situation. So many people were calling out in their native tongue, offering transportation and deals. If you've been to a foreign country, you can likely picture the scenario. Through all the noise, we remembered our reservation host who instructed us to look for the guy with the red jacket to get to our shuttle that would deliver us to our beautiful resort. The agent explained that we'd have to walk through the crowd to find that guy in the red jacket. So, we heeded his words and headed out into a crazy crowd filled with people calling out in Spanish and flashing cards and names and asking us our names and such. Still, we just looked for that one little red jacket, ignoring all the bedlam around us, knowing that would be the key to get us to our destination.

I think for many people in career transition it's the same way—you're going down a path and all these people are shouting; you hear cacophony around you. However, there is one direction out there that leads to the destination, and if you follow that—if you follow what's really in your heart and what adds meaning to your life—then you've got the roadmap to make it to your final destination.

Wright

So if I were a client of yours and you were helping me through transition, where would you suggest I start with my story?

Dampier

Good question. I like to start with the end—where do we want to go? Staying with the vacation analogy, if we go on vacation, there is a process. We don't just go to the airport and randomly decide to go to Mexico City or London or wherever. Before we ever get to the airport, we know our destination, or if we're driving, we predetermine how we're going to get to our destination.

An author writes a story with the end in mind, knowing how the story will end before chapter one is written. So it should be with our stories. If you can think about where you want to end, then the other parts begin to fill in. You can identify where you've come from, and you can pinpoint those key moments, those times that have been really important in your life along the way—especially life-changing moments.

I think if you talk to any individual about those defining moments, you'll find that it's not just moments of success or failure that are counted as "defining."

And by the way, I really don't believe in failure. That's an entirely different topic; but I'll say that failure is when things just didn't go the way you wanted them to, or that it's just feedback.

Nevertheless, if we begin to look at our struggles and our perseverance in between moments of success and failure, then we're moving in the direction of where we really want to end up.

Sometimes in life, that destination may change as we change. I heard a story of a gentleman who battled addiction issues. After he overcame those struggles through involvement with the YMCA, he made a complete career transition. His priorities shifted, and he made career choices based so that he could be involved with the YMCA and the things that mattered to him along with his walk. Often now you see people who are making changes in their careers and making changes in their lives because they do want to have more meaningful work. They want to make a contribution to society and they want to be a part of something bigger than themselves.

I think that's one of the common threads to all our stories—people do want to make a difference.

Wright

I would think that one of the first things I would think about would be what life skills are important to a successful journey.

Dampier

That's a really important question. Along the way—and it goes back to asking better questions—we have to ask ourselves "what am I really good at?" There are lots of different ways to find that out. We can ask other people for feedback. Also, there is the Myers-Briggs Personality Test, the Birkman Assessment, a Strong Inventory Assessment, and there is the DISC. There are a lot of different tools and assessments where you can get a better insight as to what you're good at, who you are, what types of jobs you excel at, and what you're interests are. If those are all aligned, then certainly you're going to be more successful in your day-to-day tasks.

Wright

So is there a process that you use for creating a roadmap to your client's future?

Dampier

There is a specific process, David, and it really starts with acknowledging that our journey begins today. It starts with taking stock of where we are through a formal assessment or by simply writing some questions and answers down: where do I really want to head, which direction do I really want to go, where do I want to end up, and then what are three or four things that I really want to have happen this year? Other questions could be: what's really most important to me now, what skills do I need in this economy (or the new economy), and how do I achieve my goals?

I ask questions about what quotes give you inspiration. I ask about the role of faith in the journey. I find that faith is a very important part of the journey for most people. Then we talk about traps. We talk about negative thinking. We talk about being human and that we are human and what that really means, how we overcome perseverance, how we talk to ourselves, and we begin to find other behaviors.

We look at common threads, principles, and values—what really gives people energy. I like to find out what they are passionate about—what really energizes them—because their passions uncover the roadmap.

Then I encourage people to really dream big dreams. It discourages me when I see that people are willing to settle at times, so I ask them to dream big dreams and to think big. Jim Collins and Jerry Porras wrote about BHAGs—Big, Hairy Audacious Goals in their book, *Built to Last: Successful Habits of Visionary Companies*. I think there are other books that have talked about dreaming big, but if people can think big, they're more likely to end up with something big or at least get further along.

There are exercises that we go through where I encourage the person in transition to ask the question "what is my true purpose in life?" It might be something that comes to mind really quickly or it might be something that he or she has to write down a few thoughts and then think about for three days or "stay in the question" as I like to say. If we think about that question for a few days or week or a month and continue to answer it then maybe we'll peel the layers back and get to something that's really meaningful. We may have to do that exercise every morning for a few weeks. But if we go through this process we'll begin to follow our hearts, follow our passions, trust our gut, and then we'll move to what I call "job sculpting." Job sculpting is a process by which we can begin to make sure our work really fits who we are and mold our work into being who we are.

I like the quote from Dr. Tony Campolo: "Your past is important because it brought you to where you are, but the way you see your future is far more important than your past." As I work with people, I think that quote is really important because they can learn from their past, but if they're dwelling on their past—and this is true in career transition as well—if they're dwelling on the fact that they just got terminated or their job was eliminated or they've been unemployed for quite a while, then they're missing some of the possibilities and the great opportunities they have to make a difference every day.

Also, I encourage people to find ways to make a difference so that they can more fully appreciate their journey while they're here—in the present. It doesn't take much to be involved in community service, to go see someone who's in greater need than you are, whether it's the Leukemia and Lymphoma Society that I've worked with or the YMCA and some of their ministry programs or St. Jude. There are people who need things that any of us—whether we're employed, not employed, or in a job where we feel stuck—can still give to their communities in many, many ways.

WRIGHT

So what if I don't have everything I need to get started?

Dampier

You start with where you are. You may feel you're missing things you need, but I would argue that you probably do have everything that you need if you'll just look within yourself to find the resources.

Wright

So what role does purpose or passion play in this journey that I'm on?

Dampier

I think passion is essential. The biggest concern for me when I talk to people is to see they've given up, and in doing so, they've allowed other people to guide them. I spoke to a career transition group just recently and could quickly tell which people had lost something inside. They were there, but they were so unsure about why they were there.

You probably know someone who's empty because they're struggling; they've lost that fire in the belly or that passion or their purpose. I encourage those people who are really struggling like that to take a step back, do some of these exercises, and focus on themselves and what really makes them happy and energizes them. Then they can at least get some momentum, purpose, and passion back. To me, this is really the key to a successful career.

Wright

One of the things I've noticed with my staff is its very difficult, especially in these challenging times, to keep them motivated. So how do I stay on this journey; how do I stay motivated?

Dampier

Many people have seen the little cartoon that has been circulated in which the big bird has the frog in its mouth and the frog has its feet and arms and legs wrapped around the bird's beak, struggling for his dear life. The caption reads, "Never, never, ever give up." I think the key is that we get the chance to live each day, and we can choose to live it. If we want to give up, we can. If we want to look for little opportunities to make steps and crawl and move forward, we do.

I think in this type of economy—since we've been going through it for more than a year now—I'm seeing more and more that people are willing to scratch and claw and crawl to continue to move forward. And as they've done that, they've found that the ability to persevere individually as well as a society is much stronger than perhaps it's been since the 1800s or the Great Depression.

WRIGHT

So how often should I check on my goals and check in on me?

DAMPIER

That depends on the individual. Certainly sit down annually and review them. I believe that the people who are the most successful are the ones who have a clear direction, and a clear path. They know where they're headed and they review their goals daily, weekly, monthly.

Just this very morning I sat down and did a check-up on my goals, and they shifted a little bit. I think we have to constantly keep our goals in front of us, and there are lots of ways to do that. There's journaling. I've seen people take stick-it notes and put them on their mirrors in their bathroom. Even if it's something as simple as eating healthy or ten minutes of exercise in the morning, moving toward something is better than not moving at all. So the more frequently we review our goals the better—though it's different for each individual.

WRIGHT

What if I'm doing everything I think I should be doing, but nothing seems to be working?

DAMPIER

That's when we need to take a step back and ask better questions. If we're doing everything—networking, shaking hands, and we're on purpose, passionate about what we're doing—then we have to go back and ask key questions. Is my model right, am I really selling to the right people, am I talking to the right people, am I sending the right message, what am I communicating to other individuals out there?

WRIGHT

I'm always interested in folks who are going through a goal-setting process, and how difficult it can be for some people. Where do I find support for my goals?

DAMPIER

Support comes in many different forms. One of the things I encourage people to do in my seminars is to assess your friends and acquaintances. Often challenging times reveal that those we thought were friends are really just acquaintances who won't provide support during challenging times.

When you're in challenging times, it's best and most important to take stock in who your true friends are, to know those people who give to us. We want to surround ourselves with people who nurture us and who also contribute to us while we can contribute to them, avoiding the people who just drain things from us. In that circle of support, there may be friends, family members, fellow church members, or others in career transition. You may connect with them through an association, a group such as a career transition group, or in a think-tank.

I'm personally involved in a think-tank of peers, for example. Peers give you sincere, direct advice. Yes, sometimes direct advice hurts, but if it's done in a caring way, those people can be supportive and nurturing. Eliminate the suckers; we've got to get those people who are negative or who are taking energy away from us out of our lives to find the support we need to find our goals.

WRIGHT

With all social media happening in our world today, I've always believed in networking, but now it's really out there. How important is a network?

DAMPIER

Well, a network is really important, and with social media, it's very easy for people to find information about us through Google, Facebook, Twitter, and other Internet sites. We have to be conscious of the messages that we're sending out there, since everything's there for all the world to see.

Our networking can actually occur in different circles. I like to think of it as a bow and arrow pointing toward a target. If we're looking down twenty yards away at the target, we'll see several different rings. There is an outer circle, a middle circle, an inner circle, and then there is a core center of the target.

So I think our network can really be described in the same way. There is core group of people who really have a major influence on our lives. I believe mentoring is a big part of being successful—especially for college people. You can integrate a variety of people into that core network. From there, you can begin to expand, to work by referral, and find people who are like-minded, who share some of the concerns, experiences, and values. Mentors can help you expand your circles and help you find success in your journey.

Let me also point out while I'm saying this, that everyone's values are really different; everyone's roadmap, their journey, and their values are different. I believe inherently that we all want to do good, but we don't all get along. This is one of the things that makes us unique as a population. So, as we're looking at our target and our network and our core network, we want to find people who are like-minded, who think similarly, and who share common values with us. Of course, it's also important to have diversity and to be able to have someone in your network who doesn't share your opinion because we learn just as much from people who don't share the same direct values and beliefs.

With social media, we have better access to people who believe totally opposite from the way we do. I think that's one of the things that balances us as a society—having different viewpoints and diversity of thought. In corporate settings, these differing viewpoints and diversity of thought make the team stronger. Imagine how it would affect your own personal network.

Wright

So how will I know when I get there—when I've arrived?

Dampier

I believe that each day we've arrived in our journey; our journey is really what makes us successful. Part of being happy with the result is knowing that we're working to get there along the way. Look at the

Olympians who have won medals. Their successes of winning medals are just fleeting moments, but all of the work that they've put into getting those medals is a great effort and part of their roadmap. Yet, not everyone won a medal, and while some might say that those who didn't win medals weren't successful, I would argue that their success was in getting there. All of us need to be mindful that our model of success is actually in the journey, not just winning the gold medal. Although the gold medal is important, we'll have to define that differently for each one of us.

WRIGHT

So why am I doing what I am doing and how do I anticipate it will end or turn out?

DAMPIER

Each individual has to ask himself or herself that question: why do I do what I do? I think that's where it starts with our roadmaps—defining what is the common thread to our stories and figuring out what motivates us to get out of bed and do something.

If we begin to look at that question and look at where we're headed, we can anticipate our needs and what the world needs. So we get out of bed to do something in the morning, and to me that's how we know what we're doing—or why we're doing what we're doing—and how we anticipate it's going to end or turn out. It goes back to our goals and our purpose and our passion. We get out of bed for something and we get to choose today what we want to do about it.

WRIGHT

As I've traveled through this process, how can I ascertain whether or not I'm on the right path?

DAMPIER

We know we're on the right path when no twists, turns, or barricades in the road alter the destination in our sights.

I like "windshield time." If I really have something I need to accomplish, then the best thing to do is get in the car, turn the cell phone off, turn the radio off, and just go down the road. Sometimes I have a destination, other times it's just about driving. With my GPS, as long as I put in an end point, I can make all the unexpected, wrong turns, and take all the back roads I want, but the system will always recalculate to keep me en route to the destination.

That's how it is on our roadmaps, our journeys. All the details of the trip may change, but our direction is still going to be recalculated if we really know where we're headed. With a clear destination as our guide, then we have the ability to adjust our course along the way.

WRIGHT

So do you think everybody defines success basically the same way?

DAMPIER

For a long time we've defined success by the gold medal—just winning. It's interesting that sometimes in youth soccer there is no score count; it's about playing the game. In the Olympics it's not just about playing the game, it's about winning the medal. In business we keep score by our finances. Now, perhaps there are new models of success, using your gifts to make the most of what you have. (I read that somewhere—I can't remember exactly who I'm quoting when I say that, so my apologies to the author of that statement, it's not mine.) How do we make the most of what we have, when we don't all have the same opportunity? I wasn't born to be an Olympic athlete, as much as I would want to be an Olympic athlete; that's just not in my journey. Yet, we all have a contribution we could make in our society, in our own unique ways.

WRIGHT

Well, this has been an interesting conversation. Transition is getting more and more difficult and more and more important in our culture. I really appreciate all the time you've spent with me to answer these questions and to really delve into some ways to answer this.

DAMPIER

Thank you, David. It's been a pleasure being with you.

WRIGHT

Today we've been talking with Al Dampier. Al is a speaker, trainer, consultant, and author. He is the Chief Executive Officer of Dampier Your HR Partner. Al injects every event that he leads, whether it be a workshop or a keynote, with useful knowledge and workable insights that propel his audiences to make positive changes in their career goals and thus in their life.

Al, thank you so much for being with us today on *Success Simplified.*

DAMPIER

Thanks, David; it's been a pleasure being with you.

ABOUT THE AUTHOR

Al Dampier is a nationally recognized leader in the healthcare industry where he has more than twenty-five years' experience with accomplishments in Pharmacy, Management, Disease, and Information Management Consulting and Human Resources.

Al founded Dampier in 1998 where he developed model programs in executive search, and conducts seminars in "Hiring the Best" and "Recruiting in the Talent War."

Dampier Payroll Solutions, launched by Al, is a professional employer organization (PEO) establishing an employment relationship with all employees, including owner(s) of the business. This turns a traditional two-party relationship into a three-party relationship and transfers the employment administration to the PEO. Services include benefits administration, payroll and tax compliance, risk management, and health and business insurance, among other services.

Al remains active in the Academy of Managed Care Pharmacy, Society of Human Resources Management, Leukemia and Lymphoma Society, Big Brothers/Big Sisters, and is a member of the board of directors of YMCA. Al was nominated for "Man of the Year" by the Leukemia and Lymphoma Society and received a Public Service Achievement Award for his work in creating a Drug Abuse Awareness Program.

Al's experience in the pharmaceutical industry, management, and human resources areas, coupled with his keen insight into the hiring process, position him as a leader in Talent Acquisition.

Al Dampier

Dampier, Your HR Partner

615-370-2977

1616 Westgate Circle, Suite 221

Brentwood, TN 37027

Chapter Seven

Your Amazing Balancing Act

By Susan Ann Koenig, JD

David Wright (Wright)

Today we're talking with Susan Ann Koenig. Susan is an executive coach and speaker who inspires and empowers successful people to move to the next level. She coaches executives, professionals, and leaders to develop skills to make their greatest contribution. She has coached CEOs and leadership teams in health care, insurance, finance, and law. With more than twenty-five years of balancing life as a lawyer, mother, and writer, Susan shares unique insights into the meaning of a successful life and powerful tools to create that life for yourself.

Susan Koenig, welcome to *Success Simplified.*

Susan Ann Koenig (Koenig)

Thank you David; I'm delighted to be here.

Wright

So is a balanced life really possible for a successful person?

Koenig

Well, David, it might be useful to look at what we mean when we say "balanced" and "successful." You know that perfect balance only exists for a split second and then we slide back out of it. So we're not going to be in that balanced place all the time. However, having a balanced life is not only possible but truly successful people find that it's essential for sustained success.

Successful people are those who focus on what's most important to them, live their lives in keeping with their values, and enjoy life along the way.

So the most important question I think is, "What is success for you?" Is it building a million dollar business, traveling abroad each year, having time with your family, or having your book published?

When we fail to look at all of the aspects that make up a successful life, we risk waking up one morning to find our wellness in decline, our relationships in shambles, and an uncertainty about the meaning of our lives. When we attend to all aspects of our success, we soon discover that intentions for our career are met with greater ease. Successful people realize that physical vitality increases mental clarity and focus, which make their professional success greater. We know that our relationships are key to supporting our professional aspirations. So balance is possible, but first you have to look at what success is for you and what balance means for you.

Wright

So what is "driven behavior"?

Koenig

Driven behavior occurs when fear drives us into nonstop action. Rather than taking time to enjoy and celebrate our successes, we push through to the next action without pausing. We might ignore our relationships, our health, and our enjoyment. Instead, our workaholic tendencies drive our decisions.

People who engage in driven behavior often rack up high levels of achievement, but at the end of the day they're asking, "Is this all there is?" They become prone to burnout and often question the meaning of all their hard work. Successful people, David, often push themselves hard. When they continue to do this with a sense of fear that something horrible is going to happen if they stop, they can have many accomplishments, but notice the joy is missing.

My client, "Madeline," a successful businesswoman, had a painful experience due to driven behavior. It was the night before her wedding. She and her husband planned to combine households after they got married. Madeline wanted to get her house on the market before they left for their honeymoon. The night before the wedding, Madeline stayed up until three in the morning to replace the grout in her kitchen tile so her house would be perfect for sale. She was so exhausted the next day that she wasn't able to fully experience the joy of her own wedding; she had lost sight of what was most important.

Explore whether or not you might be engaging in driven behavior by answering "True" or "False" to the following:

Others avoid me when I'm stressed while working.

I'm exhausted much of the time.

I work seven or more days in a row without taking a day off.

I haven't had a vacation in two or more years.

My relationships have suffered in the last year because of my work.

I miss out on enjoying activities or events because I'm so tired.

When I'm with my loved ones, my mind is often preoccupied with work. I don't know what it's like to take a weekend off without working or thinking about work.

I regularly break promises about when I'll be home from work.

I feel resentful of others who have time to have fun and do what they really want to do.

I don't schedule medical appointments that I know I need because my calendar is so full.

I don't take time to think about what's important to me in my life.

I sometimes forget to eat because I'm so busy.

I sleep less than 6 hours a night.

I don't have time to exercise because I'm working such long hours.

My family and friends complain about my work or my work hours.

I'm afraid of what will happen if I don't go to work when I'm sick.

I drink too much or use drugs to help me relax from the pressures of my work.

I break promises to clients because I take on more work than I complete.

I don't use resources I've invested in for my leisure or my enjoyment like a vacation home, a boat, or tickets to events because I have to work.

I race to take care of the next urgent matter.

I seldom having time to be proactive.

I strive to have my work be perfect.

I constantly make one more change that I think will make it just right.

If you have five or more "True" responses, you might want to consider whether your driven behavior is getting in the way of having a truly successful life.

WRIGHT

Have you been talking to my wife? I just failed your test.

KOENIG

It's true for so many of us, David. We lose sight. We know the kind of life we want, but we become so fearful of what might happen if we actually slow down to enjoy the journey that we forget to look. So looking is a good place to start and this exercise helps us to do that.

WRIGHT

I'd say it is a great exercise.

Where do we find the time to live a more balanced life?

KOENIG

Well, it's a great question because successful people are often busy people, and the lack of time appears as one of the obstacles to a balanced life. I'd invite you to consider how many ways you can improve the quality of your life by spending little or no additional time. Here are some examples:

Breathe consciously. Breathe deeply during a meeting, in your car, waiting for the elevator.

Begin to notice when you're starting negative self-talk about yourself or others and consciously stop yourself.

Start your day with an intention about how you want your day to unfold. For example, "Today will be rich with opportunities for learning" or "I have support to face any challenges that come my way today."

You would be amazed at just how making a decision like this at the start of your day can transform your entire workday.

Tackle your hardest task of the day first. This gives you a boost you can enjoy for the entire day. It also eliminates stress that we create when procrastinating on a task and the energy drain that comes from the task being incomplete.

Use your "peak energy" time of day wisely. Identify the time of day when your physical and mental energy is strongest. Plan your schedule to optimize the use of this time of day. Whenever possible, dedicate that portion of your day for tackling your most challenging or complex tasks. Save your easier chores for the time of day when you need a break or a boost.

Make different choices:

- Instead that third glass of wine, have a glass of water with a wedge of lime.
- Rather than dessert have a green tea.
- See others in a new light rather than gathering evidence about how difficult other people are. Focus on noticing their good qualities and their intentions.
- Of course, practice gratitude in every situation. Ask yourself, for what might I be grateful in this circumstance? It might be a new insight, a valuable experience, or a lesson learned.

These are all actions we can take, or better yet, habits we can develop that will improve the quality of our lives without taking any more time. Successful people know how to set goals, they know how to plan, and they know how to reach their goals. If success to you means living a more balanced life, then you want to apply those same principles to spending your time in the activities that enhance your life.

WRIGHT

I think we know that we should eat properly, exercise, and get plenty of sleep but how do we sustain this lifestyle?

KOENIG

It's so true, David—knowledge and implementation are not the same. In today' s world, we get a constant stream of information about the benefits of good nutrition, adequate sleep, regular exercise, and avoiding excess alcohol.

We know so much about our bodies and what they need. Yet even armed with this knowledge, maintaining the lifestyle is challenging for people who have morning to night commitments to work, the community, and the family. So, what's a person do?

One strategy is to develop healthier lifestyle habits one at a time. Rather than proclaiming on New Year's Day that you're renouncing a lifetime of bad habits, focus on just one habit. It may be to eat one green vegetable a day or to take two twenty-minute walks a week. Once you have that one habit mastered, tackle the next habit while sustaining the first. Start small and build.

With each one of these successive changes in your habits you'll develop increasing confidence to take the next small change. So, as your confidence increases you're more likely to take on bigger challenges each time.

Set inspiring goals to focus your attention, just as you would any other area of your life. There is nothing like SMART goals. SMART is an acronym for Specific, Measurable, Attainable, Relevant, Time-based goals to focus our attention. When we have a date to complete a promise, suddenly we pay closer attention.

You want to be sure that your goal is something that you would be absolutely delighted to reach and this is why. Getting up at 5 AM on a dark winter morning when it's twenty degrees outside to run three miles is not inspiring. Having a vision of what it will be like when you reach your goal to cross the finish line of a race will light you up. So have a goal that inspires you, because it will prevent your excuses from being more appealing than the inspiration of your goal being reached.

I'll include some examples of SMART goals I use that might inspire healthy habits, healthy actions:

I bike the Wisconsin Trail with my partner by November 15
I hike the River Canyon at sunrise by June 1
I run a 5K race by September 30

Be sure to consider what type of support will be useful to you on this journey to a healthier lifestyle. Support can be big or small. You might hire a fitness or wellness coach. It could be something as simple as asking your children to help with menu planning, teaming up with a coworker to walk with you during your breaks, joining an online support group, or registering for a yoga class with a friend. Support is vital, especially when you're making change.

Healthy lifestyle habits not only increase our effectiveness in reaching our goals, but they increase the probability that our work will not be interrupted by health problems brought on by the kind of chronic neglect of our bodies and sprit that happen when we're engaging in driven behavior.

WRIGHT

Speaking on behalf of our readers, what if people have lost sight of what brings them joy?

KOENIG

This is a sad experience that happens for many of us at some point in our life. Sometimes it's been so long since we've allowed ourselves to do that which fulfills our soul that we can't even remember what it is.

You might want to look at different areas of your life such as creativity, spirituality, or play. Recall the past times of your life when you felt happiest and ask yourself, "Did I once engage in a creative pursuit that I've long abandoned?" It might be painting or playing a musical instrument. "How do I feel when I spend time in nature whether it's near water, the woods or even a local park?" "Have I been longing to return to a spiritual community or do I find peace in prayer and meditation?"

If nothing is coming immediately to mind, you might try visualization. This can help you see what the brain can't picture. Try this exercise:

Close your eyes and relax. Take a few deep breaths. Imagine that you have no worries about time, money, or responsibilities. Picture having a carefree life where you are free to be and do anything. Where would you be? What would you be doing? How would you be dressed? Who would be around you? What would the sights, smells, and sounds be? Notice how you are feeling in this moment. Just allow your imagination to take flight. Allow yourself to be with your feelings for a few moments. When you're complete, take time to write down what you envisioned. What did you see? What has your heart been longing to unfold in your life?

You might not be the rock star you imagined in your visualization, but it might be time to take those guitar lessons you've talked about for years. While traveling around the world might not be in your budget, you could be inspired to set a goal for a trip out of the country.

It's not unusual to forget what brings us joy, but by focusing our attention on a possibility we can discover it again.

Wright

What is a "stop doing" list?

Koenig

Successful people are often surprised to hear an executive coach who talks about reaching goals, encourage the creation of a "stop doing" list. But, David, it's really a powerful gateway for people who are contributing in many directions yet are having difficulty finding the energy to devote to something that is very important to them.

Creating a "stop doing" list supports us to live our lives more intentionally. It works like this. Make a list of all the areas of your life where you're in service. Include your volunteer and social activities. For each item ask yourself, "Is this really the place of my greatest contribution at this time?" It may be uncomfortable to look at this because when you started these activities into your life, it was because they held meaning for you and perhaps they still do. They might also be enjoyable. But when we notice that there are more important things we're neglecting, it can be useful to survey all of the areas of our life to begin to ask, "Is this something I am willing to consider letting go of?"

I learned this lesson when I was in coach training. A month had gone by and I had failed to take any action to get new coaching clients. My coach asked me what I'd been doing for the last month. Of course, I had my litany of the boards I served on, my church, work, the book I was writing, and my teaching at the law school. I went on and on.

When I finished telling the tale of my overworked life, my coach asked me, "How important is it to you to become a masterful coach?"

I pled, "Oh, Coach, it means the world to me!"

In that moment I was faced with the truth. Although the causes I was involved in were meaningful, and even enjoyable, I couldn't continue to add more to my life without letting something go.

Successful people often take on new and greater responsibilities without ever pausing to examine whether it is also the time to stop doing something. Whether or not we can do it all, we need not do it all at the same time or forever.

We may not want to give up something that has been a meaningful part of our life, but it can be useful to ask the question, "Am I willing to give it up for the sake of making a greater contribution?" Just like getting out of a warm bed some mornings, we have this thought that we don't want to, but we're willing to because there is something more important to do than lay in bed. We may not want to have that difficult conversation with someone, but we're willing to do it because we know it's the right thing to do. So it is with our "stop doing" list. A "stop doing" list can be a powerful tool to move us to the next level.

Wright

How can we learn to say no when we're constantly being asked to help in areas that we really care about?

Koenig

This is real challenge for successful people because we get things done and people often seek us out when there's an important project.

A good place to start is to become very clear about your intentions for your life:

- Where are the areas that I'm going to be of service?
- What are the organizations I'm going to give my time or my money to?

- What is most important to me at this time of my life, at this season of my life?

If something doesn't fall into one of those intentions, we want to be prepared to say no. We can be clear that, while it may be a worthy cause, it's not our calling at this time.

So, first, we become clear about what is most important to us. Then learning to say no is a skill like any other—we learn it through practice and we must start small. It may be as simple as saying no to someone who wants us to go out for drinks on Friday after work when we know it's really more important for us to be home with our family, or saying no to someone who wants to schedule a meeting during our lunch hour when we know we really need to take our break at that time. Start small and practice.

Now, this is difficult for people who have made a big difference in the world by being willing to say yes. For those with a big heart and strong energy, saying yes can become a habit. But over time the ways in which we are called to contribute change. Practice saying "no" so that you have the ability to say yes to what matters most.

Anticipate how you're going to respond in these situations. Ask for more time to give a response. Offer to do something less. Thank the people who invited you, acknowledge them and their cause for making a difference.

My client, John, is highly successful "rags-to-riches" CEO who discovered the value of saying no. He's extraordinarily generous and kind-hearted, so people came to him from morning to night asking for loans and charitable contributions. His in-boxes were constantly overflowing with pleas.

Although John had had what many of us would call a very successful life of building a nationwide business, he saw that much of his energy was going to dealing with these requests. It was simply because he had not mastered the skill of getting clear on what was most important and learning how to say no.

Through our coaching, John identified a handful of boards that he wanted to serve on, and a small number of charitable organizations he valued. He began practicing saying no and letting in support to have other people help him manage these requests. Quickly, he began to feel great about his gift-giving rather than burdened and incessantly drained. John learned to focus on what was most important to him and to say no to the rest. He found himself enjoying the ability to give more than ever.

WRIGHT

Why and how do we ask for what we want?

KOENIG

Have you ever had a time in your life when you're complaining a lot more than you should be? It might be about your coworkers or the difficulty in getting new business or how you've been feeling lately. Well, complaints can actually be helpful indicators that we have some unmet needs.

When we examine our complaints closely, we might notice that there is something we want that we've not asked for. For example, if we bemoan that we're constantly tired, we may need a checkup or more sleep. If we complain that we don't have time for ourselves, we may need just a small amount of time each day for our personal restoration. If we grumble that we never have fun anymore, we may need to go to the movies or play a game with our family.

So, rather than continuing to blame our circumstances, it can be useful to get clear on our needs. Once we've identified them, we can take an action or get the support we need. Sometimes it's as simple as merely asking.

My law partner, Angela, taught me the value of asking for what you want. She's claimed that working at the law firm was an ideal situation. She felt fully supported to have a great quality of life. The truth is, she got what she needed because she was willing to ask for it. If Angela had waited for me to notice what she needed to have a great workplace, I might not have. Because she had the clarity about the kind of life she desired and the courage to ask for what she wanted, she created a life she loved.

There may be risks in asking, but there are rarely regrets. In most cases, the worst case scenario is that you'll end up exactly where you are. How often have we missed opportunities to have more of the life we really want because we simply failed to ask for what we needed or wanted? Asking for what we want is a powerful skill for reaching a more balanced life.

WRIGHT

Why are rest, rejuvenation, and celebration so important?

KOENIG

Well, David, each one of these can transform the experience of a person who is committed to having a life of sustained contribution. Let's just start with rest. Rest enables us to pause and reflect. It's a chance to recharge our physical, spiritual, and our emotional selves.

Successful people often feel uncomfortable "doing nothing." But the truth is that relaxation is an important action. When our mind is quieted and we're allowed to relax, the right side of our brain is activated. Our creativity flows more freely and we begin to open to our intuition for problem-solving and decision-making. This is why many people say that their greatest ideas come to them in the shower or while out jogging. It's because they're not working that left side of their brain, they're relaxing it, and allowing the other part of their brain to come alive.

Rejuvenation. Now, this is not the same for everyone. If you're an introvert, your rejuvenation might be a quiet afternoon on the sofa with your favorite book or journaling about the past week. For an extrovert, it might look like going to a party at a friend's or attending a conference. I get my energy from being in a group of people. So notice the difference. Rest is the more calming, less activity, and thus restorative. Rejuvenation is dependent on whatever increases your energy.

Then celebration. Surprisingly, this is something that is often overlooked by high achievers. Successful people have lots to celebrate. Yet often we've barely finished one project before we're on to the next. I don't suppose this ever happens to you with book projects, does it?

Without taking time to celebrate our successes, we can lose sight of the reason for all of our hard work and discipline. Celebrations not only punctuate the big and small highlights of our lives, they also enable us to experience the joy of the moment and to share our happiness with others.

So rest, rejuvenation, and celebration each enable us to enjoy the journey rather than land at our destination merely with relief and exhaustion.

Wright

Why do you emphasize letting in support?

Koenig

Well, if there was only one piece of advice that I could give to successful people on their journey it would be this: master the skill of letting in support. Support, David, can take a lot of different forms. Whether it's at the workplace or at home, I promise you that letting in support is essential to free you up to make your greatest contribution. The bigger the thing you're up to, the more support you need.

I recommend that you look for support from the outset rather than do what I used to do. I would wait until I was in a crisis at a critical point in a project, and then beg people to bail me out. It's much easier for others to support us when we include them from the beginning. It makes the entire effort easier. The support of others enables us to solve problems and overcome our obstacles with greater ease because everybody brings their gifts and talents.

When successful people are invited to look at letting in support, their minds might begin to resist with thoughts like:

> People will think I'm lazy, stupid, or incompetent.
> Other people are too busy.
> I volunteered for this task so it's my problem.
> If someone else helps me they'll get the credit.

When these thoughts come up, we really want to ask ourselves: Is this we want to focus on or are we willing to focus on making the difference that we're here to make?

We also forget what it means to others to be able to support us. When my husband was very ill, my friends stocked our freezer with homemade soup to make our lives easier. I had thoughts like: "Oh I'm able to do this myself," and "I can do this, I don't need anyone's help."

I saw how much it meant to my friends to perform this kind act. Their hearts were filled because they were making a difference in our lives. When we think about the times when we've supported other people, haven't we felt great? Weren't our hearts opened? We love to help others. This is the very same feeling that people have if we let them support us. We shouldn't deprive them of that opportunity.

Every year my family hosts a fundraiser in memory of my brother, Tim, who died of AIDS. In the past I prepared all the food myself. One year I decided, "Okay, I'm really learning this principle of letting in support. I'm going to ask Mom to help." I had never asked my elderly mother to help, rationalizing that she wasn't that great of a cook.

Seeing my mother's pride in having washed and chopped vegetables, you would have thought that she had been the guest of honor at this gala. "Thank you so much for letting me help you," she said. "It meant so much to me." I realized that for all these years I had denied her of the opportunity to support me and honor her son. I saw in that moment that I never again wanted to deprive people of supporting me when there was an opportunity.

There are certain times when support is particularly useful:

> You're doing something that you've never done before.
> You've a major life change.
> You're ready to move to the next level.
> You feel you're lost and you don't know where to begin.
> You have a big dream, but you're not sure how to fulfill it.

Support isn't simply delegating, although that's one good method. Support can include sending an e-mail asking someone to follow up with you. It could be partnering with a friend to get the job done. It might be picking up the phone to ask for a piece of information. Of course, working with a professional coach is an excellent means of letting in support to help you reach your goals and to move one step closer to that successful life you're creating.

WRIGHT

Considering all the information you have given us already, why do you recommend starting small?

Koenig

Especially for successful people who are tempted to make everything really big, I urge starting small. When we're learning a new habit, whether it's keeping a clean desk or getting to bed early, we are often tempted to make our promises too large. When we don't do what we planned, we feel as if we've failed because we haven't been able to fulfill that big promise. Then, we give up.

Our brains react with more fight-and-flight responses to big changes. When those changes are smaller, our emotional response is not as strong. That's why our minds have less resistance to the thought of writing one paragraph of our book than to writing the entire chapter. When we start small, we can build on our success and be encouraged to take the next small action. We might feel enthusiastic and want to promise the moon. Instead, we should consider being willing to start small so that our success can be sustained and grow over time.

Wright

Will you summarize for our readers the keys to simplifying a more balanced life?

Koenig

The keys that I've found useful in my life begin with getting clear on what is most important to this time. Focus on it, and constantly revisit those intentions and those values. Assess where you are and decide where you want to go—what are the areas that you want to see growth or change? Set SMART goals and identify the skills you want to develop. Create your action plan, put it in writing, and review it each week. Stop doing those activities that are not your greatest contribution and start asking for what you want.

Remember to pause for rest, rejuvenation, and celebration. Start small, let in support, support, support! I cannot emphasize that enough. Finally, practice gratitude. Whether it's through reflection, thanking others, or keeping a simple gratitude journal, develop the habit of exercising gratitude as a part of your daily life.

WRIGHT

Well, what a powerful chapter this is going to be. You've really given people a lot of information and a lot of great new things to try. I really appreciate all this time you've taken to answer these questions for me.

KOENIG

David, it's been an absolute delight.

WRIGHT

Today we've been talking with Susan Ann Koenig**.** She is an executive coach and speaker who inspires and empowers successful people to move to the next level. Susan has shared with us today unique insights into the meaning of a successful life, and has given us powerful tools and ideas to create this life for ourselves.

Susan, thank you so much for being with us today on *Success Simplified*.

KOENIG

Thank you, David. The pleasure was all mine.

About the Author

Susan Ann Koenig is a lawyer-turned-executive coach. She has empowered hundreds of executives, professionals, and leaders to make their greatest contribution while achieving extraordinary results. Susan custom designs coaching programs to support teams to move to the next level. She has inspired thousands as a passionate and powerful speaker. Susan is a *summa cum laude* graduate of Drake University. She holds a law degree from Northeastern University School of Law and founded the law firm, Koenig & Tiritilli, PC, LLO, where she remains of counsel. Susan received her coach certification from the Academy for Coaching Excellence and is the recipient of countless awards for her public service. Susan's passion is to bring the skills and tools for a successful life to as many people as possible.

Susan Ann Koenig, JD

Executive Coach

1266 South 13th Street

Omaha, Nebraska 68108-3502

402-346-1132

402-346-0151 fax

susan@coachkoenig.com

www.coachkoenig.com

CHAPTER EIGHT

NO EXCUSES!

BY SIRENA C. MOORE

DAVID WRIGHT (WRIGHT)

Today we're talking with Sirena C. Moore. Sirena is a dynamic young woman on the move. This infectious, high energy speaker, mentor, and entrepreneur has accomplished more than many twice her age. Despite giving birth to twin girls at seventeen years of age, Ms. Moore defied the odds and went on to become an astute, in-demand businesswoman/speaker and leader. In 2002, at the age of twenty-one, Sirena joined forces with her father and her brother to form Elohim Cleaning Contractors Inc. In just a few short years, the company has grown into a full service, multimillion construction cleaning firm.

Sirena, welcome to *Success Simplified.*

SIRENA C. MOORE (MOORE)

Thank you.

WRIGHT

So what inspired you to start Elohim Cleaning Contractors?

MOORE

What I love about our start-up story is that it's not your average story. I didn't work in the cleaning field as professional, cash in my 401(k), sell my home, join with former colleagues, and start a business. Elohim Cleaning Contractors Inc. started with a dream and a prayer.

During my last year of high school, at the age of seventeen, I found out that I was pregnant. Not only was a pregnant, but I was pregnant with *twins!* I realized very quickly that my life was about to change dramatically. My father, Theodore Moore Sr., was employed in the construction industry for most of my life.

During my senior year and immediately after graduation I realized that I needed a *job*. My father and mother encouraged me to apply for an administrative position at the construction site where he worked. While working at that particular project, we found out that there was a final cleaning contractor awarded a six-figure contract to do what my father was already doing for a nominal hourly rate. My father came to me and said, "Sirena, if you can figure out how to start a business, I can do the service and we can have our own business."

That was the epiphany—that was it! Some would say, approaching a seventeen-year-old with that kind of idea sounds pretty crazy, but my parents knew the ambition and the drive that lived inside of me. In fact, at about fourteen years old I had two goals—make a six-figure salary by thirty and be on the cover of *Black Enterprise* magazine. Those were my only two goals.

So, with no college degree and no formal business education, I got on the Internet and started researching. How do you start a business? What's an EIN number? What's a DUNS number? What do these things mean?

Finally, in 2002, with $200 in a business bank account, my father, brother, and I incorporated Elohim Cleaning Contractors Inc., and started as a construction labor supply company offering general labor to general contractors on an as-needed basis. I later enrolled in an evening course at the Women's Business Development Center while my mother cared for the twins.

My office was in my brother's bedroom at the family home. We had no money, no resources, only our faith in Elohim—God the Strong One! My desk was a brown fellowship hall folding table from the basement of the church, topped with the hutch from a broken desk. Everything was makeshift. We had three All-in-One printers because each one did one function—one copied, one printed, one faxed. This is what we started with. So you have no excuses.

Wright

Would you explain to our readers how you encourage other entrepreneurs to view success?

Moore

I encourage other entrepreneurs to view success by first identifying what success is not. Success is certainly not what you drive, it's not what you wear, it's not what you have, and it has absolutely nothing to do with tangible items. Success is simply setting out to do something and accomplishing exactly what you set out to do. I believe that it's vital for entrepreneurs—especially new entrepreneurs—to take the time to celebrate the small successes.

If last year I had a business idea and this year I have a business plan, I have a success to celebrate! My children are fed, they're clothed, they're gorgeous, their needs are met; therefore, I'm successful as a parent. So, I encourage entrepreneurs to really take the time to one identify what success is not and then celebrate the small successes in your life.

Wright

So how did you transition from a nine-to-five corporate job to being an entrepreneur? What was your strategy?

Moore

Transitioning from a nine-to-five corporate job to pursue Elohim full-time was very interesting. When my father approached me with the business idea, we didn't go right into business.

Around 2000 and 2001, I was that young, ambitious person who applied for jobs that I did not qualify for. I had enough faith to believe that all I needed was an interview. I honestly applied for jobs such as director of human resources, sales and marketing manager, and so on. I had no *clue* what these positions were, but after reading the job descriptions I believed that I was right for the job. I ended up getting a job at Morgan Stanley Dean Witter & Company (now Morgan Stanley Smith Barney). I was approached by a headhunter to move to Advest Investments, which was recently bought by Merrill-Lynch. I thought I wanted to be a financial advisor. I thank God that He had other plans for me. I worked as a financial sales assistant and I even took my Series 7 test so that I could get my broker's license.

After working there for a while, I started to realize that I was way too talented and way too creative to sit behind a desk for eight hours each day helping others build their business. In my heart I wanted to enroll in college and pursue a business degree. I was also missing out on my children's lives. I remember gazing out the window of my Center City office wishing that I could take them to the zoo or to the park on those warm summer days. I can also remember commuting to work every day by train in the rain, hail, sleet, and snow with the twins.

I went to my boss who was the top producing financial planner and simply explained to him that I couldn't stay—I really needed to resign. I enjoyed my position at the company, but it was not the right place for me. Instead of giving two weeks' notice, I told him that I was willing to stay and train the new person until he was comfortable. He fully respected my decision to leave and he decided that I would not have to resign. I would be laid off so that I could collect unemployment. My severance pay was extended, and I then enrolled in a couple of college courses.

I was able to meet expenses with my severance pay, unemployment compensation, and financial aid while transitioning into being a full-time entrepreneur. God worked it out.

Wright

So what was your strategy for the growth of your company, at each milestone?

Moore

We've always had an overall approach to facilitate our company growth at every level. That strategy is to purchase only what we can afford, pursue only the projects we want, and always negotiate payment terms.

We started out by supplying general labor on an as-needed basis to contractors. Then, we found ways to not only supply the general labor, but we understood that at the end of the construction project final cleaning was necessary. Final cleaning is more than providing the labor to remove debris. Final cleaning involves estimating and project management. Now, our job includes waxing floors, cleaning interior/exterior windows, and everything required before the facility is turned over to the owners. So, we began to identify areas to incorporate our service in every phase of construction from beginning to end.

Additionally, we recently began a janitorial/facilities maintenance division that allows us to offer ongoing services even after the construction project is complete. We specialize in high-rises, college dorms, Target/Walmart stores, various casinos, hospitals, and other larger commercial projects.

WRIGHT

So how did you manage to grow a multimillion-dollar revenue-generating business without outside financing?

MOORE

It was not our initial strategy to grow without debt; it was just our reality. We could not get a loan! I was twenty-one when the company started and I was the only stockholder. I did not own a home and did I have the type of credit history that the banks needed to guarantee the loan. My father had never financed anything except his home and he lacked an extensive credit history. So, across the board, we did not qualify! However, God doesn't call the qualified, He qualifies the called!

Our inability to obtain financing was not enough to stop us. We realized early that we had to work a lot smarter than most. We did things such as introducing each officer of the company to payroll one year at a time. I worked and held a second job for the first four years of the company, drawing only a few hundred dollars as a salary. My father's home went into preforeclosure before we were able to pay him. We made extreme sacrifices! We never financed equipment; we only purchased what we could afford. If we needed it, we waited until we could afford it so that we could own it—not lease it and not borrow it. As my father would say, "Every nickel, dime, quarter, and penny goes back into the company."

WRIGHT

Is there a particular sector or space where you see opportunity for all entrepreneurs?

MOORE

There is an enormous amount of opportunities that exist within the federal government regarding small business contracting. This has become a whole new division of focus for my company. Success in the federal contracting world can be had if small businesses take the time to learn how the federal procurement data systems work. Unfortunately, there are not a lot of organizations teaching the nuts and bolts of doing business with the federal government from an entrepreneurial perspective. With my second company, SirenaSpeaks LLC (www.SirenaSpeaks.com), I have put together training workshops, webinars, and one-day boot camps to teach entrepreneurs how to add federal contracting as another stream of revenue regardless of industry.

Here are my Top 5 Reasons why small businesses should consider federal contracting:

1. The federal government is the biggest customer in the world, spending billions with small businesses every year. Thirty-nine percent of spending is set aside for small businesses.
2. Most contracts are five years (one year plus four option years).
3. Prompt Pay Act—the government must pay invoices within thirty days.
4. They can't run out of money—they literally make it!
5. Freedom of Information Act (FOIA)—all information on previous awards becomes public information! This makes research easy.

Federal contracting for small business is like coupon-clipping—there are people in this world who have managed to save hundreds of thousands of dollars by clipping grocery coupons yet, there's a whole world of people who have no idea how it's done.

WRIGHT

So how important is time management for entrepreneurs?

Moore

Time management is the key to success. We are all given the same twenty-four hours and it's all about how you use them. Most small business owners have a family, other business ventures, church obligations, community obligations, school obligations, so we have a lot to balance. I encourage folks to first create a list of "Time-wasting Activities." These are activities that can in no way help you reach your goals such as, mindless telephone conversations, viewing friends' pictures on Facebook, watching television for hours at a time, and the list goes on. Once you identify what you waste time doing, you can now consciously avoid those activities.

Here are a few time management techniques that I use. I only accept meetings on Thursdays and Fridays. On these two days I try to schedule as many meetings as possible. I call it Meeting Marathons. So, I don't take meetings in the middle of the day, come back to the office, try to get something done, go back out for another meeting, come back again to answer phones calls, check e-mail, and so on. Those interruptions just slow down productivity. So I commit only certain days to meetings.

Within my office we have instituted something called Productivity Hour. From the hours of eleven to twelve each day there is absolutely no talking. We use that time to focus on the projects that have made it to our to-do list. Allow me to explain: people do not do projects—people do tasks, so it's important that you review your to-do list and remove the projects. For example, *Plan Upcoming Staff Meeting* is *not* a task—it's a project—so I encourage my office staff to set aside that one hour—from eleven to twelve—to focus solely on one project.

Wright

So what time management strategies do you use to get the most out of your work week?

Moore

In addition to scheduling my meetings on designated days, I also assign certain business operations tasks to certain days. For example, if I end my week with meetings, then Monday becomes my Business Development/Follow-up Day. I'll utilize this time to reach out to my clients, answer e-mails, return phone calls, and so on. Tuesdays may be

Financials Day. During this time I'm analyzing job costing, profitability, looking at monthly expenses, reviewing payroll reports, and so on.

Again, get control of your time so that you can be more productive.

Wright

So how do you set the goals or the vision for your company and how do you get buy-in from your employees?

Moore

I set the goals and vision for my company by setting aside time throughout the year to take a step back and work *on* my business and not *in* my business. I'm always feeding myself as an entrepreneur. I'm always reading, listening, researching, and watching. Each year I attend several business conferences. My favorite is a national Entrepreneurs Conference given by *Black Enterprise* magazine. I take that time away to learn and grow from the successes of other experienced business owners.

When I'm ready to introduce a new strategy or growth plan, I'll discuss it with my father, I'll run it pass my mentor, and then I write the vision. After working out the kinks and answering unanswered questions, I'll bring our key personnel together for a presentation.

Buy-in from employees comes easily when your employees have a vital position within the business operations. I've learned how to clearly define roles and responsibilities based on the company's needs while clearly communicating both the short-term and long-term goals of the company.

At Elohim Cleaning Contractors Inc. we operate as a family. We firmly believe that God the Creator, created us so that we can create opportunities for other people.

Wright

So as a young mother, how do you explain to your daughters your super busy schedule?

Moore

My daughters understand my super busy schedule. They know that Mommy works a lot, but I try to get as much accomplished during the day when they're at school so that my work outside of the office doesn't take over the time I have with them. I'm really a believer in the quality of the time that we spend instead of the quantity. To be very honest with you, during the school year they spend more time in school and in sports activities than they spend at home.

I believe that many *"Mompreneurs"* are way too hard on themselves. I tell my children that I work hard now so that we can play really hard later. Soon, retirement by age thirty-five will provide all the time that we need! Also, I involve them in what I do. The twins actually work for my speaking company—they help update the calendar, they come with me to speaking engagements, sometimes they manage the table where my products are being sold. I involve them and it becomes fun.

WRIGHT

So I guess I could go right to the horse's mouth on this one: is there such a thing as work/life balance? You ought to know.

MOORE

No, I don't think so. I honestly am one of those people who doesn't believe in work/life balance. First of all, it's hard to even determine what a work life/balance is because every day, every week is different, depending on what your work or your life consists of. There may be some weeks when the kids' extracurricular schedules are more than what I'm able to accomplish for work.

I think people should focus more on work/life management than work/life balance.

WRIGHT

What is the message you want people to hear so that they can learn from your success?

MOORE

The message I want people to hear loudly is that you have No Excuses. Everything that God has allowed me to experience has made me into the person I am today. You would think, "Oh wow, you had twins as a teenager, you didn't go to college, you're an African-American female in a male dominated industry, you didn't have money, you didn't come from a family of business owners, in fact, you came from the projects in New York." Obviously, I could have made excuse after excuse for being average. But the fact that I am where I am today, and I'm still going, means that you have No Excuses!

WRIGHT

You're now a professional speaker; how did you do that and why?

MOORE

Well, I'm a firm believer that every successful entrepreneur certainly has three revenue streams automatically. One is your core business. Then, if your business is successful, most people want to hear you speak about why it's successful, so that's a speaking business. Lastly, after you speak about it, people want to read about it, so that's a book. So now you have a business, a speaking business, and a book.

I didn't set a goal to start a speaking business at all. Honestly, between 2007 and 2008 I began to evolve into a well-known young entrepreneur. There were organizations and individuals nominating me for all kinds of awards.

In 2008, I won first runner-up for the Madame C.J. Walker Award in Philadelphia, Pennsylvania. I went to accept my award and give my acceptance speech, which was all of sixty seconds, maybe a little over a minute. By the time I was finished speaking from my heart, the entire audience was standing and clapping and shouting. After the luncheon ceremony that included public officials and about four hundred attendees, I had a long line of people saying things like, "Sirena, do you accept speaking engagements? Will you come speak at my event?" I received many invitations to speak at several venues.

The sponsor of the Madame C. J. Walker Award event was PECO Energy. They asked me to be a keynote speaker at an event they were hosting and I had no idea if I should go or not. I was somewhat thrown into the speaking business. Then I discovered my passion for assisting other entrepreneurs in any way I can because I didn't have the help and the resources I needed when I was starting my own business. Now, I have the opportunity to *Encourage, Empower,* and *Inspire* individuals around the world. So therefore, I started SirenaSpeaks LLC, and SirenaSpeaks.com.

WRIGHT

Well, what an interesting conversation. I'm really proud of you; you've done a great job. I appreciate all the time you've spent with me here this afternoon to answer these questions. I'm so glad you're in this book. I think the readers are really going to be inspired by your story.

MOORE

Thank you. I pray that the readers are encouraged to have more, be more, and do more because they have no excuses.

WRIGHT

Today we have been talking with Sirena C. Moore, who, as we have found out today, really is a dynamic young woman on the move. In 2002, at the age of twenty-one, she joined forces with her father and brother to form her cleaning contractors company, Elohim Cleaning Contractors, and the rest is history. In just a few short years, the company has grown into a full-service, multimillion-dollar construction cleaning firm.

Sirena thank you so much for being with us today on *Success Simplified.*

MOORE

Thank you.

About the Author

At the age of seventeen, Sirena Moore, a self-motivated, highly ambitious teenage mother of twin girls, entered the corporate world by working for industry leaders such as Morgan Stanley Dean Witter, Advest, and Palm, Inc. Her objective: obtain the skills necessary to fulfill her dream of becoming an entrepreneur.

By age twenty-one, with a business plan but no start-up capital, she joined with her father and brother to launch Elohim Cleaning Contractors, Inc., a full-service construction cleaning firm that provides a wide range of services to general contractors and construction management firms throughout the Greater Philadelphia region.

Armed with marketing, financial planning, organizational, and managerial skills from her previous work, this fledgling entrepreneur managed to grow her business revenue by 210 percent in one year. Her strong faith, family bonds, and ability to operate debt-free, have been her catalysts for growth. By 2008, her multi-million-dollar business was ranked number eight in Philadelphia's Top Minority Businesses, employing eighty-three minority men and women from very diverse backgrounds.

Her success in managing one of the up-and-coming small businesses in the region earned her respect and visibility within the business community and has allowed this young entrepreneur to fulfill a childhood dream of gracing the cover of *Black Enterprise Magazine* last year. Now twenty-eight, she serves as one of the youngest Greater Philadelphia Chamber of Commerce Small Business Board members, co-chairing the Diversity Committee. She is an active member of the Urban League Young Professionals, and has been named 2010 Small Business Person of the Year.

Ms. Moore is a strong advocate of programs addressing issues such as teen pregnancy, violence prevention, financial empowerment, and career development. She sits on the board of We are SEEDS, which provides an array of services to inner city young women.

Her lifestyle and accomplishments have been an inspiration to her peers and the young people she serves. Most recently, she created SirenaSpeaks, LLC, to assist other small business owners and aspiring entrepreneurs to achieve their dreams by encouraging and empowering them through her motivational talks. Her innovative techniques and ideas continue to be invaluable assets to her business and her community.

Sirena C. Moore

Elohim Cleaning Contractors Inc.

info@sirenaspeaks.com

www.elohimcleaningcontractors.com

www.sirenaspeaks.com

Sirena's Favorite Quote: *"Whatever you do, work at it with all your heart, as working for the Lord, not for men."* (Colossians 3:23 NIV)

Chapter Nine

How to Get Ahead and Stay There

By Patricia Fripp

David Wright (Wright)

Today we're talking with Patricia Fripp who was a successful entrepreneur in the service industry for twenty-four years before becoming an award-winning international speaker who has addressed audiences on four continents. The first woman president of the National Speakers Association (NSA), she received the organization's Certified Speaker Professional (CSP) designation in 1981 and their Council of Peers Award for Excellence (CPAE) Speaker Hall of Fame in 1983 for professionalism and excellence in speaking. In 1996 she received the Cavett Award, the annual "Oscar" of the National Speakers Association.

Patricia is founder and president of the largest National Speakers Association chapter, NSA of California. She is the author of *Make It, So You Don't Have to Fake It!* a practical and motivational book on personal and business success and her hit book, *Get What You Want*, has sold more than 40,000 copies. She is a contributing author to Insights into Excellence and Speaking Secrets of the Masters, along with top national speakers like Brian Tracy and Ken Blanchard.

Patricia Fripp is the star of several training videos including, "Travel the Road to Success," "Adventure in Customer Service," and, "Survival in the Workplace 2000." She is a television faculty member of the Success Network and stars in the "Bulletproof Manager" series sold in fifty countries and translated into twenty languages.

Patricia Fripp, welcome to *Success Simplified.*

Patricia Fripp (Fripp)

It's very nice to be talking with you.

Wright

Meetings and Conventions magazine says you are, "one of the most electrifying speakers in North America." What made you decide to enter the highly competitive field of public speaking and training?

Fripp

Let's step backward. As a hair stylist I arrived in America at twenty with no contacts. I had nowhere to live and I had just $500. I went to work at the Mark Hopkins Hotel; then, in 1969, I became one of the first women to go into men's hairstyling when it was a new industry.

I worked with Jay Sebring who was an innovator in men's hairstyling. He did all the movie stars' hair, and as you may remember, was murdered by the Charles Manson gang along with Sharon Tate who was one of his very good friends. I worked for his company and started demonstrating for them from 1969 until 1975.

I formed my own business in 1975 and at that point I had a product distribution business. I started traveling nationwide doing seminars for other hairstylists. My executive clientele began requesting that I speak to their individual Rotary Club, Kiwanis Club, Lions Club, Breakfast Club, etc. After a few speeches I realized that people who heard me speak came to my salon. I also recognized that this was the least expensive way to promote my business because, although I was solidly booked for fifteen years, I needed to feed my staff. So I used my public speaking in the community to promote my hairstyling business.

After a few of these talks people began asking what I would charge to give one of my talks to the various other businesses such as the Oakland Appliance Dealers and what would I charge to speak on goal-setting to the San Mateo school administrators? I decided I'd promote this—I loved doing it, it was good for business and hey, it's even paying me a little bit! Then I started letting my clients know I was available to speak to anyone at any time on pretty much on any topic.

One day I heard a professional speaker—a man called Chris Hagarty. He said to me, "Patricia, you must go to the National Speakers Association Convention." I'm a great believer that if someone you admire and wish to emulate gives you advice you don't ask what it costs, you do it. I went to my first NSA Convention in 1977 in Phoenix thinking no one was going to want to talk to me—I only talk to Rotary Clubs and hairstylists. Two things happened: one was that I was "discovered" by Mike Frank, a promoter and past president of the National Speakers Association, who booked me to speak to 2,000 people on the same program with Dr. Robert Schuller later that year. I also thought this might also be something I would really like to do.

Understand that I started hairstyling at fifteen. I signed a ten-year lease at thirty, which meant that at forty years old I would have spent twenty-five years behind a hair stylist's chair. I was still young enough to change my career—I didn't want to be an old hairstylist. I'd accomplished most of my goals—I'd traveled nationwide doing shows, I'd had my haircuts in magazines, I'd built a business, etc. Although I still loved my hairstyling business, I thought that at forty, when my lease was up, at least I would have an option. I had advised people not to quit their day job too soon—not until they were really established and sure the change was what they wanted to do.

My speaking business really took off, so by the time I was thirty-nine—the year before my lease was up—I had already sold my product distribution business to my sales manager and I sold my hairstyling business to my staff. I actually went full time as a speaker the year I was president of the National Speakers Association. At that point I was already traveling more than 50 percent of the time speaking. That was the transition.

When I went to NSA and first started speaking, my doing public speaking as a full-time occupation wasn't a consideration. If I learned the business and went to the NSA more, then I thought it could be a viable option.

Wright

It seems that success has as many definitions as people who define it, not to mention the fact that success has personal meanings as well. How do you define success?

Fripp

Success for me is really just a matter of living your life exactly the way you want to and having the freedom to do that. The only thing that ever bothered me was when I sweated cash flow. I didn't break my heart over men too much—cash flow was the important thing. It's just a matter of being in charge of your own life—making decisions and living life the way you want to.

Wright

One of your presentations is "Opportunity Does Not Knock Once." Will you tell us a little more about this?

Fripp

My presentations aren't necessarily the same because they get adapted for each audience, but the basic premise of "Opportunity Does Not Knock Once" is that it knocks all the time. We don't always recognize that fact. My formula is:

- Reflect
- Acknowledge
- Develop

Reflect back on what naturally brought you to where you are right now. For example, one thing I did as a young woman behind a hairstyling chair was that I asked questions—I was naturally curious. When I was fifteen, working in a posh salon in England with rich, glamorous women, I used to say, "What were you doing when you were my age? How did you make your money? Did you make it yourself or did you marry it?" If they made their money themselves I would ask how they did it, and if they married it, I would ask where they met their husbands. That was good market research.

Later, at twenty-three, I found myself in the financial district of San Francisco talking with business executives all day long. I used to ask, "What made you the best salesperson in the company?" and, "What did your little company do/have that a big company wanted to pay you millions of dollars for it?" What I did was use my time standing behind a hairstyling chair as a school to earn the equivalent of an MBA in business. I said to my staff one day, "You are interesting women. Why do you talk such a load of drivel when you have some of the most fascinating minds in the city sitting in your chair?" I was taking advantage of opportunity.

Once you develop a relationship with people, it's amazing how they help and support you. Once I became successful as a speaker, it was amazing how many of my salon clients took credit for helping me become a success. They would say, "Well, I started her out—I got her her first few engagements," or, "I invited her to speak to my company," etc. And I think it's wonderful when people share your success.

It's as simple as reflecting back on what you learned when you were younger and then revisiting it with fresh eyes. Then you have to acknowledge your past success because your future success will be built on the same foundation of those past successes. This means you have to acknowledge it. Many people are so overly modest that they have trouble with this. You don't have to be braggadocios but you do have to acknowledge what you have done well to lay a foundation for future success.

Then, if you want to take advantage of opportunity, you always have to be open to develop new skills and new talents. I maintain that to take advantage of the opportunities that present themselves we perhaps have to be more multi-faceted in our competence than we were in the past. I like to tell audiences that we need to be charismatic communicators who are technically competent, who have good people skills, and an abundance of healthy energy, because youth is honored. Very often, as we become more mature, we have to project that we are energetic and healthy because that gives the perception that we are a lot younger than we actually are. And then, of course, it doesn't hurt to look good.

My mother was very wise. She always said, "Of course it's the interview that counts. You have to dress up and look good so you can attract people so they can find out how nice you are, how smart you are, and how valuable you can be to them."

WRIGHT

I'd like to read a direct quote from you, if you don't mind. You have said, "It never ceases to amaze me that intelligent, well educated, and ambitious individuals frequently overlook the number one skill that is guaranteed to position them ahead of the crowd—namely, the ability to speak eloquently in public." So, why do people who want to get ahead not go to speech coaches?

Fripp

It absolutely boggles my mind and I have met and worked in companies where executives admit to me they spend more energy trying to get out of speaking engagements than it would have taken to invest in the time to become very good and competent.

It is not necessarily a natural thing for a mere mortal to stand up in front of senior management and talk. Basic training makes you more competent. I think the initial fear of it just puts people off. I have mastered it so well that I really can't totally understand why people would be so nervous; but it's natural to be nervous.

There are a lot of situations where I'm still nervous. Perhaps "nervous" isn't the right word—maybe a little apprehensive. As Bill Gove, the first president of the National Speakers Association, said, "Every time you stand up in front of an audience you risk experiencing anything from mild disinterest to outright hostility." Although those are extremes and don't often happen, public speaking isn't exactly natural. Once people focus on the benefits of personal and corporate success, of sales, etc., I think they would be more inclined to take some basic training.

Wright

Just how important are powerful presentations and speaking skills to business leaders, corporate executives, and salespeople?

Fripp

I was brought up hearing stories from my parents of how Winston Churchill got on the radio and with the power of his words got people to fight in the street. If a leader wants to inspire the sales force or anyone in the company, there is nothing like standing up in front of them and just being open, persuasive, articulate, and human—just real—without the barrier; just stand up and talk to them. Even if you have to deliver bad news such as, "We're laying off 20 percent of the sales force," people want to hear the truth from their leader. If you're talking to the financial press, and if you do it well, your stock will go up.

There is nothing that I truly believe an executive should focus on more than, along with other basic skills for leadership, being able to communicate their ideas and their passion; and it will be catching for their associates.

WRIGHT

As you were speaking about Churchill (I'm old enough to remember hearing him speak) I remembered the two greatest speakers in this nation in my lifetime, who, in my opinion, were Kennedy and Reagan. Both of them were great speechmakers.

FRIPP

Yes, and people never stop talking about them.

WRIGHT

Yes, and they're loved to this day.

You present the idea that, "*life is a series of sales situations.*" How would you define this statement?

FRIPP

Every day you have to sell yourself, whether it's internally or to your customers or in promoting your business. If you work in a company, you have to sell your ideas. You have to sell your value if you're looking for a raise. If you're a manager, you have to sell your associates to work harder. So every day we have to be persuasive. I call that, "life is a series of sales situations."

So often people want something, it could be support or help, but they don't ask for it. I would say the answer is no if you don't ask. Also, if you don't like the first answer, go talk to someone else.

WRIGHT

I know you work with entire sales teams. What do you try to teach them that others do not, and how successful have you been?

Fripp

What I hear more than anything else from attendees who work in companies where I have coached the sales team (especially when they've been through many other programs or training) is that the number one difference is that I focus on the point of view of the listener.

Most salespeople go through a formula for their presentation. For example, they say, "Hello, my name is Patricia Fripp, let me introduce you to my team: Tom, Dick, and Harriet. We're going to talk about our company. Our company has been making widgets since 1982 and we own this much of the market share. Our chairman is this person, and we've been trying to do that, and our leading technology is this, and this is who our client is, and we'd like to talk to you about what we can do for you."

I say, nobody cares—turn it all around. They know basically who you are before you get in there so why don't you start talking about them—your audience? So, for example, say, "You have an awesome responsibility. Your senior management has charged you with increasing your customer satisfaction by 10 percent and at the same time lowering costs by 5 percent." You start by talking about them and their challenges. You might then say, during the next thirty minutes, "You will decide that one of your viable options would be to partner with the Fripp Company." So, you've just turned your presentation around. It's what I call the "I/You Ratio Language." You don't say, "I am going to tell you," you say, "You are going to listen." That is one focus.

I do another thing that most coaches won't. I have extensively studied screenwriting—not that I want to be a screenwriter. There are two types of writers who know how to emotionally connect to their audience. They're in Hollywood or they write advertising copy. Advertising copy sells a picture or tells a story in a sentence perhaps. You look at a fifteen-second television commercial and you're crying. That's good, well-written copy. Listen to some of the persuasive arguments in *Westwood,* in *Law and Order*—they are compellingly written copy. Look at movies—they are compelling and make an emotional connection.

So I will look at a sales presentation or speech and I will see it, as I'm helping people, as a scene from television or movie.

I use the best principles that are relatable to speaking from Hollywood and, as I mentioned, I focus on being an audience advocate—speaking from the point of view of the audience, not my own. Even if you do have to introduce yourself, it doesn't have to be the first thing out of your mouth. Say something interesting and compelling about them, then they actually care who you are.

Wright

You've stated that a company's biggest challenge in recruiting, retraining, and motivating is its most valuable assets—its employees. You use a phrase I've never heard before, "Act-as-if-their-name-were-on-the-door employees." Would you tell our readers what you mean?

Fripp

Let me give you a specific example. My brother and I were trying to get in to see a movie. This was in New York and it was the last showing of that movie. We arrived about seven minutes after it had started. We went to the ticket booth but the cashier said, "I've closed the drawer."

She wouldn't let us in. So, being a believer in the phrase, if you don't like the first answer, go to someone else, we went to the guy taking the tickets. I said, "I know we're late; we want to get in. You can put our money in the drawer tomorrow. But let us in free, or keep the money yourself." He was honest, so he called the manager.

The manager said, "No, we don't let people in who are late for the last show."

Now, you know there were other people in there watching the show, it's not like they're keeping the lights on for us. So, as I was leaving I turned around and said, "It's very obvious you don't own this business, because the key point in business is if people want to give you money, you take it. We're trying to give you money—take it."

My point is that you've got a cashier, a ticket-taker, and a manager who had the opportunity to increase profit and serve the customer. They didn't. They weren't working for the movie house, they weren't working for the customer, they were working for a paycheck.

Anytime you take somebody's paycheck, do something positive for the company's public relations—make a contribution that will be there at least in word-of-mouth after you've left. The people in my example were working for a paycheck, and if you only work for a paycheck, you might be employed but you won't be employable.

We are living in a downsized, right-sized, re-engineered, outsourced world where wanting to be employed is yesterday's world's thinking. We need to be employable and it takes different skills. You certainly need to act as if your name were on the door, even if it isn't because if you don't, it never will be.

WRIGHT

Do you really think that today's employees can be motivated? And is it possible to expect and get loyalty?

FRIPP

Yes, and many companies do it superbly well.

WRIGHT

I hear many people in business today say that employees have changed.

FRIPP

Well, they have—they're younger and it takes a lot of training to understand how deal with different generations of people.

WRIGHT

So employees can be motivated with training programs?

FRIPP

No—you have to step backward. I remember one day when I was cutting hair in my salon and the young lady in the next station was having a conversation with a client. The client asked her, "How does Patricia motivate you?" We did have a really great act-as-if-your-name-were-on-the-door team. I had no idea how she was going to answer the question but I was really fascinated because she wasn't going to answer in a politically correct way—she would say the first thing that came to mind.

If I were telling this story in a seminar I would say, "Okay, the question was, 'How does Patricia motivate you?' and the answer is exactly what we need to run a successful business—what did she say?" I have asked various audiences this question many times. I receive a lot of good answers but often they don't give the right one. Sometimes they do immediately, but usually they don't. The answer she gave was, "Patricia only hires motivated people."

See, a training program will obviously make a difference and teach someone a skill to do the job (I don't know if it's going to change your attitude, however). You have to be careful about how you recruit. That's really difficult if you're in an area where you don't have many people to choose from. What you have to do then is take the best of the available talent and then train and encourage. The people will do absolutely anything you want them to do when they realize it's in their best interest to do it.

I remember when I was running my hairstyling salon and I wanted managerial staff. I remember saying to Evie one day, "Evie, you're not going to get rich working for me. *I'm* not going to get rich working for me for a long time; but if you want to learn how to run a small business better than anybody else, perhaps you want to work here for awhile." She was smart enough to realize she wanted to learn the business and that this was more valuable than an extra hundred dollars a month. In fact, we are still very good friends and she made a valuable contribution. I helped her and she did go into business for herself. She had been offered a job with a starting salary about double what I paid her and I would have expected her to accept it. But she said to the person offering the job, "I know you're going to think I'm crazy and I'm not going to tell you what I earn, but there is still a lot I want to learn from Patricia before I'm ready to leave."

Now, I understand in big companies it's a little different than an entrepreneurial venture; but people look at your past history—how do you treat your associates when times are tough?

Wright

Leadership is another term that many find difficult to define. How do you define it?

FRIPP

The best definition I've ever heard, and one that I use, is from General Eisenhower. He said, "Leadership is the ability to decide what has to be done and then get people to want to do it." I cannot think of a better definition myself.

WRIGHT

You often work with entrepreneurs. They seem to be a different breed of person in that they don't seem to have any problem with self-promotion—

FRIPP

Well, that isn't true. If you work with entrepreneurs, a lot of them *do* have a problem with self-promotion. People are being laid off or have left jobs—many of them have been forced into being entrepreneurs. Some adapt superbly well but others don't because they're used to having a marketing department and they're used to having a sales force. Not so much these days but in the past they were used to having someone type their letters, etc. When they have their own business they usually have to do those kinds of things themselves.

For me it was almost natural. It was part of how I was raised and then I had entrepreneurial bosses. It's probably more in my DNA than some; but no, I don't think entrepreneurs are naturally good at self-promotion.

WRIGHT

What are your plans for the future? What would make Patricia Fripp the most satisfied and happy in her personal and business life?

FRIPP

This is interesting. Just when I'm saying I do want to slow down a little—and I actually have had more vacations and more fabulous trips—I have never been so busy. This is because my business has expanded to three different areas. I still do keynote speeches but I also do a lot of sales training and a lot of executive speech coaching. Executive speech coaching is fascinating because I'm locked in a room talking to brilliant people all day long, just as I used to do when I was a hair stylist—isn't that funny? The difference is that the fee has gone up.

I have bought myself a house in Las Vegas as well one as in San Francisco. I want to keep doing what I am doing; I just want a little more down time.

I find the desert is nice. A lot of my coaching clients come to Las Vegas. So all in all, I'm quite happy and satisfied. I just look forward to a little more down time.

Wright

What an interesting conversation and what an interesting person you are. You know I've always been a fan of yours.

Today we've been talking with Patricia Fripp. She's the first woman president of the National Speakers Association and she is also a Certified Speaking Professional. She has won the designation of CPAE, which is a NSA Hall of Fame Award, for her professionalism and excellence in speaking. She also received the Cavett Award—the annual "Oscar" of the National Speakers Association. I think she knows what she's talking about; at least every time she opens her mouth I always listen.

Patricia, thank you so much for being with us today on *Success Simplified*.

Patricia Fripp is an award-winning speaker, sales trainer, and executive speech coach who delights audiences, electrifies executives who speak, and transforms sales teams. Meetings and Conventions magazine calls Patricia "one of the country's ten most electrifying speakers." Kiplinger's Personal Finance says, "Patricia Fripp's speaking school is the sixth best way you can invest in your career." She is also the author of Make It, So You Don't Have to Fake It and Get What You Want.

Patricia Fripp
www.fripp.com

CHAPTER TEN

I CAN *DO* THAT!

BY ARDIS BAZYN

DAVID WRIGHT (WRIGHT)

Today, we're talking to Ardis Bazyn, Founder of Bazyn Communications. Several life changing events have taught Ardis Bazyn patience, courage, and the importance of a positive attitude. Blinded in a car accident at the age of 20, she was required to learn a new career. Despite other setbacks, she earned a master's degree in teaching and self published four books. In her most requested keynote, "Coping with Challenges and Change", Ardis tells her personal story of viewing challenges, or obstacles as opportunities rather than tragedies. Besides her inspirational speaking and writing, she coaches people how to be more successful by setting reachable goals. She and her husband live in Burbank, California.

Ardis Bazyn, welcome to *Success Simplified.*

ARDIS BAZYN (BAZYN)

Thank you, David; I'm glad to be here.

WRIGHT

So how do you define success?

BAZYN

I define success as enjoying what you're doing in life, realizing that you might have to change your career to get to the right comfort level. You need to really be confident in whatever role you're fulfilling. If you don't enjoy your work, you're not going to do well at it, and it will be more difficult to help other people become successful. It's also important to build many and varied relationships with people in all walks of life. They will assist you in becoming successful as many of my contacts have helped me through some difficult situations.

Besides finding business networking opportunities, I've become involved in a church in whatever community I've lived. I've found faith to be a major part of my life. I always have a Friend I can trust with my problems, hurts, and personal successes. I've also become a member of several blindness organizations through the years. If I have a new task, a new computer or software program, or access issue; I can call on a visually impaired friend to ask about it.

WRIGHT

So what contributed to your professional success?

BAZYN

The key contribution to success in my professional career is my willingness to make changes as the environment changes around me. I also regularly network with a wide variety of organizations and handle many volunteer projects. I really do enjoy meeting new people and helping others to improve and succeed. I attend business networking meetings and have found Business Network International to be the best one for assisting me when I was newer in this business and learning to market myself. I also think my positive attitude and willingness to laugh at myself when I do make mistakes have also benefited me.

I do set goals, and I like to make lists of strategies for each one. I am also very flexible—if people need assistance at the last minute I'm willing to jump in. I don't hold a strict time schedule and I don't turn down a request if I can fit it in my plans.

WRIGHT

What do you think are the biggest obstacles people face in trying to be successful?

BAZYN

The key contribution to success in my professional career is my willingness to make changes as the environment changes around me. I'm a life-time learner and find new interests exciting. Since I lost my sight, it seems I've made problem solving a way of life.

I also regularly network with a wide variety of organizations and handle many volunteer projects. For over twenty years, I've volunteered on both advisory boards and board of directors for agencies and organizations. In those positions, I've learned many leadership skills and developed writing techniques that college classes can't teach. For example, I've written many articles for publications, lead seminars, and advocated for organizations before I went into the speaking and writing field.

I really do enjoy meeting new people and helping others to improve and succeed. When I was in food service management before I started my current business, I enjoyed training employees and other potential managers. I like to assist chapters and affiliates of organizations in leadership and membership building.

I attend many business networking meetings. Business Network International was the best one for assisting me when I was newer in this business and learning to market myself. I also think my positive attitude and the willingness to laugh at myself when I do make mistakes have also benefited me.

I do set goals, and I like to make lists of strategies for each one. I am very flexible - if people need assistance at the last minute I'm often willing to jump in. I don't hold a real strict time schedule and don't turn down a request if I can reasonably fit it in my plans.

WRIGHT

What do you think are the biggest obstacles people face in trying to be successful?

BAZYN

I think the worst obstacle is trying to be someone else and trying to please everyone. We like to have everyone around us happy with whatever we do, but we have to learn that it's most important to please ourselves, our immediate family, and God. Sometimes people don't set goals, and if you don't set a target, you're not going to be able to reach it. You have to have a plan of action. Otherwise, you're likely going in circles trying to make the right decisions.

Also I think it's very important to ask for help. If you find that you're stumbling in a certain area, find an expert that can assist you in that particular area. It's not beneficial to you and the people around you if you try to accomplish everything without asking for what you need. To make our businesses successful, there are aspects where specific professionals could get that project finished much faster. If we take the time to strategize about which areas in our action plan might be most difficult or time-consuming, we can then ask the appropriate consultant to handle that project.

WRIGHT

How can people keep outside influences from obstructing their progress?

BAZYN

You need to focus on your own goals and list some strategies, write them down, and keep to a timeline. You need to also keep a positive attitude. If you're not reaching a particular goal, think about why it isn't working. Look at other ways you can work around the issue(s). It is also beneficial to figure out what kinds of problems you might have in reaching each goal. If you have prior knowledge about a possible obstacle, it will assist you in thinking of how to minimize that particular difficulty.

Also, use humor to keep yourself positive. Read some chuckles, find a website that has jokes, or get a joke book. When you get frustrated, relax, take a break, get some exercise and you will have the energy to get back on track.

WRIGHT

What drives you to be successful?

BAZYN

I enjoy watching people learn from what I teach them. I like to inspire other people. And it really makes me feel good that I can help others make changes in their life. I know I want to accomplish more each time I read or hear about what others do in their lives. I say to myself "I could do that too".

Another reason I try so hard to start new ventures is because I so often hear people make comments about what blind people can't do. Most blind people can do whatever they decide they want to do. It likely will take more time and effort, but most tasks can be completed. I want to prove I can accomplish any goal I want to achieve.

A visually-impaired friend challenged me to go cross-country skiing a few years ago. I had never tried it, even though I had lived in Iowa most of my life. I found out that it was different from what I had expected. I didn't realize we'd have to ski down hills! Even with a guide beside me, it was scary the first time. However, I felt really good about finishing the three day event for the first time. I have been skiing and snow-shoeing several times now. I even broke my ankle one year when it was extremely slushy. I've found that trying new ventures keeps me feeling young and gives me the ability to tell those stories when I speak.

WRIGHT

So how do you balance your success with your life?

BAZYN

I strive to keep my life balanced- my career, family, and faith are all valuable. I plan trips to visit family. I put them in my calendar and I don't drop them even if I'm offered a good deal. I think it's important to keep family in your life and not allow your successful career to keep you from getting together with your loved ones. I also plan outings with my husband and friends. I use my work time diligently so I don't have to go outside my work time anymore than necessary. My church activities are also in my calendar and I try not to miss many of them when I need to travel.

WRIGHT

What is the message you want people to hear so that they can learn from your success?

BAZYN

I think the most important message is that people can adjust to any changes in their life. I've had lots of challenges in my life including losing my sight at the age of 20, having to change careers. One of the questions I get asked most often is "How much vision do you have?" Since I could see for twenty years, I do look at people when they talk and do have good mobility skills – probably because I picture my surroundings in my mind. Many people can't seem to fathom that a totally blind person would want to participate in many activities without a companion. Obviously, it's more fun to visit places with friends or family, but I don't wait around for someone to come with me or I wouldn't travel much at all. I learned a long time ago that I couldn't be shy. I have to ask directions often, trust that people I meet in strange buildings, bus stations, train stations, or airports will give me correct directions. Most times, people are very helpful and I just have to be patient when they aren't.

I married a wonderful man who later became multi-disabled and I needed to care for him while I was working full time, and I learned to adapt. I really struggled with the fact that I needed to ask for assistance to get everything done once David was unable to assist in my food service business or at home. I had to hire readers, particularly when I was in college. Fortunately, I could sometimes ask my daughters to help when they had time after their many school activities. When David could no longer help me with paperwork, they filled in forms for me, once I had calculated the figures for the particular form. They also assisted their father when he needed help finding an audio book to read. Gwen even learned to test his blood and give him shots occasionally.

I also had a heart attack and had to undergo a surgical procedure and follow it with a cardiac exercise program. One of the most annoying situations I had was trying to explain that I could use all the exercise equipment in the rehabilitation center. They said they were worried about liability, but they allowed eighty-year-old men and women to walk on the treadmill and they could barely walk. I was only in my forties and never had trouble using any exercise machines, but they refused to let me walk on the treadmill. I also had trouble getting them to understand I needed the articles and instructions in a media I could read: electronic Word document or audio materials. I had to insist on getting what was needed - one of many times I had to advocate for accessibility.

I had several cancer scares where I had to have surgery but each was caught in time. I think by going through those challenges, it makes people see me as being credible.

However, another message I want to share is that faith and family are important when you have challenges. I trust that God is with me and I know friends and family pray for me whenever I request it.

WRIGHT

I agree. My goodness—those are a lot of hills to climb for anyone.

So how do you teach people to be more successful?

BAZYN

I share my life story and tell them some of the techniques that I use to help me deal with the challenges in my life. People see me as I am, what I've done, and how I've done it. People then feel that they are more able to do it themselves.

In all my presentations, I use personal experiences to highlight how I've handled each situation. I use personal stories and strategies in my coaching sessions and writings as well. I encourage others to use past experiences as a learning tool - whether successful or not. Failures have often led me to many positive adaptations in my career and life in general.

I tell people that when we were raising our daughters, I adapted different teaching methods including purchasing magnetic letters and numbers that I could feel so I could teach them how to spell words. I had someone read me children's books while I brailed the stories, so I could later read them while they looked at the pictures in the books. I learned the neighborhood so I could walk them to school. Our family often went to the local park so they could play or wade in the small pool. We strived to give our daughters the same experiences that sighted parents would have given them.

I often tell people that I think my lack of sight helped my children learn to talk and be more independent. I'm sure they got frustrated when I couldn't tell they were pointing at something or were crying for food. I would just keep asking, "Do you want milk?" or "Do you want juice?" or "Do you want a cracker?"

WRIGHT

So what tips can you offer our readers and our listeners as they cope with life challenges?

BAZYN

The first tip is to benefit from the family and friends around you. If you talk to them when you're having a problem, they can either give you an idea, or they'll just be a bouncing board for you and some mental support. Another tip is to use humor to give and keep your focus positive. As I mentioned earlier, I like to laugh at myself. If I make little mistakes, I just chuckle and move on instead of dwelling on them. An example I sometimes give to women's groups is a cooking "mistake".

Once I made a simple tuna macaroni casserole for dinner. When I called the family to dinner, my daughter April said, "Mom, what is that yellow stuff in the casserole?" I checked it. I found that my husband had purchased some groceries that week and had bought a six ounce can of pineapple. Unfortunately, it looked exactly like a can of tuna. I had mixed it in the casserole instead of tuna. Needless to say, I had to fix another dish that night.

This story reminds others of blunders they've had in the kitchen. I also read a lot of jokes and keep looking at life in a humorous way instead of looking at things as always being serious.

Another tactic I use is learning strategies to cope with some of the challenges and changes in my life. I've had to learn how to use computers and different speech software and how to do different tasks in a new way especially when I first lost my sight. I had to learn how to read Braille, and learn cane travel. I had to listen to traffic when crossing streets instead of watching lights or oncoming traffic. I also had to feel whether my white cane was going down a step or hitting an obstacle in my path. It took patience and practice to travel with confidence outside my dorm each night.

I also learned to cope when I had to care for my husband. I learned how to adapt to giving him medications and feeding him the right diet. I had to learn how to study and take courses in order to get my Master's degree while working full-time and taking care of my preteens and my husband. I had to live a healthier lifestyle once I had my heart attack. With each situation, I just had to learn to adapt to different strategies, many by reading and checking various websites.

I also learned stress management, how to take good care of myself using an exercise plan to keep down my stress level. I also like to view challenges as opportunities. In each case I look at how I can learn from this particular challenge and what I could do differently. What would help me to be able to live my life to the fullest no matter what happens?

I like to find new activities to do and consider myself a lifetime learner. I always like to read new articles and check new websites to find out if there is anything new.

Developing visualization techniques is another exercise that is important to learn. Whenever I'm thinking about a new goal, I think about myself accomplishing that goal by visualizing myself in that new situation. I also think it's very important to set goals. Focusing on the goals rather than what's happening around me has helped me to move forward when I've had stressful times in my life.

When my husband was very ill and I didn't know how to handle his constant trips to the hospital, I had to leave it in God's hands and work on goals I could accomplish. I concentrated on getting my undergraduate degrees and later my Master's degree. I focused on my daughters' school activities and my business. I'm not sure how I would have managed if I didn't have other tasks to keep me focused.

Wright

You spoke of changing careers; how did you begin speaking professionally and how did you choose your main topics?

Bazyn

That is a good question to ask. When I first lost my sight, I had to change careers because that career was no longer an option. I was a proof dispatcher, which meant a lot of driving and changing ads for a newspaper. Obviously, I had to look for a new career. I decided to go into food service management, which seemed like an interesting career. I started speaking at schools when my children were really young. I told students how a person with a disability could do what they do. Later, I started talking in churches and women's groups about how much my faith meant to me. I shared how faith helped me move forward no matter what challenges I had in my life.

After speaking as a side venture for a while with my food service business, I just decided to change my career altogether. I really enjoyed speaking, especially when I realized how much it meant to the audience.

Once I decided to change careers, I went back to college and received my two B.A. degrees (in Speech Communications and Public Relations) and my Master's Degree in Arts in Teaching. I then started speaking as a professional. Gradually, I began doing more and more writing. I had written many articles, news releases, and reports for organizations and trainings. I attended some marketing sessions for speakers and decided it might be advantageous to my speaking career if I would write some books. I had previously been encouraged to write a book by a professor when I did my Master's presentation on “Meeting the Needs of a Membership Organization”.

I think the reason I chose “Coping with Challenge and Change” to be one of my main topics was because I found out early on that when I was speaking on that topic, that audience members felt they really benefited by some of the coping techniques that I had used in my life. I found that more rewarding than the responses from other topics I deliver. I do have a dozen topics I routinely cover, but I realize that anyone can identify with the coping subject. Even if they have not personally coped with some challenge in their own life, they know friends or family that have. My other topics are meant more for working in organizational settings (business, organization, or church). Since I found networking with various organizations very beneficial in my own life, I find it meaningful to help them improve their groups (image-building, board training, marketing techniques, team-building, membership growth strategies, leadership trainings, etc.).

Since I knew many organizations struggle with having the right image to attract members or customers, I decided to write a series called “Building Blocks to Success”. I wrote three books: one for churches, one for organizations, and one for businesses (which also has tips for motivating and keeping good employees). I felt my experience as a leader in churches and organizations in different parts of the country would be helpful to others. I also had owned various businesses for more than twenty years so had many skills and understanding of that arena as well. My networking with numerous types of churches, organizations, and businesses allowed me to share examples of how others could make their image more positive.

WRIGHT

What do you think makes your perspective unique?

BAZYN

First, I think that since I've overcome so many different challenges in my own life, it makes my coverage of the topic more meaningful than someone that is just using other people's examples to discuss the subject. When I give tips on coping, I use as many personal stories as possible, and listeners can identify with what I'm saying. I try to share particular situations in my life, many humorous. I particularly like to share funny incidents with my children when they were young.

One of the reasons my book series is unique is that each book explains how to make all outreach accessible to persons with disabilities: websites, seminars and conferences, attitudes, as well as products and publicity. The books identify many strategies and techniques that may help promote each type of organization to a wider audience by evaluating your attitude toward newcomers, improving visitor/customer follow-up, and developing and promoting your purpose.

The examples and observations allow each organization to critique their image as if they were outsiders, explore their current practices, learn problem-solving necessary for expansion, and investigate possible opportunities for the future. Suggested techniques may lead them to develop ongoing relationships with customers/members, employees, and other businesses/organizations. Another unique element of these books relates to marketing to all possible populations. In the business book it describes how to look at your hiring and firing methods to determine if any practices may be discriminatory and could cause you problems in the future.

WRIGHT

So why would people think your tips would help them specifically?

BAZYN

Since I've been using those same strategies myself, they can see how they have benefited me. When I'm sharing tips, I'm hoping others will think, "Hey, if it worked for her, maybe it will work for me".

They will likely notice that I do travel around the country and I tell people I just got my passport to go to Europe to visit my oldest daughter. I don't let some of the little issues that arise occasionally because I'm blind stop me. The fact that I am an established author, very active in my community, and also love to do different activities shows I do what I "preach". It seems more credible if you're actually following your own tips.

Wright

I can understand that.

Well, what a great conversation. I'm sorry about your accident that took your sight. However, it sounds like you have overcome those obstacles years ago. I can just imagine how it must make you feel helping people do the same.

Bazyn

Yes, I really do enjoy helping people. I think it's wonderful to know people recognize the benefit of my message and tips I've suggested. Even if they just ask you later, how do you do this and how do you do that? It just makes me feel like I've actually accomplished something that means a lot to people. We don't always realize our message is that impressive until we actually hear people responding to it. We tend to downplay the importance of the messages we give. It rejuvenates me to see people inspired to do more themselves in response to coaching sessions or from listening to a presentation I've made.

When I encounter groups who could use assistance, it makes me feel responsible for giving them just the right advice. I do enjoy writing follow-up articles after focus calls, giving leadership seminars, and giving guidance to those who need it. Many of my sessions with boards and individuals are conducted by teleconference. (This saves them time and money.)

Wright

Well, I really appreciate all the time you've taken with me this afternoon to discuss this important subject of success and overcoming adversity. I just really appreciate you taking this much time with me.

BAZYN

Thank you for the opportunity.

WRIGHT

Today we've been talking to Ardis Bazyn who is the Founder of Bazyn Communications. She is a speaker, trainer, consultant, and author of four books. Besides her inspirational speaking and writing she coaches people on how to become more successful by reaching obtainable goals. Ardis thank you so much for being with us today on *Success Simplified.*

BAZYN

Thank you.

About the Author

Several life changing events have taught Ardis Bazyn patience, courage, and the importance of a positive attitude. Blinded in a car accident at the age of 20, she was required to learn a new career. Despite other setbacks, she earned a Master's degree in teaching and self-published 4 books. In her most requested keynote "Coping with challenges and change", Ardis tells her personal story of viewing challenges or obstacles as opportunities rather than tragedies. Besides her inspirational speaking and writing, she coaches people how to be more successful by setting reachable goals. Ardis and her husband Kevin live in Burbank, California. Her daughter Gwen lives in The Netherlands with her husband Keith Evans and her daughter April lives in Lawton, Oklahoma with her husband Matt Gallagher and daughter Rebecca.

Ardis S. Bazyn

Bazyn Communications

2121 Scott Road, No. 105,
Burbank, CA 91504
818-238-9321
abazyn@bazyncommunications.com
www.bazyncommunications.com

CHAPTER ELEVEN

YOU CAN LOSE THE GENETIC LOTTERY AND STILL BE SUCCESSFUL IN LIFE

BY RICK GROSSO

DAVID WRIGHT (WRIGHT)

Today we're talking with Rick Grosso. There is an old saying that those who do, do, and those who don't teach. Not so with Rick Grosso. Before coming a sales trainer and consultant, Rick ran the second largest specialty home improvement company of its kind in America. Since then he has trained others to do exactly what he did so successfully.

Today, Rick has earned the reputation of being the number one sales trainer in the country in the specialty direct to consumer home improvement industry. To date he has trained hundreds of million-dollar-a-year salespeople—a milestone in that industry—with more than twelve of these people hitting annual sales of more than two million dollars and two who have actually reached three million plus in a single year.

Rick's closing techniques and methodology that he teaches has become the standard in the industry for one-sit closing.

Rick, welcome to *Success Simplified.*

RICK GROSSO (GROSSO)

Well, thank you, David; great to be here.

Wright

So why did you pick the title "You Can Lose the Genetic Lottery and Still Be Successful in Life"?

Grosso

Because I have found it to be so true. A lot of people feel that if they are not born with a certain set of skills, they will not be able to achieve the success they desire. Yet, my own life experience, as well as the experience of many people with whom I have worked, have proven just the opposite. I have worked with many people who have found success, yet they were not genetic "lottery winners"—I am also an example.

I started life as a school teacher making very little money. To supplement my income during the summer, I decided to try selling. I had always believed that I couldn't sell, and I set about to prove myself truthful. As the old joke goes, I sold a lot during my first sixty days—I sold my television, I sold my stereo. I sold everything but the prospects. Sixty days without a sale—I couldn't get much worse than that. On 100 percent commission, that earned me a great big zero, not counting expenses. Yet I wouldn't quit because I saw other people making money, so I knew there was potential. My manager convinced me to invest $500, which I could not afford, to attend a five-day sales training program. I went to class and learned the sales techniques. I turned it around and became very, very successful within my sales field and became one of the top in the country. The training not only taught me the necessary techniques, but it also changed my attitude and beliefs.

From there I wanted to become a speaker and a sales trainer. Genetically, I was the last person on earth suited for such an ambition. If there is anyone genetically who shouldn't be a speaker it is me. I have a heavy New York accent, I have terrible grammar, I mispronounce words, and I misuse words. Yet, I'm a professional speaker and have become very successful in my field. Why? It is the message, conviction, and energy that people see and hear, not my diction or grammar. As the saying goes, "What you are speaks so loudly, I can't hear a word your saying." So again, it's not what you get genetically that counts in life but what you do with it.

Yesterday, my daughter sent an e-mail to me with a quote attributed to Lou Holtz: "Ability is what you are capable of doing. Motivation determines what you do. Attitude determines how well you do it." This made me think of his personal life. Lou Holtz, the famous coach, and popular motivation speaker, was 142 pounds in college and trying to play football. Look at what he became! A 142-pound football player, third string in college, who became a legendary football coach, and has gone on to become one of the top motivational speakers in the country today, even though he speaks with a lisp.

The message is clear—it's not what the genetic lottery has given you, it is what you do with it. We all have the potential.

Wright

So what do you think that readers can take away from your story that they can relate to?

Grosso

People can relate. The more stories that they can identify with, the more they begin to believe. When they believe, they accomplish. When people understand my story and the stories of others and what we had to go through to become successful, it gives everyone the feeling that they can do it too. In sales we teach WIIFM (What's In It For Me). If Grosso, who was so bad, can make it, so can I.

When I first got started I went sixty days without a sale. My manager called me in and said, "Kid, you stink. You either have to learn how to sell or you should quit." I agreed to come up with $500 that I didn't have for the training. The only place I could get the $500 was from my father, who didn't want me going into sales. In fact, he had said, "You'll never make it in sales. Commission selling—that's not a real job. Once you fail, don't come to me looking for money." There I was asking him for money. But that training turned my life around. When you combine training with attitude and belief, look out! Things will happen.

I was young, shy, and introverted. When I finally started making it they would put me up front in a sales meeting and say, "Look at him; if he can do it, so can you.

There is an old saying, "It is not the size of the dog in the fight. It is the size of the fight in the dog." Just like in the movie *Rocky*. Rocky Balboa would not stay down. Every time he was knocked down, he would bounce back up and yell *"Yo!* Adrian!"

If you really want something enough and go after it with the right work ethic, you will find a way.

Wright

Do you have some actual stories you can share with our readers?

Grosso

More than we will have time for. But two that pop to mind right away are the stories of Mickey Harris and Ed English.

Mickey went to work for me back when I owned my own sales company. His story is almost identical to mine. When Mickey started, he also was unable to close a sale. Lead after lead, he could not make a sale. He was working on 100 percent commission for a month and a half with zero income and road expenses. There were threats to repossess his car and he was behind on his mortgage. But he would not quit. He actually came to me and asked if he could work as an installer part-time just to get some money. I told him no, that would be quitting. I believed that he had what it would take in sales and he would make it. And make it he did. Mickey not only turned around and become one of the greatest closers ever in the industry; he then became vice president for the company he's with.

Ed English had been in the business about fourteen years when I first met him during one of my training sessions, an intensive three-day camp I call "Closers Camp." One year later, he was back in the same class and had gone from $400,000 to $1.2 million. That was quite a few years ago. To sell more than a million dollars worth of anything back then was a hall of fame conquest.

When asked how, Ed gave credit to the training. The message was fantastic. By mastering the techniques we teach, he went from ordinary to extraordinary. The message is clear. It is learnable. He became one of the first people in the country to hit the two-million-dollar level and has become almost a legend within the industry, in the field that he's in now.

We tell people, "You are twice as good as you think you are, and that is only half the truth." Story after story keeps proving it.

As I said, we can go on with story after story about it, but it's what people have inside of them that counts.

WRIGHT

So what is the most important thing you believe you need to say to help others in their quest?

GROSSO

Mickey and Ed's accomplishments verify the old saying, "The proof is in the pudding." We all have the ability, we just need the training and to believe in ourselves. In our training program, we get people to believe and then back it up with a proven sales methodology they can follow—a proven success path. I use McDonald's as an example. Like so many people, I absolutely love the French fries at McDonalds. Do you?

WRIGHT

Absolutely.

GROSSO

Yet, who cooks the fries at McDonald's? It's not Emeril or Chief Jean Paul. It is usually some high school student earning close to minimum wage. Yet, the fries come out perfect every time. Why? Because of the system; nothing is left to chance. McDonalds specs the cooker used to cook the fries. There is a line on the cooker to show how much oil to put in. It only cooks to one temperature. You place the fries in a basket and press a button. It not only drops the fries in, but pops them up automatically. The fries come precut, so they are always the right size. The basket goes down and then pops up automatically. So how do you mess up the fries? You've got to do something creative to mess up the fries.

In the "in home sales" field we teach people the same thing that McDonalds does. We put them on a proven system to follow with actual scripts and presentations. If they learn and follow the system, it will work. We then drill them and test them to proficiency. When they leave, they expect to win—and they do.

One of my clients who has been very successful with the system is Gerry Rogers, owner of Mr. Rodgers Windows.

I first met Gerry when he had me incorporate my system in his company. Every night he would take me out to dinner and ask where I would like to go. Being a gourmand, I choose some of the best restaurants in the area. Little did I know that he was not sure how he was going to cover those bills. He doesn't have to worry about that today. He is the top home improvement window company in his markets, and has his own plane and pilot flying between his offices. Gerry has not only taken the Methodology, he has trademarked the slogan he created that his company operates by: "Trainable, duplicatable, transferable practices and procedures." He has taken the system and "clones" his people. As a result, he has developed a sales team that has the highest average volume per salesperson in his product field in the industry. Can you imagine close to 100 percent success rate on developing new salespeople. Why? Because it is trainable and duplicable!

Wright

So what other keys do you feel are vital for achieving one's dreams?

Grosso

Again, I keep coming back to belief and determination.

In sales, as in all of life, you will perform proportionally to your self-esteem and self-confidence. That is easy to say, but the trick is how you get other people there. That is why in sales a proven success path and methodology is so necessary. A system that is "Predictable, Repeatable and Transferable" is essential to success. Results and knowledge builds self-confidence.

Once we get people to that point, we preach to them, "Never be satisfied." When you are green, you are growing. When you are ripe, you rot. If better is possible, then good is not good enough. Keep reaching and stretching. That is what makes life exciting.

In his acceptance speech, upon being inducted into the basketball hall of fame, Michael Jordan said, "Limits like fears are often just an illusion."

Recently I flew to Seattle. As the plane was descending, I had a spectacular view of 14,408-foot Mt. Rainier. That view reminded me of an article I had read many years ago that had inspired me. It was about a guy, Don Bennett, who had climbed Mt. Rainier. Don Bennett had only one leg. When asked how a one-legged man could climb Mt. Rainier, he replied "One hop at a time."

What are our limits? Look at what the Don Bennetts and Lance Armstrongs of this world have accomplished. What can we fulfill?

Wright

So of all of the people you've trained and certainly many, many of them are very successful. What are the most common characteristics that you find in winners?

Grosso

We just quoted, "When you are green, you are growing. When you are ripe, you rot." Winners are constantly striving to be better—they're never satisfied. I go into a company to do a training seminar and the owner will often say, "Gee, the number one salesmen I have might be a problem. Do you think we should have him in there? He'd probably be a disruption." The owner couldn't be more wrong. The number one salesperson is the one who asks the most questions, who takes the most notes, and who is most eager to get new information and knowledge. Winners are never satisfied; they're constantly striving to become better.

It amazes me to see people spend hours and hours practicing their hobbies like golf, and yet don't practice perfecting skills that they use to make a living. They don't work at becoming better at their chosen profession. If they were to put the same time and effort into increasing their professional skills, how much better could they be? Again, if better is possible, why don't we keep getting better? In sales, as in all skill professions, we need to constantly keep striving to get better. School is never out for the pro.

Another characteristic of winners is that they have no patience. Patience is an excuse for procrastination. They act—they're not willing to wait. They make things happen, and will persist. Successful people are very determined. People quit because they think they will lose or fail. The winners persist because they expect to win. Vince Lombardi once said, "The Green Bay Packers never lost a football game. Once or twice a year they ran out of time." He had them believing that if they could have played longer, they would have found a way to win.

Winners not only expect to win, they know it is up to them to make things happen. Michael Jordan always wanted to take the last game-deciding shot. He wanted the ball. A reporter once asked George

Bernard Shaw what was the most exciting thing that ever happened to him. Shaw replied, "Things don't happen to me, I happen to things."

There is a great book that came out recently titled, *The Art of Racing in the Rain,* by Garth Stein. The theme of the book is that the car goes where the eyes go. Wow, that's powerful—the car goes where the eyes go. Isn't that life? Life will bring us whatever we focus on. Where are your eyes? Where do you focus? What are your thoughts? Where your eyes go is where life will take you.

Winners love what they are doing; they take great pride in what they do. Here's the beautiful thing: the better you get at things in life, the more enjoyable they become. You should love what you do professionally. That's why so many highly successful people never want to retire. Work should not be a four-letter word. It should be exciting—the thrill of achieving a goal, the rush, the high. It is the ultimate adventure. I always tell my sales trainees that the three greatest feelings in the world are:

- Sex
- A bowl movement
- And a sale!

And not necessarily in that order.

Wright

It's been said that the Millennials—the people who are graduating now and coming into the workplace—have that "you know me attitude." How important do you think work ethic is?

Grosso

Work ethic is vital. The car might go where the eyes go (that's attitude), but if you want to race a car and don't know how to drive, you are going to crash.

If attitude and belief are two legs of the stool, then work ethic is the third leg. I have always said that there is an ocean between saying and doing. But the concept that you pay the price of success is laughable. You don't pay the price—you enjoy it. If paying the price is that dream car, house, education for your kids, let's pay it.

Michael Jordan was cut from the high school basketball team. He wasn't good enough. Instead of quitting, he decided to win. He set a practice regimen to practice dunking. Can you believe that Air Jordan couldn't dunk? He practiced dunking a thousand times a day. He started from one foot away until he could do it a thousand times in a row, then two feet, three, four, etc. Now is that talent or work ethic? It is amazing how talented you become with the right work ethic. Tiger Woods practiced hitting three thousand balls growing up. No one has ever hit three thousand golf balls a day. The average pro hits a thousand. Tiger had the best work ethic ever in his profession.

We gave examples of Mickey Harris and Ed English, Mickey couldn't close. He memorized all of my materials, and today not only can he teach them verbatim, but he has also expanded on them. Ed's story is identical. So are they great salesman, or people with a great work ethic?

The motto of the Marine Corps is "The more you sweat in peace, the less you bleed in war." It is amazing how talented we become with enough sweat!

Wright

Do you think it's necessary to make personal life sacrifices in order to become successful?

Grosso

That's a great big *no*—absolutely not.

I remember an article I read in the *Wall Street Journal*. It asked top CEOs in America the same question about making sacrifices in their personal life. The vast majority—80 percent—said that they would not miss a child's ballgame or play. This did not mean that they didn't work hard, but for important events in their family life, they were there. Remember the old saying that the tail doesn't wag the dog. The reason we want to become successful is for a better life. We don't want to become the tool of money—we want money to become our tool to allow us to do the things in life we want.

The concept that you have to sacrifice your personal life to succeed is an excuse—an excuse to rationalize.

I love the story of the man who always took his work home from the office and didn't have time for his children. Finally, his little girl said, "Daddy, if your work is too hard to finish at work, why don't they put you in the slow class like they do in my school?" No one ever said on their death bed, "I wish I had spent more time at the office."

To me, a great family life is always quality over quantity. How many people work nine o'clock to five o'clock and when they come home, what do they do? They walk into their house, grab a beer, turn on the television to watch someone else do something exciting, and complain that they never caught a break.

Don't let the tail wag the dog. Don't become the tool of money. Nothing is more important than family.

Wright

How important is it to have patience in striving to become successful?

Grosso

Winners are not patient. They expect things to happen now; they want results now. We said before that patience is a poor excuse for procrastination. Understand that there is a difference between patience and persistence. Persistence is not being willing to give up. If we waited until we were ready to start a new endeavor, we would probably never leave home.

Thomas Edison failed a thousand times with the light bulb; he wasn't patient but he was persistent—he wasn't going to give up, no matter what.

When I was young I read every success and motivation book I could find. My favorite was *Think and Grow Rich* by Napoleon Hill. One of the stories in the book tells about a man named Darby. Darby went to California during the gold rush to seek his fortune. He found a rich vein of gold. He staked his claim, went back to Pennsylvania, and held a meeting to raise funds so he could go back and mine it professionally. He raised the necessary money and went back and started mining. Then the vein of gold disappeared. He drilled hole after hole, but could not find the vein. Finally, broke, he sold the rights to his claim for the junk value of the equipment and went back to Pennsylvania. Meanwhile, the person who bought Darby's claim drilled a new hole six inches from Darby's last drilling and found that elusive vein of gold.

Darby went on to be the most successful insurance salesperson of his time. When asked why, he said, "I'll never forget I once stopped six inches short of gold. Don't stop short of gold."

I went to high school with a fellow by the name of Paul Costa. In high school Paul was six feet, four inches and weighed about two hundred and forty pounds. He played fullback and seemed unstoppable. He received a full scholarship to Notre Dame and couldn't make it as a fullback because he was too slow; but he wouldn't quit. He had them red-shirt him so that he could spend five years on the team trying to find a spot he could fit in. Then he tried as a tight end, but couldn't make it as a tight end, either. Yet every summer I would see Paul back in Port Chester at the park, running, working out, and lifting weights nonstop. Finally, he bulked himself up enough so that he went back and was drafted by the pros. Paul went on to become an All Pro guard for Buffalo, blocking for a guy named O.J. He couldn't make it as a fullback, couldn't make it as a tight end, went through five years in college very low in the draft, but ended up all pro. He wouldn't quit—he knew what his goal was, knew what he wanted, and he kept working to find a way to accomplish it. He made things happen justly.

Wright

So what is the biggest, most important sale that you have ever made?

Grosso

That is what this chapter has been all about. The most important sale that I or anyone could ever make is to sell yourself on you. Until I started believing in myself, I was on the road to nowhere. When I didn't believe, I had no self-confidence—I was lost. I didn't think I could make it. That thought was in my head. That was where my eyes were going. It wasn't lack of work or effort. The harder I tried, the worse I got. When you expect bad things, bad things happen.

I use an example in my training. I ask everyone to close their eyes and then I repeat several times: "The dog is not chasing the cat. The dog is not chasing the cat." I then ask them to open their eyes and tell me what they saw in their subconscious mind. They all answer that they saw a dog chasing a cat—the exact opposite of what I was saying. The reason is because the mind cannot go away from a negative thought. The mind actually pictures that negative thought and leads you right to it. If you are on a golf hole with water and say, “Don’t hit it in the water,” the mind sees the ball going splat! When we change our thinking, we change our lives. The Olympian is taught to visualize himself going over the bar. The golfer should picture the putt going in the hole. Perception truly is reality. When you change your perception, you change your life; you change your results. Life is a self-fulfilling prophesy—it goes both ways, you get out of life what you expect.

I remember many years ago when I was young, the great Norman Vincent Peale was speaking to an audience and he said, “How would you like to know how much money you’re going to make in five years? How many people would like to know that?” Of course, everybody in the audience raised their hand. Then he said, “I’ll tell you exactly how much you’re going to make five years from now. You’re going to make exactly what you believe.” That’s so true of everything in life. As the book says: As You Think It, So It Should Be Done unto You. Think about it: if you think you’re happy, you’re happy, regardless of circumstances around you. Health, wealth, and happiness are all a state of mind—you can control that state if you choose to. So choose to.

I love the story of the rider in the desert at night. All of a sudden, a herd of riders comes down upon him. They tell him to dismount and to reach down into the sand and pick up a hand full of rocks. They then tell him to stick the rocks in his pocket, to mount his horse, and ride all night to the east. When the sun comes up he must reach down and take the rocks out of his pocket, and then he will know both happiness and sadness at the same time. He rides all night, and as the he dismounts and reaches into his pocket, all of the rocks and grains of sand have turned into diamonds. And he remembers the words, “You will know both happiness and sadness”—happiness because the stones turned into diamonds and sadness because he didn’t pick up more stones. Yes, let’s be thankful for the diamonds that we have, but how many more stones can we pick up?

I say go for it, that’s what it’s all about—go for it. There is no fun in safety. You can do it. To the one who believes all things are possible, all these quotes from the book have meaning.

We only have one life we know we're living for sure in this existence, let's make it great, let's make it exciting, let's make it fun, let's make it worthwhile, let's never look back and say, "Boy, I would have, I could have, I should have, if only, someday."

Wright

Well, what a great interview. I really do appreciate you all the time you've spent with me and answering these questions. I've learned a lot here today and I know that our readers will.

Grosso

Thank you, David; I appreciate that. You know I once saw a quote that read, "The greatest tragedy of our times is going to your deathbed with the greatest music still within you," and we don't ever want that to happen. So let's go for the gold. Let's not wait for things to happen—let's make them happen. I do not know about reincarnation. I do know that this is the only life I am living right now. Let's make it exciting. Let's make it great!

Wright

Today we've been talking with Rick Grosso. Before becoming a sales trainer and consultant, he ran the largest specialty home improvement company of its kind in America. Today, he has earned the reputation of being the number one sales trainer in the country in the specialty direct-to-consumer home improvement industry.

Rick thank you so much for being with us on *Success Simplified.*

Grosso

My pleasure.

About the Author

Rick started life as a school teacher. To supplement his income, he started in sales in a multilevel organization. After a rough start, Rick went on to become the fourth and youngest person ever to become a member of their exclusive Chairmen's Club in an organization of more than eighty thousand salespeople in twenty-eight countries. Rick then went on to become Vice President of their Italian operation, and then President of the Spanish Corporation, which achieved a record sales volume of more than one million dollars during its first month in operation. Upon returning to America, he started his own replacement window company, and in just four years became the second largest replacement window company in America. That success allowed Rick to follow his dream and become a professional motivator and sales trainer, specializing in home selling. Rick has become recognized as the top sales trainer for closing in the home improvement industry today.

Rick Grosso

4000 N. A1A, Ste 602
Ft. Pierce, FL 34949
772-359-7918
rickgrosso@aol.com
www.rickgrosso.com

CHAPTER TWELVE

ON THE BACK OF A COCKTAIL NAPKIN

BY CHUCK BEAN

DAVID WRIGHT (WRIGHT)

Today we're talking with Chuck Bean. Chuck wasn't very interested in school; instead, he went to work as an industrial laborer and quickly understood the value of hard work and return on investment. In short order he moved through the ranks, working in sales and marketing management, eventually becoming a senior executive of a major corporation. In 1998, he formed Baxter Bean & Associates of Calgary, Canada (of which today is CEO), along with Bean Dental, Baxter Bean Creative, and Stand and Command.

With more than thirty years of solid business experience under his belt, today Chuck spends his time doing two things: traveling the world listening and understanding people and cultures, along with coaching and training some of the most successful businesspeople in the world. Chuck is a no nonsense guy who believes in basic business strategies. His processes and ideas are easy to implement and they provide lasting value and return on time invested. He believes that everyone can be successful.

Chuck Bean, welcome to *Success Simplified.*

CHUCK BEAN (BEAN)

Thank you.

WRIGHT

So what do you mean by "on the back of a cocktail napkin"?

Bean

Well, David, I think that everybody needs to have a set of operating strategies or mantras. They should be powerful enough that they can be remembered and recited quickly, they should be comprehensive so that they will conjure up immediate action in the stakeholder and they should be simple enough that they can be written on the back of a cocktail napkin.

Wright

Will you tell me what they are?

Bean

I have nine of them—nine simple strategies—and I will list them and go through them one by one. All of them are very specific to business management, although they certainly can be applied to life management as well.

Wright

Wonderful. Would you take me through the meaning of them and how they apply to business?

Bean

Absolutely. The first one is *don't debate the past, debate the future* and points to the challenge of people wasting time on non-essential items.

What I have found throughout the years that I have been coaching and working with people, is that we can get caught up arguing about what should have happened, however, it makes better sense for us to focus on where we are going, not where we have been.

As an example, look at a football team; they have a very limited amount of time to get into the huddle and call the next play. They have to focus on the end game, and if they get caught up in the last play, they can't set up the future play. In fact, football is a great example of any business. There are plenty of failed plays, along with lots of offensive and defensive challenges. Great teams put the failures behind during the game and only focus on the positives.

Football coaches do the same—they only focus on future opportunities and continually modify their game based on that. When the coaching team starts arguing about past issues on the sidelines, there is a strong likelihood that the game will be lost.

I see it in business all the time, be it at the boardroom table or in strategic planning sessions. Business teams literally get caught up in debating and arguing about what should have been done. I'm not saying we shouldn't look at the past, but it should be to study, not debate.

When I see a businessperson spending valuable time focusing on the past, I find a way to steer him or her back to looking forward. It is simple as that.

Wright

That makes sense. What you are saying is that people waste too much time focusing on things that they cannot change.

What is your second strategy?

Bean

I'll bet you have heard this before: put your own mask on first, then assist those around you.

Wright

I have heard that a thousand times before, every time I get on a plane, but not in relationship to life or business.

Bean

I've been using this mantra with business managers for decades now. It means that you can't help someone else if you're not looking after yourself. It is easy to get caught up doing other people's work or looking after other people's problems. Good business leaders understand that they have to look after themselves first.

Actually, I like to say that there are four ways we can help ourselves first. The first is physically—making sure we're in good shape, we have a physical presence, and we're strong.

The second is emotionally—we are tuned in, we make those emotional connections we need, and that we keep our sense of humor and passion.

The third way is intellectually—we remain in the thought and planning process.

The fourth way is spiritually, which relates to your ability to tap into your creative juices and creative energies.

I think it makes great sense for anybody who wants to be successful in business, or at home for that matter, to understand that those four quadrants are critical. We should continually challenge ourselves to have greater levels of competency in all four areas.

I also think we have to be careful that we don't check out in any of those four areas. We can check out physically by letting ourselves go, living an unhealthy lifestyle, etc. We can check out emotionally, meaning we are present, but not really engaged. We can check out intellectually by failing to be part of the thought process. Finally, spiritual check-out usually manifests itself as a lack of self-actualization.

It can be lonely at the top and good leadership requires an awareness of these challenges.

Wright

Do you have a formula to help avoid checking out?

Bean

First and foremost, be self-aware and engaged to the potential of falling off the wagon. Next, take the time to exercise and eat healthy. There are plenty of experts out there who can assist in that area. Having good health is foundational to our ability to look after ourselves; without it we will struggle. Thirdly, laugh a little and try not to take difficult situations too personally; but rather, see them logically. If you can't do that, fall back on exercise. It is amazing how much more in control of emotional situations we can become when we walk up five flights of stairs or go for a walk or run.

If you find yourself in an intellectual stupor, unable to think things through, or if you hit a wall, find a funny movie to watch or read a good book and make it a point to take a break. And finally, if you find yourself mentally sapped and unable to be creative, try stepping away and going back to the plan. In other words, anytime you find yourself bogged down, don't keep grinding forward. Instead, step back for a moment and physically, emotionally, or mentally breathe.

WRIGHT

You mentioned in our pre-session that the third strategy was to *encourage creativity*. I find that very interesting. Do you really believe that we're not creative enough in today's business environment?

BEAN

I think we knock creativity out of our children at a very early age. Not that I'm here to knock the education system, but we do take children and we put them into an environment where we take away their play factor. We steer them into chalkboard learning and by the time they're adults they've been conditioned to do a lot less play and a lot more tactical learning. Ultimately, for many of them, when they become adults working in a grown-up world, they are conditioned to not work independently and to avoid being creative. It is actually a disconnect.

WRIGHT

What can we do to correct it?

BEAN

I am a big believer in structure and process; however, I really do believe that we need to encourage play in the workplace. I find good managers who run good businesses generally have employees who are not scared to talk to them about new and crazy ideas. The managers then put these ideas into action.

Throughout the years, the majority of good, sustainable ideas I have seen take hold in businesses have been started from the fringes—many times from people just "kicking it around" and playing with it. Innovation, after all, is not the exclusive domain of someone with a particular role or title. Innovation can happen anywhere and with anyone. In fact, I caution all of my clients to never think about whether or not their competitors will copy their great ideas; rather, they should think in terms of *when* they will copy their ideas. Even worse, they will probably not only copy it, but will also innovate on it. Rather than waiting for that to happen, my advice is to let your people be creative and play around with as much as possible, so that they can bring on improvements as a matter of course, rather than as a matter of cost.

And there is an additional point to all of this. When we encourage creativity, it establishes a base level of accountability. As time moves on, it evolves into expectations and through creating expectations we establish respect, which leads to loyalty. Show me a manager who doesn't want loyalty and I will show you a manager with limited scope and a limited life span. Most people crave loyalty and the solution is right before our eyes.

Wright

It sounds like a math equation—accountability and expectations equals respect and loyalty. I love it! What comes next?

Bean

Well I don't want to sound too Zen, but here it is: *friction is meant to polish*. This statement speaks to the fact that we should be looking at all situations and learning from them. Many people have a tendency to "shoot the alien" so to speak, so that when something new comes at them and they're not sure about what it is or what to do about it, they ignore it or they gun it down rather than stepping back and taking a serious look at it, and asking, "Okay, what is this, why is it here, and what is this all about?" The key here is to try and learn something from whatever is presented to us and to not disregard or discredit someone or something just as a matter of course. This is one of the most powerful mantras that we can have. If we can adopt a strategy of continual curiosity, it can open up millions of new doors.

Wright

I agree with what you are saying. Curiosity is an attractive quality in people. What is number five?

Bean

Empower the stars, carry the strugglers and shoot the stragglers. Yes, this is harsh but it is a message for anyone who has to manage a group of people—volunteers, a sports team—a business, and so on. I draw on this operating strategy from my years of observing people on teams and in the workplace. I really do believe that there are different types of people who work in the workplace and it is the leader's responsibility to understand organizational structure and the people working for him or her and how they fit.

If you look at my first illustration (below), you will see three circles, each representing the keys to an effective organizational model. Throughout the years I have developed my thinking around the fact that the higher your awareness of, and your capability in, each of these keys, the stronger and more effective your organizational or corporate culture will be.

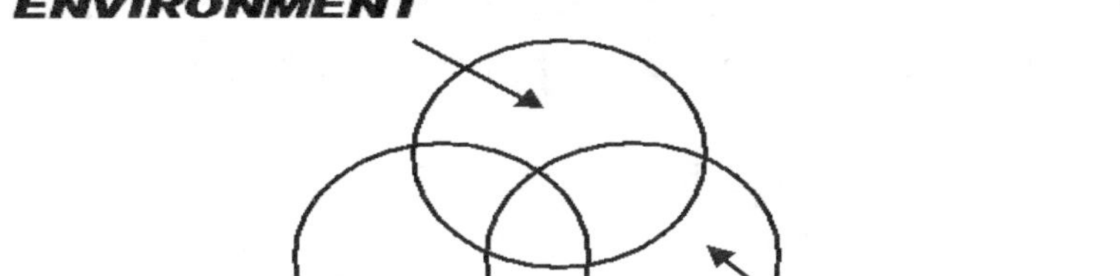

Operating environment refers to products and services, the economic "impact" competitive challenges, and such. It is the most difficult to control and this is why all great leaders should practice some sort of safety strategies. We can predict and prepare for environmental threats and opportunities, but we cannot control them. Physical, financial, and proprietary discretion is the key to success here.

Process refers to your day-in-day-out standard operating procedures. Wherever possible, smart leaders will develop processes that people can follow to ensure consistency in output. For any leader this is the easiest to control and your return on both investment and time investment is generally maximized through process implementation.

People are the wildcard. Ask any good leader and he or she will tell you that people are the most valuable asset; however, under their breath leaders will also tell you that this is not always true of *all* their people. It is the leadership dilemma—finding people who are motivated and then spending the appropriate amount of time with them to ensure that they are effectively utilized. And in all of this, we find this statement of empowering the stars, carrying the strugglers, and shooting the stragglers. When you put all of this together and you create a standard of excellence for each of them, you raise the bar on your company culture.

So specifically to the people component, the only real way to deal with this is through watching them.

WRIGHT

Are you referring to observational behaviors?

BEAN

Yes. You've got to see them in action and apply the stars, strugglers, stragglers model. If you look at the second illustration, you'll see that we identify three groups of people based on observational characteristics. It provides insight into the way they conduct themselves and their approach to taking action both in life and certainly in business, and mates this with skill sets.

Attitude / Conduct

Skill Level	STARS +Problem Solving + Resiliency and Responsibility	STRUGGLERS - Problem Solving + Resiliency and Responsibility	STRAGGLERS - Problem Solving - Resiliency and Responsibility
CAN TEACH	Mentor	Player	Redeploy
CAN DO	Player	Apprentice	Redeploy
CAN'T DO	Apprentice	Redeploy	Remove

The first group we call stars. They have great problem-solving skills along with positive resiliency and responsibility. My experience tells me that those are the two attributive or conductive sets that are most valued, whether you are looking for a partner, a boss, spouse, friend, etc. Nothing is more attractive than a person who can solve problems, handle rejection or disappointment, and take responsibility. When we have people with both sets we have people who can be motivated. They will source out problems and solve them or when given a problem they will solve it. When they have to take a punch or when something goes wrong, they have great resiliency and they take responsibility for their actions.

In the second category—strugglers—we find people who are usually missing one of those skills; typically it is problem-solving. They will be resilient and they'll be responsible, but they have a tough time solving problems. These are people who have had challenges, been knocked down, and find solution-seeking difficult. They sometimes struggle with resiliency and responsibility. The upside is that it is fixable and with some management and leader intervention they can be saved. They can turn into great contributors. It will take time, but it can be done.

The third group—the stragglers—are missing both skill sets. They can't solve problems, they have difficulty with resiliency and responsibility, and quite frankly, for a manager, this is a big fix. They can seriously slow you down. We've got to recognize that the stragglers—the people who pull you back and don't want to contribute—shouldn't have a home in your business.

If you then consider skills under three headings: can't do, which simply means that they are not trained for the moment; can do, which indicates that a person is able to perform job functions on his or her own with minimal or no supervision, and finally, can teach, which means that these are people who are so good at what they do they can teach others, you can quickly establish those who are worth investing in, those who need additional development, those who are over their heads, and those who have to go.

I know this is tough and I know this is harsh, but I ask every manager who works with me: do you have the three or four years it's going to take to turn someone around, and is it the right thing to do to hang on to people who are sinking your ship?

Wright

This is tough stuff, but it makes sense. When it comes to observational behaviors, how do you make determinations for people you are hiring fresh?

Bean

I am a big believer in three thoughts on this: fit, feel, and science. When you are meeting candidates to join your team (and by the way, I am referring to any team, from line positions to senior executives), use this strategy:

Fit: do they have the skills and capacity—ability to grow—for your group?

Feel: what does your gut tell you about the person? Does the candidate stir up positive emotions in you?

Science: for me, that means testing. I have been using testing systems for years. We have a great one that we have developed in-house as well. Using this model significantly lessens the risk of making a bad choice.

There is a difference between checking references and a background *investigation*. Nobody applying for a job will ever give someone bad references. Don't waste your time with them. Successful managers will dig deeply into a candidate's past to determine patterns that can be duplicated going forward.

WRIGHT

When we talked earlier, you mentioned that point six was for young people. Why do you say that? *Every job sucks sometimes, so get one that pays well.*

BEAN

Yes sir, and it is not just for young people, however, it is probably most appropriate for them. I have harped on this point all of my life. We all need money. In fact, we live in an environment where we need wealth to both survive and to enjoy the finer things in life. We tend to be motivated in a hierarchy of three drivers: wealth, achievement, or recognition. This being said, not everyone is motivated by wealth as their key driver. I think it's a shame to see someone work somewhere and not get out of it what he or she should financially.

All jobs suck at times. I don't care if you are the president of a world-class corporation or if you're working as a sweeper in a factory—all jobs suck at times. Things get bad, people are miserable, it goes on and on. So seek out something that is going to give you a return that you in turn can take and do whatever you want with. If you want to make your money and then give it away after, do it, but be sure to look after yourself financially first.

WRIGHT

I can certainly agree with you, Chuck. I have heard of people quitting good jobs over what were traumatic, yet temporary difficulties. In retrospect, if they had just held on they could have seen them through to a better ending.

What is number seven?

BEAN

Beware of the riptide.

WRIGHT

You must spend time in the water, beware of the riptide. This is intriguing. Are you saying that there are times when you get sucked in and pulled off shore so to speak?

BEAN

Correct. If you watch waves on the beach, you'll see that they arrive in blocks, generally a group of easy waves, followed by rip. Some people say that they come in sevens. So when the waves are calm, there is not much danger, but when the waves are strong that's when people get hurt. This happens in business all the time. I think a smart business manager understands that something could go wrong and will not get caught up with success after success after success without having some sort of a contrarian view of all the initiatives. Business owners especially need to be aware of the "founder syndrome" (I will comment on later), which can be a real challenge.

WRIGHT

Point eight is introspective—*a step back can be a step forward.* It seems to speak to the need for people to be willing to take a step backward while also relating to the riptide point as well. Am I right?

BEAN

Great leaders learn that a step back can indeed be a step forward. Basically, it means that we shouldn't get caught up with the concept that *our* idea is the only idea.

I mentioned founder syndrome earlier, which is created when people who have developed a great idea can't step away from it. My theory on this is pretty simple: when businesses grow, they go through four stages. They start off as small small, they become big small, then they move to small big, and then they become big big. The process of running the business changes. When you're small small, you may only be a single person or very small group. Your idea is owned by the small entity and you have a two-legged policy manual. Decision-making is simple—if you don't know what to do, just ask the boss and almost no consensus or politics are involved. What dictates the move to big small is the addition of people. At this point, decision-making becomes more complex, with more people in sponsorship and stake positions. Politics start to play a role. Consensus can be needed.

When you move from big small to small big, the world changes. This is typically where founder syndrome is pushed to the wall. Leaders are forced to have to engage more people and give room. Failure to do so may end up in good people leaving, or in worse cases a dictatorial management situation. Smart leaders will understand this and let teams be engaged in decision-making. This is big on so many fronts. It creates better succession, buy-in, engagement, and so forth.

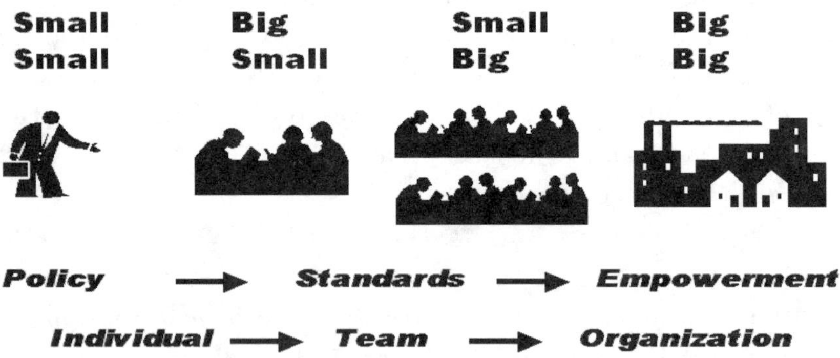

When a leader can successfully make the leap from big small to small big, the next step to big big is easy. By this time leaders have created management teams that are empowered and can run things based on shared visions and values. If you look at the illustration above you can see that dynamics change as well. The company will move from policy to empowerment, and from being individually managed to being organizationally managed. And yes it can work, but it takes work! And here is the warning. If you don't follow this model, you may still succeed personally, however, once you are gone, what you have built will probably not. That, David, is the consequence of founder syndrome.

The challenge around this is it can be a step back for people and a step out of the way in order for the entire business to move forward. If you want to grow your business and have succession, a great leader has to understand that he or she will have to hand it off to someone else one day. Whether a founder is the founder of the business or the founder of an idea in the business, he or she needs to step back and let other people take over at some time.

Wright

And all of this relates to the founder syndrome?

Bean

Yes it is. The founder syndrome is a challenge that people have when they believe they own an idea or concept and it has to be that idea or that concept and they can't let go. In fact, many owner operated businesses have been stopped dead in their tracks by founders not willing to let go and let others move ahead.

Wright

I've never heard that term in all these years. That's a good one. I'm a founder of ideas and companies; you're scaring me here. I need to do some stepping back, I guess.

Please tell me your last point.

Bean

My final strategy is to *worry about being satisfied.* I think that we never really "arrive" and that if we think we have arrived, we should probably worry about it. My wife always tells me not to get too caught up in my successes and to always be grateful. This is sage advice. So the idea of "wow, we've arrived, we've made it," should always be tempered with, "where do we go from here?"

WRIGHT

So with these nine topics, do you have a summary or an action plan that you can put together for people who own companies or for use as individuals?

BEAN

I would recommend to anyone to follow the lead from these strategies and adapt to them to your approach in business and in life. Circle them with your vision, mission, and values. Simplified, vision is "what you want to be when you grow up," mission is how you are going to get there, and values are the guardrails that keep you on track during the journey.

It is always lonely at the top and the reason is simple—most people don't like to put in the work that it takes to stay at the top of their game. The greatest leaders of history have very similar characteristics. They are persistent; they stick to their vision and values, and they focus on their best skills. They delegate those things they recognize that they do poorly; they give these tasks to others who have the right skills to accomplish them. They are humble, they don't over-blow their own horn; but rather, allow those around them to flourish. They are curious and they focus on learning. Finally, and maybe most importantly, they constantly reinvent themselves. They don't just lead change in others, they lead change in themselves.

We don't need a four-hundred-page plan for all of this; all we need is a simple strategy. The key is to find something and make it simple, make it easy—a back of a cocktail napkin will work just fine.

WRIGHT

When you pointed out "shoot the stragglers," I remember years ago I was raised as a Christian. A leadership guru told me, "David, you can't reach down into the muck of life and pull up people who do not want to come; there are too many that need and want your advice and services." I always thought that the others needed more because they don't understand, but it took me years to understand his point and that he was right and I was wrong.

BEAN

Great thoughts, David. I mean, really, do you have the time to help everyone? That's the challenge. I think that if our objective is to simply help people then go for it. But if you're running a business or a team of any kind, most leaders don't have the time to take those people who are just simply not interested in being a part of it and push them along. I have seen too many businesspeople spend 80 percent of their time with the impossible when they really should be spending 80 percent of their time with the possible. That's the difference.

WRIGHT

So what you're saying is that people waste too much time focusing on things they can't change, right?

BEAN

Absolutely, and that's nothing new.

WRIGHT

That's true—it's not new, but you would think people wouldn't do that but I do it a lot and many of my friends who own businesses do, too. As a matter of fact, with all the training we get in leadership today, you would think that you would never work on your weaknesses but work on your strengths. Most people I see, however, are still working on their weaknesses, and I don't get it.

BEAN

The key to overcoming the dilemma of spending too much time on the impossible, non-reparable, or on weaknesses, is to take a logical view of things and follow models. Models give us a structure to follow, and that is important. Without models, we will hang on to bad people, bad processes, and bad ideas because we are emotionally invested in them and we can't dump them. It is like buying a stock at $10 and hanging onto it all the way to twenty cents. We feel personally vested.

Use a model to determine your sell position and watch what happens. You won't think that you are vested, you will now think that you should run away—fast!

Wright

I've done exactly what you're saying so many times. These things are deeply ingrained in many of us and in our heart but I tell you, you have certainly made it a lot easier today. I really appreciate the time you've spent with me here. These nine points are extremely intelligently put together. I have never thought about them in that way before, so I appreciate your sharing them. I know our readers will, too.

Bean

You're welcome and thank you for asking me to participate in this great project. One final thing: don't complicate it—keep it to the back of a cocktail napkin.

Wright

Today we've been talking with Chuck Bean of Baxter Bean & Associates of Calgary, Canada. I think he knows what he's talking about, and I'm listening. I hope that our readers will, too.

Chuck, thank you so much for being with us today on *Success Simplified.*

Bean

Cheers.

About the Author

Chuck Bean is the President of Baxter Bean & Associates Inc. along with divisions, StandandCommand, Baxter Bean Creative, and Bean Dental. Bean's companies provide services in business coaching, consulting, and training in areas such as strategic planning, leadership development, sales development, communications, and teamwork. Chuck provides practical consulting and coaching, and his workshops and lectures are educational, informative, and always engaging! He works with business professionals and leaders around the world helping them grow their businesses quickly and profitably without giving up their personal lives and core values.

Chuck Bean

Baxter Bean & Associates, Inc.
205, 5th Ave SW, Suite 700
Calgary, Canada T2P 2V7
403-703-9525
chuck@baxterbean.com
baxterbean.com

CHAPTER THIRTEEN

AUTHENTIC SUCCESS

BY PHYLLIS HAYNES

DAVID WRIGHT (WRIGHT)

Today we're talking with Phyllis Haynes. As a speaker, facilitator, trainer, and moderator Ms. Haynes is in demand. Her work has taken her to many countries and across the United States. Her roster of clients include the United Nations, NCAA, NFL Players Association, Ernst & Young, Columbia University, AT&T, and many other organizations. Her knowledge of global media, new media technology, and cross-cultural communication encompasses more than twenty years of experience in television and production. She is also receiving attention for her video biographies and interviews of accomplished individuals who may not have received the media attention they deserved. Dr. Russell Ackoff, Professor Emeritus of the Wharton School, is among her favorites.

She is well known as the former co-host of WOR-TV's *Straight Talk* and as a former network correspondent for ABC's *Evening News* with Peter Jennings, and *Good Morning America*. She is also the producer of the award-winning documentary titled, *AIDS: The Facts of Life*. It received an American Film Institute Award in the category of Health Education.

Phyllis was invited to the European Union by the Hellenic Foundation to bring her work to the emerging marketplaces of Central and Eastern Europe. As a result of the invitation, she delivered programs on communication skills and new media in Athens, Greece, Bulgaria, and Romania. She also served on the faculty of Emerson College in Boston, teaching at the graduate level in Boston and in Maastricht, the Netherlands. She served as President of the International Society for Panetics a scholarly organization based in Washington, D.C., devoted to reducing suffering. She is a partner with InterChange Consultants, a producer for Studio 1 Think-Tank, a working mother, and happily married wife.

Phyllis Haynes, welcome to *Success Simplified.*

PHYLLIS HAYNES (HAYNES)

Thank you so much, David Wright.

WRIGHT

So why is it important to assess accurately what we think it means to be successful?

HAYNES

Success is one of those over-used words in our society. The meaning of success for each human experience is as different and unique as our individual fingerprints. Because people are bombarded with images, attitudes, and displays of so-called success, they are confused and they tend to think about success in terms of media portrayals (e.g., fancy furniture, fancy cars, and large, high maintenance homes). Those are great things, but are not true indicators of success. Identifying true personal desires and desired results, will give us a more authentic experience of success.

Our parents probably have shared with us what they think success means based on their lives and the times in which they grew up. They influence us and guide us but success for us must be determined by our own experiences and the realities of the times in which we must live and work. Real success is a matter of our own perceptions. Of course, we must consider and evaluate our parents' viewpoints but then work to understand our own. Even if parents are not pushing in a given direction, children can pick up patterns, interpretations, perspectives, and attitudes. In any event, we have to respect our parents, love our parents, but move beyond their interpretations. It's important that we overcome this, go beyond those perceptions, and do the investigation to find out what we think success is for us. So even as parents, when we have children, we need to be conscious that as we develop them toward their successful lives, they're going to be living in a different universe and a different time.

Success is a fluid state, not a fixed point in time. Sometimes people decide that it's going to be one particular thing that will make them successful. With this kind of object fixation, people will move Heaven and Earth trying to get to that one thing. Of course, what happens when they get there or obtain that one thing, is that they discover it doesn't make them feel successful.

Scholars are even suggesting that even the rate of change is greater now than it has ever been—change itself is at an accelerated pace. So as a result, our fixed notions of success must become more fluid. In this fluid investigation and fluid interpretation that we need to make for ourselves, we may find the stream of feedback, indicators, evidence, ideas, and thoughts that give us a true sense of success.

Wright

So would you tell our readers what led you to this understanding of success?

Haynes

I began to realize this perspective when I worked as a journalist and television host. It was a fascinating time for me; I was on television almost every day of my life after I graduated college. I worked at night at a television station and then through graduate school. I worked full-time at WPIX-TV in New York and then WOR-TV. At WOR-TV, I had a talk show that was on every day, six days a week, one hour each day. I interviewed some of the greatest people who have ever been on our planet, wonderful people. I had the opportunity to talk with so many celebrities, business leaders, government heads, and award winning writers.

The sad part about being in television, sometimes you meet someone who is your hero and you discover that he or she is abusing tranquilizers and alcohol, and that they're terribly depressed. I'm not going to name names, that's not the business I'm in; but it really struck me that some of these successful people didn't feel successful at all. They were lost. There were book award winners who couldn't write unless they were absolutely drunk. There were people who came for an interview that if they didn't have their drugs before the interview they couldn't do it. It was an amazing education and a look into the lives of people. Some of them I came to know on a personal basis.

Now, of course, the other side of this—the real eye-opener—was those individuals who didn't need any of those things. There were people who were profoundly happy, maybe not with as much as some of the others, but they were profoundly successful in the eyes of society. They were wise and at peace and didn't seem to need alcohol or medication.

Let me give you some examples of those positive figures: Studs Terkel, a very wise and witty man. Harrison Salisbury, a regal and philosophical journalist. Maya Angelou, a stately poet and writer who overcame challenges in her early life. Harrison Salisbury was fantastic as a writer and traveled the world and loved people. He always talked about the richness of his life. It was an amazing opportunity to talk with him.

Maya Angelou just resonates wealth and peace and joy. She expressed deep satisfaction with her life. She said that she did not dwell on all the losses and tragedy; she turned those tragedies and losses into great writing. She really made an impression. When I think about her and some of the other people I mentioned earlier who were absolutely miserable, she was the exact opposite. So I decided to learn from them and ask questions like, "What was it that made you successful? What gave you so much peace?"

The characteristic that they apparently have in common is that they seem to be playing by their own rules. Maya Angelou said, for example, that she liked to do all of her work early in the day and then have the rest of the day to do whatever she wanted.

What a refreshing idea that was for me. That idea had never occurred to me until she said it. I was raised with the Benjamin Franklin model. According to Franklin there is a time for work and a time for rest. You divide it according to eight hours each, which is one good way toward success and I understood that because it was my parents' way. But no one had ever said to me, "I get my work done by twelve noon and then I play for the rest of the day." Then, I began to discover that it was just like learning a new word. When you learn a new word, it shows up everywhere.

I started meeting other successful people who had the same understanding. They had managed their time, so they worked hard, got their work done in the first part of the day, and they did whatever they wanted to do with the rest of it. Now, there were exceptions made for guest appearances at a banquet or when they had to give a speech, but for the most part, their daily lives were run by their own time values not some imposed schedule.

Michael Korda, author of the bestselling book *Power! How to Get It, How to Use It,* was another person who played by his own rules. I had a chance to talk with him He loved horses. He wanted to get his work done early in the day. He liked having time work for him instead of his having to work for time.

So that was one of the things that really struck me—successful people who *had their own values and made their own powerful use of time*.

Then I found a teacher who taught me how to master time. Now, of course, you never really "master" time, but you learn to partner with it, work with it, and have it reflect your values. That teacher was Burton Geyer. He had a system called Workability. Workability laid a foundation for me to understand that 1) my relationship to time is what will determine my perception of success, 2) if I don't get things done, I'm never going to feel successful, and 3) if I don't get things done in a way that allows my life to feel free and open and positive, I'm not going to feel successful. No matter how great your success, you're going to feel like you've been in a struggle. That's not success.

Burton Geyer taught me to have a peaceful relationship with time. He advised me to never arrive to a meeting five minutes before it is to start, panting and running because I'm almost late. He told me to walk into the meeting as if I'm strolling in; even if I arrived a minute before, always come into my meetings in a place of peace. The real solution is to avoid being late as much as possible, plan a certain number of minutes before you get to where you're going. Again, you'll feel successful just because you're not in that panting, worrying, stressed way of being that so many people have because of the fast pace of life.

The second point is *focus*. There's not much to say about focus except that not many people achieve it. Focus is a matter of understanding that what's in front of you—the present moment—is what's important and not being distracted. Focus is being able to take in the big picture—the picture right in front of you. Just like an excellent driver, you need to approach your life in the same way. Some people are walking around with their eyes open and their feet on the ground, but they're not focused.

The third point is *staying in the present and not being reactive* to mistakes and what happened in the past. Some people are filled with regret and there is almost room for nothing else. They're so filled with the past. They have no ability to look at the moment and take it in; they are in a state of reaction.

I owe this understanding to Robert Fritz. Robert Fritz is the author of many books. *The Path of Least Resistance* is his most famous book. In fact, he said that people need to be able to be in the present and not be reactive because when you are reactive you are acting unconsciously. You need to choose your actions, make decisions in the present, look at what you want to accomplish, and not let reaction guide you.

Reaction is something that is part of our makeup; we have a survival mechanism. The fight or flight mechanism is a matter of biology, so you really can't overcome it. What you can do is learn to observe it and subsequently choose not to be sucked into reaction. This particularly applies to identifying opportunities. If you are not focused, present, and managing your reactive state, you may miss opportunities that show up right in front of you.

The next point is being *engaged.* Now, this is a controversial one. There are many interpretations; people are going to have to find this point for themselves. There are great quotes, including this one: "Nothing great was ever accomplished without enthusiasm." Some people think that having a struggle built into your life will make you more likely successful. Others say keeping a positive attitude and being terribly enthusiastic will make you successful. I think it's a personal choice. I have found that being engaged is such a rare skill that I find business deals happen for me just because I was paying attention and listening. Being engaged is a step above being present. It means paying attention to the person you want to have that job interview with or the person with whom you want to make a business deal or the one to whom you want to give important information. It means listening for opportunity.

I also work with many people on a one-on-one basis and some in groups. When you're giving a presentation, listen to those who are listening, don't listen to what you're thinking in your head. Stay focused and be present with the audience. There is a wave of information coming even from the silent person in front of you, or from a silent group. You can feel the energy of a group. If you pay attention to that information or that person in a job interview, your deal will more likely occur because you are not stuck in your thoughts. Most people can't do this—it is a skill and it's almost a "ninja" skill. You need to be able to listen outside of your head, not to just what is going on inside.

If you can do that, you can reach more people because you're not thinking about what you're going to say next or what others are going to think or how you look. All of those are your thoughts that take you away from the possibility of discovering what's needed next. Most people are not paying attention too, so if you go into an interview or into a job or into any circumstance and you're completely engaged, the person you interact with will have a rare experience with you that he or she may have not had in a long time, if ever. Now, I do not mean entertain, that is not being authentic. If you are authentically interested in what other people or a group has to say and the way they are functioning, they will be with you.

Wright

So what are the classic misconceptions of success—why are these misconceptions pervasive?

Haynes

The classic misconceptions of success are perpetrated by Hollywood and television. The power of imagery has had a profound impact on what we see as successful. We've always had misconceptions about success but they were limited. The growth and global influence of visual and audio media have given the world a superficial, visual display of wealth and its trappings. This imagery misleads and entertains folks and sets many on a disappointing path. Success isn't something that you can show easily. You can show a fancy sofa, you can show a fancy car, and a really decked out night club, but you're not showing the consciousness inside.

Despite this, Hollywood grabbed onto the trappings and mythologies of success, and over time, during the twentieth century, the trappings of success became the benchmarks of success. Many people lost their way in the same way that boats get lost on rocks. Some people even reached those benchmarks and lost their way. Now, in the twenty-first century, we have some extraordinary examples of people attaining the outer layers of wealth but are deeply impoverished on the inside.

Tiger Woods apologized for his behavior with so many women outside of his marriage saying that he felt "entitled." I won't spend any time judging the morality of his actions, that is a personal issue. What Tiger Woods reveals is that, again, success is not a single point or accomplishment in time but a whole inner state of being. He acted on what he thought others did when they had success.

Athletes, actors, and politicians have often been caught acting out the Hollywood theme of cavalier behavior with irresponsibility as an indication of their success. Hollywood is not the main problem. The problem is a lack of understanding that real wealth is within and is a place of mindful fortitude. When someone has a sense of self, these misconceptions that are everywhere have little impact. I am not making a case for having nothing or that there is something wrong with wealth, but if you don't have the real wealth of self, then the things money can buy will have you! I don't want to be one of those people who says, "Don't enjoy things around you. That's not what I'm suggesting, but you don't really need those things to experience deep fulfillment and deep satisfaction."

A recent example of that is a company, Tom's Shoes. Tom is a man who has given away to poor children around the world one pair of shoes for every pair of shoes he's sold. He decided, after seeing how happy those children were, to live a simpler life on a sailboat, with less in his life. He says, "I realized I don't need that much stuff to be happy." Now that is a short version, you need to go check out Tom's Shoes on your own.

Misconceptions are easy because they are so showy and obvious. You should be suspicious of obvious displays of wealth because they are usually accompanied by a deeply troubled spirit.

People who are truly successful are often the ones behind the scenes. Perhaps they are enjoying the sunshine or enjoying their children or grandchildren or giving their money to universities. Now, it's alright to know what you want. If you want a fantastic yacht and throughout your life you've dreamed of having a fantastic yacht, then work toward it—do whatever it takes to get your yacht, but with integrity.

I can think of the Hollywood stars I've interviewed who have thirty-two-room houses and they've never even occupied every room they have, they don't know the staff members who run the house, and they wonder why their stuff is not around or is missing. That is not success. That's an obligation. A successful life is balanced.

Wright

So why does understanding these misconceptions really matter?

Haynes

Because when you know what "your success" is, you can claim it. You'll more readily identify it in the pile. When all that stuff is removed from before your eyes, what you really want will be reflected back to you. Now, you will learn some of this by experience. Some of us have to actually taste things.

A wonderful food critic gave me a very helpful idea during an interview on my show. I was describing something that I didn't like to eat. He said that doesn't mean anything. He went on to say, "It is not that you know what you like, it's that you like what you know." Light bulbs went off for me. So I understood that I needed to broaden my base of experience and understanding to get beyond my own misconceptions, taste things, try things in moderation, travel, talk to people, and find out more.

When you educate yourself and experiment, you will truly begin to know what matters to you and what you desire. Knowing what you truly want helps bring about an authentic self. You won't waste time with what doesn't matter.

Wright

You talk about three key behaviors. Would you share that with our readers?

HAYNES

The three key behaviors are: immersion, attraction, and understanding.

I don't like to talk too much about poor childhoods. I had great parents but we didn't have a lot of money. I spent my early years in Bedford Stuyvesant in New York. Some people called it a ghetto, some people called it a slum, but it was a great place to grow up. I didn't know much beyond my day-to-day life experience.

When I went to college, I didn't have the life experiences that so many of my fellow students had. What became important for me was to learn by immersion, not just by reading. Reading was terribly important, but actually going to museums, going out into the world, and having personal experiences were key ingredients to learning. That is why working in television worked so well for me as a career. It allowed me to go into places, go into the marketplace, and surround myself—immerse myself—with experts and with those actively engaged in so many areas of work and business.

I even created a radio show on NBC local radio that was designed to help me learn about the marketplace. It allowed me to immerse myself. The program was called *A Matter of Money* and it allowed me to ask experts any question about the market or the financial world. I didn't set myself up as an expert, I just told the truth—I wanted to know more about the financial world. And I got answers.

Sure, there were things I could do at a small level and at a large level but I put myself into the environment of the financial world by doing many interviews and conversations and combined those with reading on different subjects. I did so well that I became a television reporter on the Financial News Network, the predecessor of CNBC.

The point here is that if you want to have something or achieve something, wrap yourself in it! If you want to know how to cut diamonds or work with gems, immerse yourself in that world. Join a club, join an organization, become a member of a group doing activities related to your desire. I continue this practice and find it rewarding all the time.

Another example of this practice of immersion is my participation in the International Society for Panetics, a scholarly group devoted to ending suffering in the world. They actually understand that suffering may not end, but they want to reduce suffering for as many people as possible. This was a way for me to immerse myself with thinkers—with people who care about the world. And not just from the emotional aspects, but from the scientific and research aspect.

I needed that immersion because it was not part of my education. I have a Master's degree in Political Science. Joining this group gave me an opportunity to look at application of theories, not just classroom study.

Sometimes putting yourself in your areas of interest means that you pop right out. You might discover that it doesn't work for you. That is the good thing about immersion—you can discover your true desire and direction faster than you would by just sitting in the classroom. I do recommend class work but adding the experience of getting involved speeds the learning process along.

Attraction really is a huge concept. Most people misunderstand it because it's such a popular term used in so many books and television shows. The law of attraction is really about having your being operate at its highest frequency.

You cannot attract and sustain wealth and success if your being is out of whack. The idea of taking care of yourself is one of the most important and simple success actions that so many overlook. You need to make sure that you balance your body, because we are made up of energy and all of our cells work together.

Using just the brain means that the brain is not working effectively. You will attract and recognize your desired outcomes more easily when your body is in tune. You could not drive your car with a flat tire or if it were missing a spark plug, yet so many people will run their brain energy with their whole bodies running on poor nutrition and without stimulating, life-building exercise. I know there are examples of unhealthy millionaires but they are not experiencing success at the highest level. That is why so many keep seeking more and more money when they are impoverished in so many other ways. You will attract to you the level at which you are functioning. If you are not functioning at your highest level, you will not be able to attract to you those opportunities that will be pivotal in putting you where you want to be. You can't also read yourself accurately.

There is an old book written by Spencer Johnson called *A Minute for Myself*. I thought it was the best book on the subject of attraction, even though it never really talked about attraction. It did discuss how you will accurately perceive the world if you take time for yourself. If you do not take time for yourself, what you see will be inaccurate. What reflects back at you when you haven't had adequate sleep, proper nutrition, and proper exercise is a troubled world and you won't know that it's because your own screen and your own filters are damaged.

So attraction has to do with making sure your own attractor—your body, your being, your essence, your thoughts, your actions—are all in integrity so that the energy you radiate is at the highest possible level and you recognize your treasures when they appear.

Understanding is the third key. You will gain understanding when you are constantly working on personal development—reading, being willing to adjust, and learning. Again, Robert Fritz, who was one of my great teachers, talks about flexibility. Some great teachers suggest that we "be like bamboo," and be able to bend, not just physically but mentally. We need to be flexible, to look at a situation and change and move with that change, not hold on for dear life until all is lost. I know everyone has had a minister, a rabbi, or a teacher who has told this story but I'm going to include it here because I think it is so relevant.

The story is about a tremendous flood. There was a minister in a chapel. Some members of his congregation came by in a boat and said, "You know, you really ought to come with us; we've got some rowboats. We'd like for you to come with us."

"No," he replied. "God's going to save me."

Then another boat came by and offered to help but, the minister said, "No, I'm just going to stay here. I know the water is rising, but I know God's going to save me."

The water continued to rise and then a helicopter came by. Someone used a megaphone to call to him, "Minister, please come with us!"

"No," he said. "I'm going to stay right here; I know God is going to save me."

By then he was on the top of the building. The water eventually covered the building and he drowned. He reached the pearly gates and asked, "God, why didn't you save me?"

"Well," God replied, "I sent you two boats and a helicopter but you just wouldn't budge."

It's one of my favorite stories. I laugh every time I hear it. But it really is indicative of how people are when they think they're on a path and they're not looking at what's happening around them. They won't budge and they'd rather stay stuck. So being flexible, being able to read your environment, making your decisions effectively, and changing with what is required would be the third key point on what's needed to be successful.

- Immersion
- Attraction
- Flexibility

Wright

So what do you do if you find yourself headed in the wrong direction?

Haynes

Create and adjust. These are the powerful words offered by Robert Fritz. If you are headed in the wrong direction, get still and reflective and don't go into reaction mode. This will increase your chances of finding the course of action that is right for you. Change course, thank yourself, thank the universal force. Thank whatever your beliefs are—your spirit, your God, whatever your perspective is. Be thankful that you've discovered the need to change, and change. Practicing gratitude is a way of acknowledging where you are. So many people miss the joy of receiving what they have asked for because they move to the next desire without noticing that they have reached what they wanted.

Some people think success is a straight line up a chart but it's not. It's a jagged line up and down. Author Morty Lefkoe presented this idea to me in a lecture. It makes sense that all actions have frequencies like radio or particle waves. Why on earth do we think that success will not have many little downward turns and sometimes great downward turns before we get where we want to go? If you understand that all of our actions are engaged in fluctuations, you won't be terrified of moving forward, you'll understand that sometimes there's an up and sometimes there is a down. You'll just take it in and you'll have a greater view of it. You'll learn from the down parts. You'll be a constant learner, not a constant reactor.

That's what you do when you find yourself going in the wrong direction. If you're still going in the wrong direction, make a list of people you can ask for accurate feedback. Assemble a mastermind group as suggested by Napoleon Hill. Don't just have "yes" people around you or people who criticize unnecessarily.

My father was marvelous telling this to me. He said, "Do you want a parent who is going to say yes you're sweet all the time? No. You want a parent who is going to give you honest feedback." That's how my father was—he wasn't cruel, he wasn't harsh, but he gave me advice and would say, "This is better, try this." You need friends like that. You need mentors like that—people who will give you an adequate and accurate reflection and feedback. That is going to keep you on course.

WRIGHT

So how do you choose these models of success?

HAYNES

You choose these models of success by going back to the benchmarks that we mentioned before. Are these individuals true to their own values? Are they living in an authentic way? Are they focused? Are they in the present? Are they engaged in their lives? Do they have a larger sense of the world? There is one other piece that I always use as my indicator: Is the individual engaged in philanthropic endeavors? That's a very important piece—is the person giving back to the world? Now that doesn't always mean giving money. Philanthropy is not an activity just for the rich. In many of the developing places in the world, when the measurements are taken of what is being contributed, the poor people in those areas give a far greater percentage of their income than we do, relatively speaking.

Being philanthropic is an indicator of one's true sense of worth and your true sense of wealth. If people are doing that, then I want to be in the same space with them, I want to help them give, I want to understand what motivates them to give, and I want to give. That's really a very important part of the whole piece. You can give your time, you can give your intelligence, you can give your experience, and you can give your old good clothes (don't give anyone anything that you wouldn't wear). That's another good piece. But definitely give away what you can give.

Wright

So why is mindfulness important?

Haynes

Mindfulness is a skill. I'm glad you brought it up at this point because mindfulness is a practice. It is something that few people have. When you're with your spouse, are you really mindful of who he or she is? Do you take in everything about him or her? Do you listen carefully or are you reading the paper while your spouse is talking to you; are you otherwise distracted? Mindfulness is looking at the world in a quiet fashion. I don't want to use the word Zen because Zen is a word that has been misunderstood. It isn't necessarily a practice where your body has to ache because you're sitting still for long periods of time. Mindfulness is the ability to observe and be observant without judgment.

Mindfulness is not holding your breath, it's not chanting. It's simply being quiet and observing. You know you're there because suddenly flowers have brighter colors, the sky is clearer, your eyesight is clearer, and sometimes you can feel or hear your own heartbeat. It's a discipline that, in my opinion, makes simple success realized. I can't adequately assess my success without this mindful state. In short, you cannot have success without pausing and quietly taking it in.

These are things that may be individual for each of us. My daughter wanted a dog. I never really wanted a dog but I got a dog and now I love the dog. Holding my dog, listening to the dog's heartbeat, having the dog lying on my heart and now I hear the two heartbeats, at that moment I experience great joy. A glance from my wonderful husband, a hug from my wonderful daughter, these are things that give me a thrill.

When I was younger I would probably have laughed if someone told me that this is success. I would pay attention somewhat, but I think I have paid attention enough now to discover that it is true. I want to share it with people so they don't waste their time on unnecessary endeavors.

There isn't anything better than what is already here for us in terms of fresh air, beauty, preserving the Earth, and being a part of that—that is success. Mindfulness gives you a chance to be in that success.

Wright

So how do you use assessment or gratitude-tracking?

Haynes

There are many ways of doing gratitude-tracking and assessment. Some suggest that you write in a journal every day things that you are grateful for. I think it involves taking stock in whatever way you choose to do it. In some of the twelve-step programs, taking inventory is reviewing your situation carefully. That is another way of taking stock. But it's important to be conscious about yourself.

So many people are like houses with fantastic furnaces. You've got this fantastic, efficient furnace and it's freezing outside, but you don't feel any heat. The reason is because all of the windows are open and the heat is escaping. That's what happens when people don't take stock of their accomplishments, of their day-to-day successes, and of the things they're grateful for. They actually don't experience their success because they're so busy focusing on the next thing and the next thing and the next thing, they lose the feedback, they're not adequately tracking the successes they have had.

I suggest that you make a list each day of what you want to do and keep it simple. Burton Geyer suggests writing it in simple sentences with a verb at the beginning and then a command. Go to the library might be one. Then, at the end of the day, if you went to the library, mark it off. That is a form of simple success. The more of those things that you check off, the more you will begin to have a quantum experience of success. Success can be realized with simple, small steps of tracking your actions.

Success is not a big, full, sweeping action. It may be for some. It might be a big deal that comes through. But most things are a result of many small, clear actions. So writing those actions down each day and honoring them, listening to them, and allowing yourself to choose—not react but choose. For example, I like to do art projects with my daughter or play the piano with her. So I might not choose to do the final piece of book-balancing that I was going to do that day, but I guarantee you, the next morning I will complete it.

So it's managing your time, managing your actions, choosing to be in those actions, tracking those actions by honoring them, by noting whether you have done them or not, and by not having unrealistic desires. Some people put down so many things but they don't realize there are only a limited number of hours in the day. You need to consider, are you delegating—do you have someone to help you?

Even in those times in my life when I didn't have lots of income, I've always had one person, even if it was a graduate student, working with me for a few hours once a week. It made a huge difference in the progress of my projects. I found it exhilarating to provide real work for someone else and to take on the consistent responsibility of being organized and delegating work.

WRIGHT

Help me understand the difference between "whole success" as opposed to "one-dimensional success."

HAYNES

This is a great and important question. Human beings are made up of many different components. You are not just what you do, you are not just what you have, you're not just who you're married to, you're not just who you are the parent of. Your beliefs, your values, your day-to-day experiences, your digestion, your exercise—all the things that make you who you are—have levels of success. Having a balanced chart of success in all of those areas is much more realistic in terms of success than success in only any one of those areas. How many people do we know who in fact are multimillionaires in the global marketplace, but they hardly spend time with their families. That's not whole success, that's one-dimensional success.

Whole success is having a balanced life—your health is in intact, your spiritual relationships are intact, your sense of yourself is intact, you are running your own race, not the way someone else thinks you should run it. We could go on and on, it's an individual choice for you. You'd have to put down the components for you as to what the whole of you is. But assessing what makes you feel fulfilled and tracking and honoring that information is most important.

Then, when you have that other kind of financial success, or you win the Academy Award, everything doesn't go out of whack as it seems to do in Hollywood for so many people because they don't have whole success.

Wright

What part does keeping your word play in being successful?

Haynes

Your word is something given to you. What separates us from the animals is our ability to speak, our ability to speak may, in fact, be what helps us to create, to write, to speak, and to think in language. When we give our word to someone or something or to ourselves and we violate it, we are violating a fundamental human component and it registers with us. So the next time we go and make a promise to ourselves, the mind says, "Oh, wait a minute, you didn't keep your word the last time, what makes you think you're going to keep it this time?" So keeping your word is very important.

My father always taught me to keep my word. When he died, I found a piece of paper in his pocket. It read, "God takes no pleasure in fools, if thou giveth thy word, keep thy word." You can imagine that made a permanent and lasting impression on me.

I want to be clear that if you give your word and you cannot keep it or it's not appropriate to keep it because circumstances may have changed, what you do is you honor it by cleaning it up, clearing it up, and speaking the truth. If you promise to be somewhere and you cannot do it, you call ahead, you keep the slate clean, and you don't allow broken words and broken promises to pile up. There are times when the word with yourself is more important than anything else. What have you promised yourself? That is where keeping your word is absolutely important.

Wright

You talked about giving money according to other people's needs. Why is philanthropic endeavor the true indicator of success, in your opinion?

Haynes

One of our illusions in this life experience is that we are individuals. We are individuals but we are part of a global community. When one group is ill or not functioning, it affects the whole. If we are strong enough and have been blessed enough to have something—a piece of wisdom, money, extra food, clothing—it is our responsibility to look out for those who do not have it. There are all kinds of political arguments about this question, but we are a holistic organization. If we, for example, poison the river in one part of the Earth, in the long run it has an effect on the rest of us. When we breathe the air, we're not just breathing air that is right above our heads; we're breathing the air that comes from the poisoned areas in the rest of the world. We have to keep our world clean, we have to take care of our brethren, and we have to take care of those who cannot take care of themselves. We have to live as a global citizen.

So philanthropy is not just your individual giving, which is great, it is your consciousness that we have a partnership with others, and we're in this journey together, we're on this spaceship—Earth—together. If we don't give, it sends into our consciousness a kind of artificial feeling, a feeling of isolation that is not real. We are all breathing the same air, our fields are being plowed by people who are poor and who need our help. We need to have a better consciousness about how everything works together as a whole, and then we have to give furiously to keep it together to make sure it works.

It goes beyond politics; it goes beyond watching our own backyard. Sure, we need to take care of our families and our own well-being, there is nothing wrong with that, there is enough to go around. I'm not afraid of extraordinary wealth, I think people can enjoy it and still make a difference in the world, but you cannot do it and not be conscious about what's happening in the world around you. That's why philanthropy as a way of being is a key step to success. I think the consciousness you must have of the world outside your own will cause you to learn so much that you can't help but be successful. There is always a payoff but it is best to give without expecting the payoff. Keep your focus on how your contribution will help the planet, how this will help your neighbors, and how this will help your world!

WRIGHT

Well, what a great conversation. I've learned a lot here today about success. Some of the things you've said I've never considered before, and for that I'm very grateful. I know our readers will get a lot out of this chapter.

I really do appreciate all the time you've spent with me answering these questions. Thank you for being so open.

HAYNES

Thank you for the opportunity.

WRIGHT

Today we've been talking with Phyllis Haynes. She is a speaker, facilitator, trainer, moderator, and author. As we have found out here today, her knowledge of global media, new media technology, and cross-cultural communication encompasses more than twenty years of experience in television and production.

Phyllis, thank you so much for being with us today on *Success Simplified*.

HAYNES

Thank you.

About the Author

Phyllis Haynes is well known for broadcast interviews and insightful conversations with world leaders, thinkers, and innovators. As a speaker, facilitator, and consultant on global media, new media technology and cross-cultural communication, Ms. Haynes offers her clients the benefits of her more than twenty years of on-air experience including *ABC's Evening News* and *Good Morning America*. She also appeared daily on the one-hour news and talk program *Straight Talk* on WOR-TV. She produced the documentary Aids: *The Facts of Life* with Susan Sarandon, Iman, and James Taylor, winning the American Film Institute Award in the Health Education category.

She is a speaker and facilitator in demand. Her clients include the United Nations, Columbia University School of International Public Affairs, Ernst and Young, NCAA, and NFL Players Association, Stony Brook Medical School, and the Conversation Among Masters (the most prestigious organization for master coaches). Phyllis was invited by the European Union and the Hellenic Foundation to bring her work to the emerging marketplaces of Central and Eastern Europe. As a result of the invitation, she delivered programs on communications skills and new media in Athens, Bulgaria, and Romania. She also served as a professional specialist on the faculty of Emerson College in Boston, teaching at the graduate level in Boston and in Maastricht. She has been an active member of the International Society for Panetics since 1995 and a founding board member of the Coach Initiative, an organization designed to give pro bono coaching to nonprofit organizations whose missions are to help humanity. Ms Haynes has an MA from New York University in Political Science and works to create illuminating conversations that will advance the human experience.

Phyllis Haynes
Studio1ThinkTank
800-482-5152
networkproducer@gmail.com
Studio1Network.net

Chapter Fourteen

Staying Motivated For More Than A Day

By Deb Cottle

David Wright (Wright)

Today we're talking with Deb Cottle. Deb is founder and president of World on a String, a company focused on enhancing people's lives through inspirational seminars, workshops, coaching, and professional speaking. With her proven four-step GUTS formula, Deb has successfully motivated individuals and groups to take action in moving through transitions. She established herself as one of the highest-ranking female executives in the Chicago television and advertising industry. During a twenty-year career in that field, Deb worked with national clients including Anheuser-Busch, Coca-Cola, Humana, Ford, Sears, and Oprah's Harpo Productions.

Deb currently lives on Amelia Island, Florida, with her creative director husband, Stan Cottle, and teenage son, Connor.

Deb Cottle, welcome to *Success Simplified.*

Deb Cottle (Cottle)

Thank you, David, for inviting me to be part of this exciting new book, *Success Simplified.* I'm honored to be included with this prestigious group of speakers/authors such as Dr. Stephen Covey, Dr. Tony Alessandra, and Patricia Fripp.

Wright

Well, great. So where and when did you get your start in the advertising industry?

Cottle

My advertising career began in 1985, after securing a job as an account executive with a television production company called Telemation Productions in suburban Chicago, where I grew up. Interestingly enough, my uncle, Bill Hamilton, was a client of the company and he encouraged me to apply for a sales position there. Since having had sales experience in other industries, and acting experience in films and commercials, it motivated me to learn more about the entire production process in order to sell the services.

There was just one small problem—they weren't really looking to hire additional salespeople! But persistence finally paid off. After several months of calling weekly to request an interview, the opportunity finally opened up. The general manager of the company called to inform me that *both* their sales manager and "star" sales person had quit that morning. My interview was scheduled for that same afternoon.

After working hard to convince the executives at Telemation that I was a quick learner and would put 110 percent effort into the position to make up for my lack of experience, I was hired as their new account executive.

Needless to say, with having GUTS to persist on breaking into this industry, coupled with expecting a positive outcome, it happened. The company offered me a low base salary with the promise of commission based on my ability to establish new business. My first year commissions were almost double my base salary, so the commission structure seemed to work out well for me!

In the meantime, one of the staff directors, Stan Cottle, swept me off my feet and we were married a year later.

My first big success was bringing in a multi-year, multimillion-dollar client, Ford Motor Company, to shoot its commercials on our expansive sound stage and on location around Chicago. It took me three years to land that account. Just when it felt like it wasn't ever going to happen, I gave it one last push, and we were finally awarded the business! National clients such as Coca-Cola, Humana, and others followed and my account executive position turned into a sales manager position in a short amount of time. That's when it became even more rewarding—hiring, training, and motivating sales people!

My career continued on a path of moving up and into senior management positions within the Chicago advertising/production industry. By networking and becoming involved with related associations such as The Women's Advertising Club of Chicago (as Board Member and President), and Women in Film, I was able to gain more knowledge of the business that helped move me to the top in my field.

Soon I was getting invitations to speak to people in advertising agencies, industry associations, and corporations about motivation, sales and marketing techniques, and other relevant subjects.

These speaking opportunities revealed my true passion—using my voice to communicate to others about how they can improve their lives. This revelation began my transition from management in the advertising industry to speaking to groups about self-improvement and motivation.

Yearning for an environment better suited to creating these messages, we transitioned to Amelia Island, Florida, just north of Jacksonville. This is my husband's hometown and truly a slice of paradise. We wanted our son to grow up in a small community and be surrounded by family, and for all of us to enjoy a more relaxed lifestyle. Both Stan and I can run our businesses from anywhere, so why not choose a beach community as home base?

WRIGHT

So how did you further your professional speaking?

COTTLE

David, even though I was very comfortable with giving sales presentations and seminars in my industry, it was important for me to gain more knowledge in the speaking profession. A friend recommended an organization called the Professional Speakers of Illinois (PSI), and the National Speakers Association (NSA). After joining both, I learned the tools of the trade through NSA conventions, seminars, monthly PSI meetings, and local speaking workshops. In fact, that's how I met Patricia Fripp—Patricia was a keynote speaker at an NSA convention. I've also taken her full-day workshops in both California and Florida. My philosophy is that each of us can improve our craft by learning more in our area of interest or expertise, and by having role models. Patricia was mine in the area of professional speaking.

Two other factors helped me to grow as a speaker. One was hiring a professional speaking coach, Sandra Schrift from San Diego. We talked via phone monthly for several years. I still consult with Sandra to this day—twelve years later. The other factor was getting listed in speaking directories. The American Advertising Federation (Washington, D.C.) was the best one for me. This national organization represented advertising clubs nationwide, and clubs utilized this directory to hire speakers for their meetings, workshops, and conventions. That opportunity allowed me to travel all over the country—and it was very exciting!

Wright

So what's your most requested speaking topic?

Cottle

Believe it or not, my most requested topic is "How to Stay Motivated for More Than a Day: Utilizing the Proven Four-step GUTS Formula." This easy formula was created years ago, and is routinely updated and customized per audience. I've found that most people appreciate simple tools and concepts, especially when they prove to be effective.

Wright

What exactly is the GUTS Formula?

Cottle

The GUTS Formula is a four-step daily routine that is so simple to follow. This process fits beautifully into the theme of this book, *Success Simplified.* It's a formula that anyone can practice to help make his or her life work better. That's what it's all about, isn't it? How can we live a better, easier, and more fulfilling life with less stress and frustration?

I have found that most people who attend motivational seminars or listen to motivational programs get all excited and want to conquer the world right then and there. But, after a day or two (or sometimes after just a few hours) the motivation begins to wear off. The biggest challenge is to find ways that will help us *stay* motivated for longer than the moment.

After studying the lives of successful people for more than twenty years, and experiencing trials and errors in my own life, I have found that successful people tend to have the GUTS to overcome obstacles and move beyond negativity.

Other less successful people seem to just give up. It fascinated me to see what the successful ones did to remain positive, especially when the odds were obviously unfavorable.

The result of those observations is a simple four-step process that I call the GUTS Formula.

WRIGHT

Would you explain to our readers what the four steps are?

COTTLE

Sure.

WRIGHT

I imagine GUTS is an acronym.

COTTLE

It is, David. Based on our time that we have today I'm going to go through it quickly and give you the *Reader's Digest* version. In workshops and coaching sessions, it is a more involved process that is customized to the group or individual. Basically, the formula starts with the acronym GUTS:

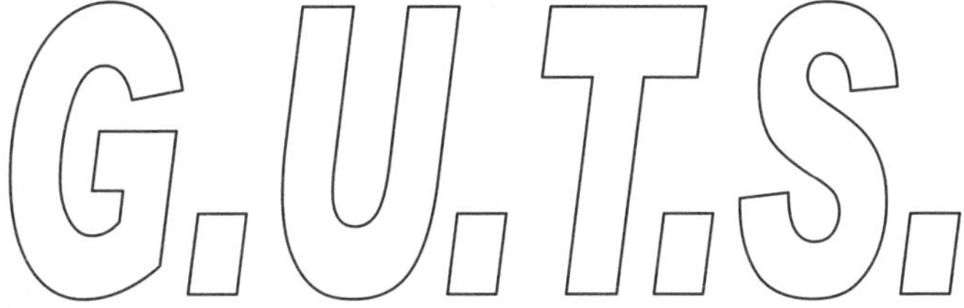

G Gain Knowledge

Each of us can take responsibility for deepening knowledge in our workplace, hobbies, or personal life in order to learn and grow. In our chosen field of work, it's extremely important that we find ways to become an expert in our field, or at least become more knowledgeable. This is good for two reasons: First, it boosts our own confidence level when we know more about a particular subject or profession. Second, it gives us a competitive edge. When clients are making a choice among various vendors and salespeople, they typically choose to do business with those who are leaders in their field. Anyone can easily become a leader by earning additional credentials and designations and taking more classes or seminars in his or her industry.

For example, my father, award-winning nature photographer Len Messineo, conducts his own photographic nature lecture series, exhibits his photography in several galleries, and has five nature DVD products on the market. Even at eighty-five years old, he continues to take classes in photography to increase his knowledge and stay current with the ever-changing photographic tools and technologies. He is a great example of the G—Gain Knowledge, and living proof that we are never too old to learn new things!

U Use Positive Affirmations

This is what psychologists call self-talk—statements that we declare on a regular basis that can truly work to define our outcome in life. If we focus on stating more positive statements, we will see more positive results in our lives. This is not rocket science; these are things that most of us have either heard about or even do already. The challenge is to become more conscious of the words we use, and what we declare to ourselves and others.

If you aren't saying positive statements or affirmations most often, then the opposite may be true—saying negative statements either about yourself or about others will attract more negative experiences. The subconscious mind doesn't know the difference between a statement that is true or false. It simply responds to statements that are said most often and those fueled by the strongest emotion. So, we are always attracting situations about which we have the most intense feelings—good or bad!

For example, when it comes to money, we often say things to ourselves and to others that are self-defeating, such as: "I can't afford it" or "I'll never have enough money." Much of that programming comes from our upbringing and what we were taught to believe and think about money. My mom used to make statements like, "Who do you think we are, the Rockefellers?" or "Do you think we're made of money?" or better yet, "Do you think money grows on trees?"

It's healthy to reflect back on experiences in our past, but it's more important to learn ways to change any negative programming that can hold us back from the good we desire.

Just recently I documented the progression of a new money-attracting affirmation I set for the year 2010. That affirmation is as follows: "Money flows from unexpected places, and I am open to the opportunity." By really focusing on that statement every day, my goal was to attract money that didn't come from the usual sources.

Soon, I found myself paying more attention to alternative money sources, and making sure that this specific money-attracting affirmation was repeated with passion every day.

A couple of weeks into this experiment, I received a letter from a law firm stating we had unclaimed funds due to us from the State of Florida. Now, for years we have received this sort of solicitation, and thought it was a scam. The letters went into the trash along with all the other junk mail! But this time, since my mind was more focused on attracting money from unexpected places, I decided to pay attention to this particular letter, just in case it *was* true!

Our accountant checked into this unclaimed money offer, instead of calling the firm that sent us the letter because the firm wanted a fee to collect the funds due to us. Believe it or not, there were indeed two claims in our name, totaling more than $12,000!

After filing some paperwork with the State of Florida to confirm our identity, we were informed that our claim was valid, and the payment process would take anywhere from thirty to ninety days. I still wasn't 100 percent convinced that we would ever receive the money, but I continued to focus on the affirmation, "Money comes from unexpected places, and I am open to the opportunity."

Two checks arrived in the mail within sixty days—one for $11,953.71 and the other for $478.42!

This is compelling proof that you can use positive affirmations on a daily basis to attract things you want into your life, *if* you are open to the opportunity, believe that it's possible, and persist in that belief!

T Train Your Thoughts

The National Science Foundation states that we generate about 60,000 thoughts per day. If we're thinking positively only half the time, that's about 30,000 positive thoughts. But what about the remaining thoughts that aren't as positive?

What I teach people is how to concentrate on converting thoughts that are negative into constructive, positive thoughts. It's unrealistic to expect us to be positive all the time, but I'm sure you'll agree that most of us can use some improvement.

Here's one of the techniques that you can use when you are having a negative thought: Say out loud either the word "Cancel!" or "Stop!" to discontinue the negative thinking pattern. Then quickly replace that negative thought with a positive one. This is a simple way to increase the number of positive thoughts you have each day. This may sound overly simplified, and it is, but it requires conscious effort to do on a consistent basis. The good news is that each of us has control of our own thoughts!

Famous former football coach Lou Holtz believes "Life is 10 percent what happens to us, and 90 percent of how we react to it." Have you noticed how differently people can react to the exact same news? Whether it's a health issue, loss of job, or other unsettling life experiences, choosing how we handle the situation can make an impact on the outcome.

Ralph Waldo Emerson claimed, "We are what we think about all day long." Once you begin catching your negative thoughts and replacing them with positive ones, you will begin to see how the results of your positive thoughts continue to manifest good in your life—all because you've learned to train your thoughts.

S Set Realistic Goals

Most people don't spend enough time setting goals, or they set goals that are so unrealistic to achieve that it's almost impossible to accomplish them. I recommend starting out by setting goals that are achievable and easy. Once you start having success in realizing your goals, you will build more confidence and attract even more success. Success breeds success.

Also, make sure your goals are very specific. Some may be short-term goals, while others may be something to accomplish long-term. But, the most important part of the process is to write them down. You will not get the same results if you just keep them in your head. Writing goals down encourages you to make each goal very specific, prioritized, and with realistic time frames.

Once written down, practice visualizing yourself already having accomplished these goals in your mind. Remember, your subconscious mind doesn't know the difference between what is real or what is imagined. It just brings to you what you see in your mind most often. So, you can visualize yourself in a new job, a new location, or enjoying a new lifestyle! Then give it focused energy to accomplish it. With enough repetition and practice, you begin attracting those desired experiences into your life, mostly because you Set Realistic Goals.

Wright

So what other strategies do you use to stay motivated for more than a day?

Cottle

Here are *ten* easy tips that can help anyone stay motivated for more than a day.

1. Identify a role model and follow their life story to learn what they did to become successful. Find and work with a mentor who relates to your industry or your goals.
2. Fill your mind with uplifting reading materials and listen to inspirational music. Learn more about the power of the mind and what it can do for you.
3. Spend quality time with just you. Take yourself on a date, go to the movies, walk on the beach or in other natural settings. Watch funny movies. Laughter is great therapy.
4. Keep a gratitude journal to record what is going right in your world and what you are grateful for. When you're in a down mood, take time to reflect on the good you already have in your life. You will find there is much to be grateful for.
5. Meditate daily to help clear your mind of negative thoughts.

6. Spend more time with positive-thinking people, and less time with negative-thinking people. Sounds simple, but it's not easy.
7. Learn new things on a regular basis. Get out of your comfort zone!
8. Focus on your family and good friends. Build stronger relationships with the people you love.
9. Do something for someone else as often as possible, even if it's just sharing a smile or giving words of encouragement. Write out personal cards and send them to people for absolutely no reason. Tell them you're just thinking about them. Call friends to hear about their lives and don't dwell on yours. That will actually make you feel better.
10. Find a place that makes you feel better just by being there. Immerse yourself in that environment and note what makes you feel good about that location.

We all have such a place in mind. Stan loves to walk on the beach where he recharges his batteries. Believe it or not, mine is hotels, especially luxury hotels. First of all, they're beautiful, normally having a great view of an ocean, gardens, or impressive streetscape. Just sitting in a hotel lobby perks up my mood. In addition, it is expected of hotel employees to be gracious and accommodating to visitors and guests. You are almost guaranteed a positive experience!

Wright

So how about your volunteer work—how has that influenced your personal and professional life?

Cottle

In the past, I volunteered primarily for industry-related organizations that gave me more exposure, experience, and influence in the advertising/production community in Chicago. All that changed when our family moved to Florida. My focus evolved from a professional purpose into a richer, more personal purpose in volunteering with non-profit organizations and mentoring two high school students. It's so rewarding to volunteer in areas where giving of your time, talent, and treasure is truly appreciated.

But above all, I think my involvement with Rotary has taught me the most about the value of volunteerism. As past President of The Rotary Club of Amelia Island Sunrise, I've learned a great deal throughout the past few years by connecting with Rotary's community—locally, nationally, and internationally. Their motto is "Service Above Self," and through that philosophy I've learned how to put other people's needs first.

Rotary is not about building your business, but rather about building business relationships in your local community to help others who are less fortunate. It's also a great opportunity to take on leadership responsibilities within a structured organization. I believe that when you volunteer for any kind of non-profit group, doing good things in your community and in the world, it is like making deposits into a spiritual bank account. It's not about money; instead, it's more about enriching and nurturing relationships and making others' lives better. You build up a spiritual bank balance by making regular deposits.

As an example, through Rotary our family hosted an exchange student from Belgium. When we first met, Kevyn spoke mostly French, so we struggled to communicate. Yet, during the nine months we hosted Kevyn, we became very close as we shared our differences as well as our similarities. The fact that his English improved dramatically certainly didn't hurt. It was a great growth and learning experience for all of us, including our son. Being an only child, Connor was able to experience having an older brother for a while.

And, we were able to help guide Kevyn's future as if he were our own son—something we continue today, even though he's now in the Netherlands. It was an enriching experience that our family will always treasure!

Wright

So what tools do you use to reach Kevyn and your clients throughout the world?

COTTLE

While I still do a fair amount of traveling, one of the best new ways to reach out to distant clients is through an online video and audio conference service called Skype. I'm a big fan of Skype, a free service that is downloadable from the Internet. Once you and the client download the software, you can have a "face-to-face" conversation right at home or office. This assumes, of course, that the people on the other end also have Web cameras. Most laptops nowadays come with a camera already installed. It is such an advantage to be able to see each other and connect on a more personal level, and to gauge body language.

WRIGHT

Tell me about your "Inspirational Evening Events."

COTTLE

World On A String is producing Inspirational Evening Events that include inspirational music, motivational talks, and sometimes guest speakers or experts in a particular field. Even in the pilot program, it was obvious that people not only wanted to be inspired, but they also wanted to hear real-life stories about those who had accomplished their dreams and goals. Basically, the format is a true multi-media experience that includes visual effects and video clips to provide an enhanced experience for the audience.

The first Inspirational Evening Event evolved from a coincidental meeting (or maybe not so coincidental) with a young lady named Ruby Garza.

My belief is that people are put in our path at the right time for the right reasons. We just need to pay attention to these opportunities that arise and consider why we are guided to meet a certain individual or experience something that is unplanned or unexpected.

Let me illustrate a most recent example of finding opportunities in unexpected places by being open and aware. Last fall, a young woman named Ruby Garza came to our house with our regular cleaning professional to do some work for us. She was brought in as a temp on this particular day to help expedite the job. Ruby had never been to our house before. As soon as she stepped through the door I knew there was something about her that I really wanted to explore. She was wearing a bandana, had braces on her teeth, and seemed very sad. She hung her head, avoiding eye contact, and didn't engage in conversation.

But for some reason I was really focused on getting Ruby to talk with me. I asked if she wanted to listen to music while she worked, and we started a conversation about music. Gradually Ruby opened up and we began talking about what kinds of music she preferred. Ruby explained in detail how music increased the serotonin in the brain, and how important music was for the soul. Her knowledge of music was unexpected and surprising.

After more discussion, Ruby explained that she was a singer/songwriter who specialized in inspirational music, based on stories taken from her own life. Ruby used day-to-day struggles as a basis from which to write, but then turned her negative experiences into inspiration and hope.

You can imagine my excitement to learn that Ruby had a special gift! As we talked more, I learned that she had been writing and singing since she was sixteen years old and had been a finalist in the Mid-Michigan Idol back in her hometown. Immediately, I asked Ruby to participate in my first Inspirational Evening Event the following month.

Would you believe I hadn't even heard her sing yet? But there was something special about Ruby—a deep longing to get her music out into the world and to inspire others to overcome their own struggles in life. We scheduled a rehearsal, and her music was indeed inspiring.

As a fascinating sidebar about how things really do happen for a reason, I later learned that earlier in that same day we first met, Ruby had packed her bags and was planning to move back to Michigan, effectively giving up on her dream to make music. In fact, she had planned to leave immediately after the cleaning assignment at my home. Bags were packed and ready to go, but because Ruby found someone to believe in her, and in her goal to get her music out, she decided to stay and work even harder toward this goal.

Think about how many times we overlook or judge people or their situation without getting to know them or discovering their inner passion and soul. I was very blessed to have found Ruby that day.

Wright

So what does the future hold for Deb Cottle?

Cottle

The future is exciting, David! In addition to producing a "Music and Motivation" audio series, I'm also developing a video series called *Women with GUTS,* from the adaptation of the GUTS formula. It's targeted toward women, as it features those who have beaten the odds of becoming successful in spite of their upbringing or other negative influences in their lives. This program will present several positive role models to all women, in an interview-based, documentary-style program that will be offered as downloads as well as on DVD.

Wright

What a great conversation. I have really learned a lot here today and took copious notes as well so I won't forget it. I really appreciate all the time you took today to explain what you're doing and to talk about very important things like networking and the importance of volunteering. I'm especially interested in your GUTS Formula—what a great and simple system to follow.

Cottle

Thank you, David! I appreciate the time you've taken to talk with me also.

Wright

Today we've been talking with Deb Cottle who is founder and president of World On A String. Her company focuses on enhancing people's lives through inspirational seminars, coaching, and her professional speaking business. We've also been talking about Deb's GUTS Formula, with her proven four-step process. Deb has successfully motivated individuals and groups to take action and move through transitions.

Deb, thank you so much for being with us today on *Success Simplified.*

Cottle

It was a pleasure. Remember to stay positive, and look for opportunities to help and empower others!

About the Author

Deb Cottle is founder and president of World On A String, a company focused on enhancing people's lives through inspirational seminars, workshops, coaching, products, and professional speaking. With her proven four-step GUTS formula, Deb has successfully motivated individuals and groups in major corporations, associations, and non-profit organizations to exceed personal and professional expectations.

She says, "It is up to us, as individuals, to create innovative ways to live more enriching lives. Having found my own direction, I am passionate about helping others find the GUTS to reach their fullest potential."

On her Web site, www.worldonastring.com, there is additional information on speaking and workshop topics. Motivational products are also available such as: *Success Simplified* (book), *Music & Motivation* (CD), and *Special Moments* (DVD). *Women with GUTS!* (DVD is currently in production. Stay tuned!

Deb Cottle

World On A String, Inc.

118 Sea Marsh Road

Amelia Island, FL 32034

904-261-2712

deb@worldonastring.com

www.worldonastring.com

CHAPTER FIFTEEN

TAKE COMMAND—LOVE THE LIFE YOU LIVE!

BY ELIZABETH TRINKAUS

DAVID WRIGHT (WRIGHT)

Today we're talking with Elizabeth Trinkaus. Elizabeth is the owner and founder of Pinnacle View, a unique and innovative Life Enrichment Coaching Company. She is a Master Life Enrichment Coach and International Speaker who has been consulting with individuals and corporations for more than twenty years in a perpetual quest to promote harmony of thought and vision.

Elizabeth's proven techniques have helped thousands of clients uncover blocks and take action to achieve success in their personal and professional lives. She teaches her clients that great success happens when you recognize the power to change your thinking and design your life from within.

Elizabeth was a contributing author for *Conversations on Success,* which also featured Deepak Chopra and Mark Victor Hansen. She created the video, *The Most Powerful Ingredient for Success—Do You Have It?* Her local and international speaking engagements and retreats inspire audiences to believe in themselves and take charge of their lives.

Elizabeth, welcome to *Success Simplified.*

What were your thoughts when you were asked to be included in our *Success Simplified* book project?

ELIZABETH TRINKAUS (TRINKAUS)

My first reaction was a big "Yes" because two days prior to receiving this invitation, I was sitting with my pups during a morning meditation, thinking I would like to be included in another book. My next reaction was facing the irony of the situation—the notion of success being simple was not modeled to me growing up and had been a very foreign concept.

My family lived in Connecticut until I was eight. At that point my father decided to go on a spiritual quest. We loaded up in our "champagne mist" Buick station wagon—my mom, my two older brothers, our three dogs, and me, with Dad at the helm—and headed out to destinations unknown. For years this involved lots of travel and living in different states and Nova Scotia.

My father was a brilliant architect and designer. At a young age, I witnessed his commitment to excellence through many accomplishments. My childhood perception, however, was that despite these accomplishments, he was always waiting for "our ship to come in." It never did. He would land great contracts, but we were never sure when and if another would come along.

After many years of observing and cheerleading, I realized that just because this was his story, it didn't have to be mine. I have to say it was very freeing to let go of the notion that success was somewhere "out there" and one day it would land on my doorstep. I let go of the old familiar story, but I was desperately in need of a new definition of success for myself.

With the help of mentors and coaches, I began the slow process of redefining success. I discovered that success isn't random—something that luckily appears—rather, it was something I could create within and around me, offering a new awareness with opportunities galore.

This led me to thinking that perhaps many of us have needed to re-define success for ourselves, to move away from a definition that caused us to live only in the future, rather than loving and creating a life we live now.

WRIGHT

What would you say has been the biggest contribution to your success?

TRINKAUS

Even though, in his eyes, Dad's ship never came in, he and my mom were huge advocates of believing in yourself and doing what makes you happy. This helped kindle dreams of creating my own business. It was scary starting my own firm, not knowing if I could pay the bills week to week, but my parents' emotional contribution carried me through the lean years. I loved the work I did and the life I was creating around me. I never stopped believing that I would succeed, even though there were many days when I didn't know what that would look like and I had no idea how.

Wright

Elizabeth, what is your definition of success simplified?

Trinkaus

For so many years, I believed that success was something I had to work really hard for, something "out there" that I had to achieve, to get, to possess—something that would validate me as a person. It was such a relief to finally discover that success is an inside job made up of choices we make to design the life we want to live. It's empowering to know that the choices we make are ours and we can always make new ones. Success is here and now—an ongoing journey that brings fulfillment to the present moment.

Can we simplify success? I know we can. My definition of success is taking command and loving the life we live! By taking command, I mean being willing to take charge of our lives through real action. Recognize what isn't working, what old patterns you are holding onto, and rewrite our own success story.

I've worked with many clients who, from the outside, appear to have everything and, according to a typical Western cultural definition, are successful. But deep within they weren't happy, and what kind of success is success without happiness? This brings me to the second part of my definition of success—loving the life you live.

To love the life you live, you must love and believe in yourself and do your best to create a life that is fulfilling. We deserve to love the life we live, take command of it, and experience true success.

I've watched so many people move from living a life of chaos and disillusionment to taking command and designing a life they truly enjoy. They didn't think it was possible for them. So I urge our readers to stretch beyond what they typically think possible for themselves and be open to the miracles in store for them.

WRIGHT

What would help our readers determine what success is for them?

TRINKAUS

I encourage all our readers to define success for themselves, perhaps redefining an old definition that may be the cause of not feeling successful and happy in the first place. My generation was brought up to believe that having the "career, husband/wife, house, kids, and two-car garage" was success. Many of us achieved some variation of this but didn't feel satisfied. So we strove for more, thinking that it would give us the feeling of the success we longed for. We were spinning our wheels.

We have so much available to us, and many don't know how to create a true feeling of success. Our culture teaches the, "I'll be happy when—" I'll be happy if—" success scenario. However, millions have discovered that this just doesn't work. We filled in the blanks again and again and found ourselves still seeking that feeling of true success.

Again, success is taking command and loving the life you live. It's really not about possessions and achievements. All those things are great, but they don't cause us to love the life we live. To the readers I ask, what do you need to love the life you live? How do you begin to go about this? Is it even possible? Absolutely. Begin to set yourself free with your new definition of success.

WRIGHT

Elizabeth, what are some steps one can take toward this new success?

TRINKAUS

Caring for Self and Restoring Your Energy

Our energy is restored when we remember to take care of our self. It may sound silly, but many folks are running so fast that they forget the most important ingredient—themselves. Caring for ourselves is an imperative component for success. Without it, we won't make good choices, won't stop to listen to what we need, and we will simply be living in what I call the unconscious whirlwind. This state causes us to run on an empty tank and wonder why we aren't happy. Then we try harder and often become depressed or sick. I've worked with clients who thought, "If I do more I'll feel better." So they keep trying. Balance is the key. When you take care of you, your performance will speak for itself and you will feel better.

Dr. Christine Northrop notes that a mother must first feed herself before she breastfeeds her baby. That is simply how nature operates. Our culture tries to go about it the opposite way. Are you trying to give from an empty cup?

One successful action step toward restoring energy is finding a hobby. This takes your mind and energy away from everyone else and focuses it back to you. I have clients taking up or returning to activities such as piano, photography, stamp collecting, repairing pinball machines, and arranging hiking and golfing trips. You have to make time—take the time. This is crucial to filling your own cup.

Other ideas are scheduling walks, evenings out with friends, volunteering, or finding a comfortable spiritual outlet. Take the time to determine what fuels you and do it!

As Stephen Covey so brilliantly states in his Habit 7 in his book, *The 7 Habits of Highly Effective People,* we must "Sharpen the Saw." Sharpening the saw refers to creating a balanced program that restores and renews your soul, reenergizing your greatest asset—you. As you renew yourself, positive change occurs.

Take care of you, love you. We need to teach ourselves. We learn to love our self by letting go of old misperceptions, self-judgment, and criticisms. When we do this, it shifts our whole paradigm.

Pay Attention to What You are Telling Yourself

Dr. John Hagelin, a quantum physicist, states that medical science recognizes now that our body is a product of our thoughts, and our thoughts and emotions determine the physical structure and substance of our bodies. What we tell ourselves—our "self-talk"—either fuels or depletes us. Pay attention to when your harsh inner critic whispers—sometimes yells—"you're not doing enough, you're neglecting this or that," or "it's just not good enough." These incessant thoughts rob us of the enjoyment of life.

But there's great news. It's possible to turn down the volume on this critic and rewrite the stories we tell ourselves. I do it myself and have witnessed hundreds of people who successfully learned to pay attention to what they are telling themselves. They chose to tell themselves something different and got a totally new outcome—the one that is success based.

Chances are, if you are reading this, you are motivated, you work hard, you care about performance, but you rarely reward yourself. Rewarding yourself is an example of a new story we can live into. Inner acknowledgement of a small or large goal reached is a form of positive self-talk that is light years away from the harsh inner critic. It is so easy at the end of a workday to think about everything you *did not* accomplish. What would it be like if, instead, you focused on—even rewarded yourself for— the work you *did* accomplish? How would you feel? Your energy level would increase and you would start to experience success in expanding cycles.

Practice the Art of Being Present

"But to be aware of little, quiet things, you need to be quiet inside. A high degree of alertness is required. Be still. Look. Listen. Be Present" —Eckhart Tolle.

I was working with a client on the issue of work/life balance. He described his life as complete chaos. It went like this: "When I'm working long hours, I feel bad for my wife and kids. When I'm home, I'm wondering what e-mails I should be answering. If I'm playing a round of golf, I'm feeling guilty for not being home." He described how dreadful and dissatisfying it was to live this way. We talked about the concept of being present. This concept is difficult for most us because we live in a fast-paced, fast-food, full-of-distractions culture.

Practicing the art of being present means bringing your focus to where you are in this moment right now, rather than thinking about the past or the future or where you think you should be or what you think you should be doing. I call being present an art because it is a skill that is the result of learning and practice. Being present focuses you and your energy on the only moment you can experience—the right-here-and-present moment of now. You are no longer scattered or torn by the past and future, by here and there. Being present puts us in the driver's seat without distractions and allows us to be more effective in whatever we are doing. This is part of achieving success, of taking command, and loving the life you live.

The practice of these tools now allows my client to have both feet where he is instead of one foot here, and one foot there. He experiences greater satisfaction as a result of his new focus. Practice this—it's magical and has the impact of a deep, satisfying breath.

"We get lost in doing, thinking, remembering, anticipating—lost in a maze of complexity and a world of problems. Nature can show us the way home, the way out of the prison of our own minds."—Eckhart Tolle.

Wright

Any other steps you would like to mention Elizabeth?

Trinkaus

Work that Body

Work that beautiful body so it will continue to work for you. If you're already working out regularly, great; you know the benefits that come from it. If not, you lose out on those benefits, so why cheat yourself? Why deny yourself the success energy that comes from working your body? You know you want it, and maybe you've even tried to start working out many times. So what? Now is the time to resist any urge to self-talk out of it. Start now. Remember, success is taking command and loving the life you live, and this includes your body.

It's common that even though we are motivated in our head, our body is likely telling a different story. "I don't want to get up and go for a walk." Expect that, and do it anyway. Be brave in the discomfort of doing what you don't want to do at that moment. Go for the end result. Not only does your body feel g-o-o-d physically afterwards, but your mind gets a great psychological boost. It's saying, "I did something good for me. I'm proud of myself for dragging my butt out of bed and going for a walk!" It will get easier and easier, I promise, because your body will be saying, "Yes!" And the cool thing is, when you exercise regularly, you are much more inclined to think about what and how much you eat.

Eat Nourishing Foods

As much as possible, choose foods that make your body sing. Have you ever walked out of a sushi restaurant and thought, "Ah, my body loved that meal; I feel so satisfied without that stuffed feeling"?

Don't get me wrong, on occasion I love a burger and fries meal. Sometimes I'll throw in a chocolate malt, too. And, I walk out of that restaurant going, "Wow, that was twenty-eight minutes of bliss, and now I can't move!" The body works hard to digest its goodies so be conscious and caring about what you put into it. Bottom line: take great care of your body with your choice of food and exercise. It will repay you. I promise.

Wright

I know you are a big advocate of balance in life. Why is this so important?

Trinkaus

We live in a world that is often out of balance, and we try to make it, force it, to work. Living in balance is like going from a congested, polluted city to sitting by the seashore—an experience of not thinking clearly to clarity and true vision. It's easy to notice when we are in or out of balance. The art of being present will take you there; you can quickly sense balance or the lack thereof. Take time to notice if your thoughts about yourself and your choices are in balance. Are they fueling you?

When we make choices to achieve greater balance, we get immediate and positive results. This is key to our health, our happiness, and peace of mind. Ultimately, balance is also the foundation of success. So again, I encourage us all to look at where we are out of balance in our lives. Is it our thinking? Our work? Our personal life? Our relationships? All of the above? Whatever the imbalance is, name it and begin to take action to restore balance in your being. When you do, you take command and love the life you live. You experience success.

Wright

In your twenty years of Life Coaching, what are some of your favorite success stories or statements that you have heard from clients?

Trinkaus

I created a Work/Life Balance Immersion Program, and here are a few quotes from clients who have made the choice to take command of their life:

"Wow. What a great way to start the day this morning. I've had more energy all day long! It is amazing how powerful self-talk (in a negative way) and visualization (in a positive way) can be.

One of my favorite most recent comments is, "The *acceptance* that I can only do ten of the one hundred things on my list *is freedom.* I had to experience it to believe it. I'm actually doing more by focusing on doing less!" This thrills me not only because this is going to make amazing changes in his life, but he is a model to his team at work and his family at home.

He continued to state, "I'm extremely excited about what I can do now. It's so simple. This calm feeling allows me to think through things and come up with answers." This taking one thing at a time mentality, even though there are ten or more things coming at you, is a wise choice that is actually a gift you can give yourself.

Another favorite success story is a woman who recognized she was living through the eyes of her paralyzing past—her wounded inner kid—and decided to do something about it. We all have "inner kids" that are carrying a story about what happened to us at a particular age. So if we merge with an inner eight-year-old who can't let go of the story "I never do it right," that struggle will consistently show up in our adult life until we name it and heal it. It shows up as the adult working toward some unattainable goalless end, because that's the earliest pattern the kid in them remembers.

Healing comes from separating from the kid, letting him or her know it was just the story from their past, their tribe, and the truth is that their best is enough. We need tell ourselves the truth—you fill in the blanks for yourself.

Another client went from living a life of fear with chronic panic attacks, to designing the life she had dreamed of. She now has a college degree, her own business, rich social/spiritual network, and is constantly saying, "I can't believe it, I love my life now."

When life is challenging, clients often think the answer is to work harder. When they start to think differently toward win-win-win fulfillment, they are amazed. Thinking it has to be hard is a thought pattern they can choose to change. When we expect ease, we get more ease. It doesn't mean everything is always easy, but the power to shift our thinking during these stressful times causes us to be proactive and is a great empowering life tool. Try it. Play with this new way of thinking; it really works.

Wright

Elizabeth, if you had to pick one main ingredient for success, what would that be?

Trinkaus

The main ingredient for success is paying attention to what you are telling yourself. This is what allows us to be present, to restore our energy, turn down the voice of the critic, and make good choices that bring the results we long for. Thoughts create feelings. How do you want to feel?

Most of us are programmed to think about what we don't want in life—chaos, confrontation, debt. This lowers our energy level.

What we focus on, we manifest in our lives. We want to visualize the positive end result. Athletes use visualizations all the time. They see themselves winning and then create the training program to fulfill that vision. The cool thing about visualizations is that the body goes through the same physiological responses if you are thinking about sitting at the beach or if you are actually on the beach. Your muscles begin to relax, your breathing is deeper, and you become thirsty for a margarita! Again, visualize the end result. Feel your joy. Feel your power. Dr. Alexander Graham Bell said, "What the power is I don't know, I just know it exists."

W. Clement Stone said, "Whatever the mind of man [or woman] can conceive and believe, it can achieve."

Create a life that makes you feel good.

Wright

Summarize for me, Elizabeth, the steps that will remind us of simplified success.

Trinkaus

I love the summary because we are familiar with much of this; we just all need to be reminded. And, if we are reminded at just the right time, it really lands powerfully and we commit to taking the steps that are necessary to take command of our life.

Some great reminders include:

- The quickest way to finding balance and joy in your life is being good to yourself
- Pay attention to what you are telling yourself—release the critic, affirm the truth
- Be willing to do things differently
- Practice the art of being present
- True success happens when we take care of ourselves so that we can take great care of the journey around us
- Do things that restore your energy
- Take charge of your thoughts
- Be grateful
- Remember that "your best is enough." It is. This is your freedom ticket
- Embrace the idea of attempting something significant that takes you out of your comfort zone
- We deserve to love the life we live

The following quotes are also helpful reminders:

"Are you bored with Life? Then throw yourself into some work you believe in with all your heart, live for it, and you will find happiness that you had thought could never be yours"—Dale Carnegie.

"Success is not the key to happiness. Happiness is the key to success. If you love what you are doing, then you will be successful"—Albert Schweitzer.

"You can either live your life as though nothing is a miracle or as though everything is a miracle"—Albert Einstein.

Thank you for the invitation to be included in this book.

WRIGHT

Elizabeth, thank you for your time. You play such a positive role in people's lives. You are truly a catalyst for change—change that brings contentment and peace to the soul—the thing we all so desperately long for.

I think it's incredible how these insights have the capacity to not only inspire but transform so many lives. What if we did *take command and love the life we live*? The world would be a much happier and healthier place. I know great things will come from your contribution. Again, thank you for shedding light on genuine success.

About the Author

Elizabeth Trinkaus, owner and founder of Pinnacle View, is an intuitive Master Life Coach bringing more than twenty years of experience to individuals, couples, families, and corporations. She has designed an accelerated coaching program that brings a wealth of knowledge and yields commanding results for her clients.

Elizabeth's other creations include:

- Co-author of Conversation on Success, with Deepak Chopra and Mark V. Hansen
- Work/Life Balance Immersion Program, Fortune 500 Company
- Employee Importance Program, Taking care of your number one asset—your employees
- Mighty Isis Club, ongoing workshops and retreats that inspire women to experience life-affirming shifts
- Life Enrichment Spa Series, wellness retreats within spas
- Guest Columnist for American Spa Magazine, creative ideas that inspire spa employees
- Retreat Designer and Presenter, customized soul-inspiring getaways

Elizabeth Trinkaus

Pinnacle View
Chapel Hill, NC
919-968-1620
et@pinnacleview.net
www.pinnacleview.net

CHAPTER SIXTEEN

USING THE PLATINUM RULE

BY TONY ALESSANDRA

DAVID WRIGHT (WRIGHT)

Today we're talking with Tony Alessandra. Tony, when we decided on the title of *Success Simplified* for our latest project, you were one of the first people we thought who exemplified success. You've built a successful company by helping other companies achieve market dominance in their industries. Where did it all start and why did you choose your profession?

TONY ALESSANDRA (ALESSANDRA)

Well, David, it's hard to put a finger on where it started. In my opinion, where my attitude and aptitude for success started was when I was a little kid. As strange as this may sound, I grew up in the projects of New York City, right in Manhattan, in the Chelsea section of New York City; my father was a New York City cab driver. We lived in the projects, which is the lower income area of the city; there were several of these areas.

One day I was in the playground of the projects. The projects were four large high-rise buildings, all small apartments. In the middle of these four buildings was a little playground. Some kid, older and bigger than I was beat me up. That was my first fight. So I went upstairs (I think we lived on the sixth floor) crying. My father happened to be home and asked me what happened. I really believe that this was a turning point in my life—one of the big turning points. When I told him what had happened, he said to go back down and fight that kid again, that I'm living in New York City and if kids really feel that they can beat me up, they're going to bully me and it won't be safe for me. I said, "No, no, no!" I was crying and I was afraid. And, are you ready for this? He took off his belt and said, "You're either going down and fight that kid again or you're going to face the belt." Well, I knew the belt, so I said, "All right, I'm going back down." With that motivation and after just being beaten up by this kid, I went back down and I beat him up.

Now, within a day, one of his friends came by and challenged me to a fight. Remember, this is only my second real fight. I fought this kid, again knowing what happened with that other kid, and I beat him up. What that did was to give me a confident attitude and I carried myself with confidence. As a kid, all the way through high school, I never lost a fight, other than that very first time. I had a reputation. It's almost like the gunslingers in the Wild West—the fastest gun. Kids would come from other neighborhoods to fight me.

When we finally moved to Brooklyn, New York, my cousin would bring kids home from his school to fight me because he was proud of me. I was in a Catholic school and he was in a public grammar school. The reputation I had of always winning a fight allowed me to carry myself in a very successful way. So that was my first start. It prompted kids to not put peer pressure on me to do things that they may have forced other kids to do. They stayed away because of that.

When I went through school, I actually was quite a good student. I earned very good grades in school, though I was a troublemaker, mischievous, and a "wise guy." I didn't go out looking for fights, but I was a class clown, so I'd get in a lot of trouble with my teachers. Even though I irritated them and I got detention every so often, they gave me a little bit of leeway because I did well in school. This was another thing that led to this concept of success. So it was the street fighting, my grades, and then sports.

I found that I had a natural aptitude toward sports. I excelled in baseball and football. I never wrestled competitively in my life until I went to college. I went to the University of Notre Dame, and they didn't have an intercollegiate wrestling team, but they had intracollegiate or intramural wrestling. It involved all classes. It wasn't freshman against freshman, it was freshman, sophomores, juniors, and seniors—anybody—as long as you were within a particular weight range. Someone pushed me into wrestling because he had heard my stories about street fighting. So I entered the tournament and won a gold medal in my weight category, even though I had never wrestled before. The dominoes kept falling that way—one success after another.

I graduated Notre Dame and went to grad school at the University of Connecticut. When I was there and graduated with an MBA, I decided to take on a teaching position. I taught two years at Susquehanna University and one year at Cal State Fullerton. After three years as a college teacher, I decided that I wanted to make teaching a profession, so I enrolled in a doctoral program to earn a PhD in Marketing in Business at Georgia State University.

This was a major turning point because one of the senior professors on the senior faculty at Georgia State University, in the Department of Marketing, was a gentleman named Dr. David Schwartz. Dr. Schwartz, it so happened, was author of one of the three books that I believe had an enormous impact on my life. Those three books were: *30 Days to a More Powerful Vocabulary, Psycho Cybernetics by Maxwell Malts,* and *The Magic of Thinking Big* (by Dr. Schwartz).

The first book helped me improve my vocabulary and my articulation skills. The second book was about the mechanics of the mind. And "thinking big" was a subject that intrigued me.

So, when I went to Georgia State University Dr. Schwartz became my Doctoral Dissertation Chairman and it so happens he was also a motivational speaker. He was my role model and became my impetus to enter the field of professional speaking.

While I was a doctoral student (1973 to 1976), when I finally got all my course work out of the way (in 1974) and was working on my oral exams, my dissertation was when I started doing outside consulting, training, and speaking, which was because of Dr. David Schwartz being a role model. I earned my doctorate in the spring of 1976 and I taught for another two and a half years at the University of San Diego. That's what brought me out to California. I started doing speaking part-time in the fall of 1974. In December 1978, I left teaching to go into speaking full-time, beginning in January 1979.

I was a good speaker and I continued to be a good speaker until the winter of 1981. This was another major turning point in my success. There was gentleman named Bill Gove who was the first President of the National Speakers Association. I did a one-on--one weekend coaching, speaker/coaching session with him.

During that weekend he pulled me to the side and said, "Tony, when you are not trying to speak you are this playful, mischievous New York City Italian personality. But when you try to speak, that professorial style comes to the forefront. It's not working for you. You're trying to do a style that isn't your natural style. What you need to do is let more of that playful New York City Italian style come to the forefront."

I have to tell you, this was the major turning point in my career. Once I went that direction, I went from good to very good and, in fact, by the summer of 1985 I was inducted into the Speaker Hall of Fame. That's how big a turn around it was in my career.

So those were some of the success forks in the road, where if I went one way or the other way it got me to where I am and got me into professional speaking.

Wright

What a coincidence—back in 1973, Paul Myer introduced me to two of the three books you mentioned. They made an indelible impression on me. My favorite speaker of all time was Bill Gove.

Alessandra

And he really was good, wasn't he? I likened Bill Gove to the George Burns of public speaking. He had that style and it looked so easy to do, but it wasn't. He was so good; he was a master of his craft and we really miss him.

Wright

Absolutely. I talked to him just months before he died. I tried to get him to do a coaching session, but he wouldn't because he didn't leave his house anymore. What a great speaker.

So it's been my experience that people get excited to achieve their goals and their dreams. You've been one of the most successful speakers in America for years. How did you learn to get people to listen and to create excitement in them?

ALESSANDRA

Well, I think there are at least a couple of things here and there, and might be more. One is that no matter how important and how practical the message might be, if it's delivered in a dry way, you're not going to get people to listen to it. You have to make education entertaining.

I'm a storyteller and I knew this from the time I was a kid because I would tell stories about things that happened to me. When I was telling these stories I would have groups of people listening and I'd have their rapt attention. I should have realized that I was a natural, gifted storyteller. I could tell the story but in a compelling and funny way. Once I brought that technique to the platform I really got people's attention. They love to listen to stories, especially stories that leave them with a learning point.

Another way to get people to listen and create excitement is to bring it into their world. What I do before I give a speech is to do a lot of information gathering and research with either the executive or the meeting planner. Sometimes I phone some of the attendees and ask questions like, "Will this fly? Is it relevant? Am I using the right language? Do you use different language?" And I try to make it real for them.

Let me give you a good case in point. In the summer of July 2008 I gave a series of three speeches for a group called the Pampered Chef. They're owned, at least partially, by Warren Buffet. It was started by a woman named Doris Christopher in 1980. In 1995 they brought me in the first time to give a speech and it went well enough that they brought me back again 1998. So I did two talks for them. Ten years later they were looking for another speaker. They asked all of their highest executives which speaker they would like to bring back. I'll tell you what they told me. My name kept coming up over and over again, so they brought me back.

When I spoke to them again I wanted to do two things: I wanted them to give me the names of five people who were in my session in 1998 and I want to ask them two questions: 1) What did I do in 1998 or how did my talk in 1998 influence their career and their success? 2) What would they like their people to hear from me?

So I called each of those five people and they gave me the answers to those questions. I told them to make sure they came up to me at the various sessions, because I was doing three separate talks.

At each of these sessions there were approximately four thousand people in attendance so they couldn't fit them all in at one time. Pampered Chef sells high end kitchen equipment and utensils—everything from cookware to knives, to baking equipment to little gadgets—and they do home shows. So what I did was to say, "Would you set me up to go to one of the shows so that I can see what's changed and what's new, how it's done, and how they interact with the people—with the women who are there?"

I don't do this for every speech—not to this depth—but because this is such a good client and I was going back for the third time and doing three programs to thousands of people, I wanted to go the extra mile for them.

I have to tell you it really does make a difference. When I can tell stories and give examples that let them know I really know what they do, they know I've gone the extra mile to learn their business and they're going to take my message much more seriously.

So that's how I get people to listen. I tailor the message to them by doing my homework and I tell stories, making it entertaining. I describe it as making sure that they take their medicine, which is a key concept, but the medicine is wrapped in candy.

Wright

You're the founding partner of the Platinum Group that's based on "the platinum rule." I know the golden rule but can you tell us what the platinum rule is?

Alessandra

The platinum rule is a little twist to the golden rule. Everybody knows the golden rule, which is do unto others as you would have them do unto you. I believe in that rule and I follow that rule 110 percent when it comes to values, ethics, honestly, and consideration. There's no better rule to live by. However, when it comes to one-to-one communication—whether it is simple conversation with family and friends, a sales situation, customer service, managing, motivating, counseling, coaching employees—the golden rule itself can backfire. The reason is that maybe not everybody wants to be treated the same way as you do. The world today is all about diversity—gender diversity; generational diversity, Gen X, Gen Y, Baby Boomers; personality diversity, outgoing, shy, right brained, left brained; ethnic diversity, Italians, and Germans, and Americans; religious diversity, racial diversity. There's a lot of diversity today, and the golden rule of treating people from your point of view is not as relevant as in the past.

So that's where the platinum rule came into being. (I have the federal trade mark for the platinum rule). The platinum rule is to do unto others as *they* would have you do unto them. In other words, treat people the way that they want and need to be treated. It's no different than that age old saying, "When in Rome, do as the Romans."

I learned this firsthand when I moved from the New York/New Jersey area to Southern California. When I moved to San Diego I treated people in San Diego according to the golden rule—I treated them the way I wanted to be treated. I treated them as if they were New Yorkers. Well, it backfired. I came on too strong, too fast, too aggressive, too impatient. Even when I asked people to do things that under any other circumstances they would have willingly done, they dug in their heels, and they stonewalled. It wasn't because of what I was asking, it was because of my approach. I simply rubbed them the wrong way.

So that's what the platinum rule is about. It is a concept involving adaptability. Adaptability is your ability to change your approach or change your strategy or situation to match that of the person you're dealing with.

Wright

So if we're determined to use the platinum rule, can we actually discover what makes people tick—their strengths and weaknesses, likes and dislikes?

Alessandra

Absolutely. In fact, I've spent all this time—since 1976 when I was in the doctoral program at Georgia State—doing research, writing, and speaking on the subject of the platinum rule. If you go to platinumrule.com or even platinumrulegroup.com (there are two different sites) or even to Alessandra.com, any of those sites will show my lifetime of work in this field.

The platinum rule is based on a behavioral style—a four-style model—not unlike other models such as DISC or Social Styles or True Colors. It basically says that people have a dominant pattern of behavior. It's not their only pattern but it's a dominant pattern of either being a director, a thinker, a relater, or a socializer. If you really keep your eyes and ears open, watch what people do, listen to what they say and how they say it—their verbal, vocal, and visual behaviors—they will actually tell you how to treat them.

What I teach people to do is to be able to pick up these signals—these signs, these cues—quickly and effectively. Make two simple distinctions: is the person coming across right here and now as opposed to more open or guarded? And is the person coming across, right here and now, more direct or indirect? When you can make those two distinctions, you will know how to vary your pace and priority. You will know if you should go faster or slower and focus primarily on the relationship or the task. I'm simplifying it here, but that's the model. It truly is a model to use to get that ah-ha moment.

Many of the companies I speak to have incorporated this philosophy of the platinum rule. Now, they may not use my terminology—director, thinker, relater, socializer. They may use the terms driver, expresser, analytical, amiable. They may use the DISC assessment but the basic concept is that people are different and if you can understand where they're coming from, right here and now, you can actually get on their wave length.

Let me just give you one final example here. My dominant pattern is that of the director—no nonsense, fast-paced, a little bit more guarded in the use of my time, I don't like people to waste my time, I've got a lot to do, but from being Italian I'm generally open in terms of telling people about what I feel and think. But generally, in a business setting I am a director, a driver, a dominant, bottom line, no-nonsense, Donald Trump type of guy. When somebody calls me, let's take one person in particular, my partner in the Platinum Rule Group, his name is Scott Zimmerman. When Scott calls me, I can see on my caller ID it's Scott. Depending on what's going on with me right then and there when he calls, I may answer the phone, "Yeah, what do you want?" Now he knows I'm in my director mode (he's really good at this). He'll say, "Tony, one thing and it's going to make you money—" It's a quick call and he hangs up.

Another time he might call, I know it's him and I'm in a little bit different mood where I don't have time pressures, I'm not working on a deadline, I'm feeling pretty good, I'm caught up, and I don't have to leave the next day for a speech. I might answer it, "Tony's Pizzeria what kind of toppings do you want?" Then he says, "Oh, give me some anchovies and some mushrooms," then we laugh and he'll say, "What's going on over there?" So you see, it's a little bit more upfront schmoozing before we get down to the reason he calls.

This is what this concept is about. We can get into things like left brain, right brain, outgoing, shy, time disciplines, time flexible. All these aspects play into whether somebody is more direct or indirect, more guarded or open. Once you understand where people are coming across at that particular period in time, you know what their dominant style is, you know what makes them tick—their strengths, weaknesses, likes, and dislikes.

Wright

Let's get back to helping big companies build market dominance. Do you start at the top with management or with company employees to implement successful strategies?

Alessandra

If it's at all in your power you always want to start at the top. If you start at the bottom, people are going to be looking up the hierarchy at the top people. If the top people are not behaving in the way you're asking the subordinate people to behave, they're going to say, "Hey, this is not supported by upper management. This is a do as I say, not as I do." You've got to get upper management involved and it's got to be pushed down from the top—the people at the top have to model what they're asking the employees to do.

Wright

So what happens when good employees want to hang on to the strategies of the past and resist change? Is it best to terminate them and move on or do you really believe it's possible to modify their behavior over time?

Alessandra

I am a trainer and as a result I believe you can modify behavior, but let's talk about that because there are two questions here: what about people who want to hang on to the strategies of the past? What you need to do is make sure that when you're asking people to adapt to change, a lot of people simply focus on what you're asking them to change, and they make such a big deal about it. What you need to do when you're introducing change is to explain not only what's changing, but how many things are staying the same. In any organization, in any family, in any environment, when you're creating change, probably 80 to 95 percent of what they're doing stays the same. You're usually only asking them to change a fraction of the overall picture. When people see this, it can feel a little more comfortable. Then you need to explain why the change is important, what's in it for them, what they will get out of it, and then you have to ask them to make that change over a period of time. If people can't or won't modify their behavior, do you terminate them, or do you change?

Remember the groundbreaking book called *The One Minute Manager*? Ken Blanchard wrote that book and in it he said you set a goal and when people are moving toward the goal you reward them. When they don't move toward the goal, reprimand them. However, what I really believe the purpose is that when you set goals or behaviors you want employees or children or students (this applies to anybody) to change behavior, when they're moving in the right direction, at the right speed, at the right pace, toward the change, you reward them. You reinforce, you coach, and you give them pats on the back so they keep going in the right direction.

All of us in the training business know this old saying, "Inspect what you expect," so you want to make sure that when you're asking for things to change, or you're asking for a particular type of behavior that people know you're going to look for it, you're going to inspect it. When they're moving in the right direction at the right speed, you reward them, and when they're not (at least the first and maybe second time) you retrain. Now, there comes a point where if retraining is not working, you've really got to explore terminating, because maybe the person just can't do it or isn't getting it or doesn't want to do it.

WRIGHT

As President of AssessmentBusinessCenter.com you offer 360 degree assessments. Explain to our readers what this is and how it helps people.

ALESSANDRA

Well there are a lot of what they call online assessments, and online assessments measure people's behavior. People's behavior can be their leadership style, their selling style, their behavioral style, and/or their emotional intelligence. These assessments require that you go online and answer questions. We call it an assessment and not a test because a test connotes there are right and wrong answers, where an assessment measures where a person is.

At my site—assessmentbusinesscenter.com—I have probably twenty-five different assessments that measure everything from diversity and cultural awareness to emotional intelligence. It includes various four-style models such as the Platinum Rule, True Colors, DISC, Social Styles, leadership, sales, and so on. What we try to do in some of these are pre-tests and post tests. For instance, let's take either leadership or sales because those are two very interesting ones. We have somebody take the leadership or sales assessment and typically it is a 360 or multi-radar assessment. People take the assessment in terms of how they think they're performing in all these different categories—selling skills or leadership skills. Then we ask them to send the same set of questions to representative groups of people.

So let's say for leadership we would have them send it to their managers, the person they report to, to their peers that they work with but don't supervise, and to their direct reports. We will see a composite of answers as to how these various groups of people actually perform that behavior.

So we see the test subjects' behavior and we then look at how others see their behavior to see if it's better or worse. We do the same thing with sales, but with sales we don't do quite the same thing. A salesperson answers questions on how they do on the various aspects of selling and then asks their sales managers, their fellow salespeople, and the key group—their customers or clients. Then we put the manager/leaders or the salespeople through a training program. This could be a seminar run by somebody like me, a live program, or a self-study program (such as an e-learning program) or an audio video learning program. When they finish the program we give them between thirty and ninety days after the program to implement some of these newly learned skills and behaviors. Then we have them go back again, answer the questions themselves in view of how they think they're performing now, and then go back to that same group of people and ask them, "Rate me now." It is then when, hopefully, we see improvement as a result of the training program, the live program, or the self study program. This tells us how our training and learning is hopefully positively affecting behavior.

The assessments I build are not just my assessments. I have an assessment platform, which is a technology platform I developed in 1996 for my Platinum Rule assessment. That's when my Platinum Rule came out, and I was hoping to sell more books, but then all the sudden people started coming to me, Brian Tracy, Ken Blanchard, The University of Phoenix, HRD Press, and so on. They would ask, "Would you put my assessment on your platform? Your platform is so technologically advanced. So, that's what I do. Actually it's now become a bigger business for me in terms of revenue than my speaking business.

Wright

Tony, it seems as though you're not only a speaker but you've got these other businesses that seem leading edge to me.

Alessandra

It is, and again, let me just go back David. I have a strong education background, I have a PhD in Marketing I was a college professor for eight and half years, and when I went into professional speaking, one of my biggest frustrations was how to change people's behavior in a one-hour speech? I can motivate them, I can give them a tip here or there, but when I leave, if you go to education theory and brain theory, within two weeks they've lost probably at least 75 percent of what I've told them.

I've always been looking for ways to make education and learning and training stick. That's why I formed the Platinum Rule Group and that's why I got into Assessment Business Center. I even became chairman of a company called BrainX.com, and it is a cutting-edge e-learning technology that doesn't just take people through self-paced e-learning, it creates learning mastery. Learning mastery is the ability to remember, recall, and effectively use the material you've learned. A lot of e-learning programs simply have people go through, and as long as they can pass a test at the end they're happy, but a week or two later could they pass that test again? With BrainX they would pass the test because the technology is cutting-edge.

I'm always looking for things like the Platinum Rule Group, Assessment Business Center, and BrainX.com. Are you familiar with the terminology Customer Retention Management (CRM)? It's a database program like ACT and Goldmine. These programs take all your customers and clients and put them in a database so that you can keep in touch with them.

The problem with that is you can have a thousand people in your database and all of a sudden going through your database and by accident you see a name and, for instance, you say, "Oh, David Wright, Insight Publishing. I haven't contacted him in a year; I should have stayed in touch with him."

We created a new system called Cyrano. It's a play off the concept of the play and the book *Cyrano De Bergerac*. The site is called TheCyranoGroup.com and our software is automated software. So let's say that after today, David, I put you in my database and I ask you a couple of questions: David, if I were to stay in touch with you, what are some of the things you would like me to send you information about? Your answer might be leadership or sales or time management or self-development. Either I can ask you four or five quick questions or I can say, "Would you mind if I sent you a link to click on and would you mind simply answering the four or five questions there?" What that does is put you in my database, not just as a name, but now I know some things about you. Every time I send you information, it only involves the subjects you clicked on. You have the option to unsubscribe, but it also gives you the option to update your preferences. You can always update your interests, goals, and so on. The system will automatically whatever from every source imaginable such as all of my colleagues in the National Speakers Association.

Thousands of articles go into my system and then we click off what the article is about. Now if that matches what you are interested in, it will send you, eventually, that article. I can also send the article to you based on your style—director, relater, thinker, socializer. The program will tailor the intro to you about this article. Every day that my system automatically sends things to people, including birthday and anniversary greetings, it will send me an e-mail that lets me know who was sent e- to and what was sent. This way I can't be blindsided by someone calling me three or four months from now saying, "Hey, Tony, thank you for that article; it was great!" And I won't wonder what article you're thanking me for. I might say, "David, yes, I know you like golf and I came across that article and I knew you would like it."

In fact, if I come across an article, let's say a really creative article on retirement or on sports or whatever you're interested in. I can scan it in to the Cyrano system and then click on retirement, or golf, or football. I can ask the program to find all the people who are interested in that subject and my system will pull up all the names. I can then send the article to them.

Wright

Sounds like that's a practical application of the Platinum Group.

Alessandra

Yes, it is. In fact, my partner in the Cyrano Group, Scott Zimmerman, is the guy who developed this whole system. I'm always looking for ways that I can take what I teach and preach, and put it into a practical, successful, cutting-edge system. That's where PlatinumRuleGroup.com, AssessmentBusinessCenter.com, BrainX.com, TheCyranoGroup.com, all that come into play. I'm always looking for ways I can deliver learning in a digital format that's cutting-edge.

Wright

On another subject, business owners tell me that customer loyalty is a major problem for them. They cite everything from the changing attitudes of their customers to the World Wide Web/Internet. How do you teach companies to retain their customers and build loyalty?

Alessandra

What I teach people to do is to start this process of customer loyalty and customer retention in the prospecting stage. They should do this whether they are doing outbound prospecting, cold-call prospecting, or whether they are getting their prospects from referrals.

Step 1—Profile their top 20 percent—their most profitable and most loyal customers—and then start seeking referrals of prospects who fit that profile. That's the first step.

Step 2—In the actual face-to-face selling process, make sure that they are selling the right solutions to the customer's needs.

Step 3—When it comes to the after sale service, make sure they stay in touch with their customers so that they are constantly exceeding the customer's expectations, creating as many "moments of magic" as possible for those customers and "wow" experiences, and to ultimately develop deeper businesses and, in some situations, personal relationships with their customers so they can convert them from repeat customers to an apostle. An apostle is a raving fan, a business advocate, someone who is out there in the marketplace preaching the gospel for us, somebody who is giving us good word-of-mouth referrals. We don't even have to ask for them. That's the ultimate in customer loyalty.

I teach people four sets of skills:

1. Marketing skills so they can do appropriate prospecting, targeting, and niche marketing,
2. Selling skills so they match solutions to real customer needs,
3. Service skills so that they're constantly identifying, managing, and monitoring customer experiencing so they can exceed customers' expectations,
4. Relationship skills so that we can convert our customers into apostles.

WRIGHT

You've written about creating value for customers and creating emotional attachments with them. Will you tell our readers some examples of how that might happen?

ALESSANDRA

Well, the key thing in creating value is making sure that during the information gathering stages of a sales process, we truly find out what the customer values—what's important to them, where it hurts, and where the pain is. For example, if we were to sit down three or six months from now, after you start doing business for me, and as we're sitting here, reflecting back on the last three, six, or twelve months, you might tell me, "Tony, doing business with you was an incredibly positive decision." David, what had to happen during those three, six, or twelve months to prompt you to say that to what you'll tell me are your expectations, how you are determining the success of our relationship, and how I created value for you with my solutions.

Now, creating emotional attachments is converting repeat customers into apostles. I've got to tell you that 80 to 100 percent of what we do to create emotional attachments has to do with our quantity and our quality of communication. That's one of the reasons we created The Cyrano Software at TheCyranoGroup.com. We would have the right quantity and quality of communications. The messages are targeted specifically to the individual and his or her likes, dislikes, needs, goals, and so on, even to the products that the individual purchases.

WRIGHT

I have been in the sales industry more than fifty years, and I've read a lot, but I don't think I've ever come across the concept you are talking about. It's called "collaborative selling." Would you tell us what that is?

ALESSANDRA

Collaborative selling is moving away from the more traditional approach where it's telling, selling, persuading. I've got to tell you, that's where I cut my teeth when I first learned how to sell. I mean, I sold door-to-door. I learned how to use all the tricks and techniques, the psychology, the closing techniques, and the overcoming objections skills. This simply taught me how to make sales, not how to make customers. Collaborative selling turns that on its head.

In the early 1970s when I was a college professor, I had the good fortune to be able to get any sales books ever written for free. I got hundreds, and I truly mean hundreds, of books and I poured through them looking for a better approach to selling. Quite frankly, it was rare when I found a tip or technique or skill here and there. I really had to go outside of the sales literature into management, coaching, and counseling. I had to go into psychology and psychiatry and pull ideas from those sources.

The concept of collaborative selling was that, I'm not selling—we are helping each other discover and solve your problems. Instead of persuasive skills, collaborative selling relies on questioning and listening skills. It requires exploring the customer's needs. With collaborative selling, we're talking with the customer and sharing ideas about what the customer's problems and needs are. What are their goals and missed opportunities? When you're looking for potential solutions, talk about the options and the various things you can do to help them, and talk about the tradeoffs.

Basically you are helping the customer to build the solution, whenever that's appropriate. By the way, it's not appropriate in every sales situation with every product, but in many situations, if I can talk about options and trade-offs with the customer, and the customer helps me through this collaboration process to build the solution, it's very difficult for a customer to say no to a solution that he or she helped build. That's what collaborative selling is all about.

Wright

I have quoted you many times, but one of the most insightful statements I've heard you say to date is that people don't buy because they're made to understand, they buy because they feel understood. Will you explain what you mean and how we can best help people to feel understood?

Alessandra

One of the things we've done in collaborative selling is to establish guiding principles. The sale begins when the customer says yes. One of those principles goes to the crux of collaborative selling—we're not selling, we're helping; we're not telling, we're asking. People don't buy because they're made to understand all the features and benefits of your product, they buy because they feel that you understand them and their needs and you're tailoring the solutions to those very specific needs. It gets beyond the telling and selling to problem-finding, problem-solving by way of asking and listening. It's an entirely different mentality. People don't care how much you know until they know how much you care.

Wright

Finally, Tony, what's in store for you in the immediate future? Do you have any new projects? Do you have any more mountains to climb?

Alessandra

I'm continuing to go down this path of the Internet, technology, and digital delivery of material as opposed to having to send materials in the mail. In fact, a project I didn't mention to you before is called Just In Time Sales Solutions (JITSS). I've teamed up with an award-winning film maker and we've created five-minute or less, bite-sized sales scenarios that address very specific sales issues.

For instance: How do I deal with the issue of a customer saying my price is too high or "I want to think about it"? I'm on screen for less than a minute setting the scenario about how to do a proposal, high price, asking open-ended questions, and the funnel technique. I'm only on screen describing these issues for less than a minute. Then there is an approximately four-minute actor role-play. The actors actually show you exactly how to do what I'm teaching. The viewer is not reading or listening to something or watching me tell you how to do it, the viewer is actually watching it done. It is being role modeled the way it should be done in five minutes or less.

Then we've put it into a database so that you can search for it and then click on it and you have that five-minute or less role model of a just-in-time sales solution to your problem.

I've even gone further with my assessments and added more. The software we've used is TheCyranoGroup.com.

I'm doing all those things and doing less speaking. I'm reaching more people through the Internet and the digital media than I could in a lifetime giving live speeches.

Wright

Well, what a great conversation, Tony. I have followed your work for years. I really do appreciate all this time you've taken with me today to answer these questions. I have learned a lot and I am sure that our readers will.

Alessandra

I really appreciate your thinking of me and including me in this project, David. If another project comes up in the future where you think I can provide some benefit, you give me a holler—I'm here.

About the Author

Dr. Tony Alessandra has a street-wise, college-smart perspective on business, having been raised in the housing projects of New York City to eventually realizing success as a graduate professor of marketing, entrepreneurship, and business. He is an author and hall-of-fame keynote speaker. He earned a BBA from the University of Notre Dame, an MBA from the University of Connecticut, and his PhD in Marketing from Georgia State University.

In addition to being president of Assessment Business Center, a company that offers online 360 degree assessments, Tony is chairman of BrainX.com, a company that created the first Online Learning Mastery System™. He is also a founding partner in The Cyrano Group and Platinum Rule Group, companies that have successfully combined cutting-edge technology and proven psychology to give salespeople the ability to build and maintain positive relationships with hundreds of clients and prospects.

Tony Alessandra

www.alessandra.com

CHAPTER SEVENTEEN

LESSONS FROM A SPORTS MIND

BY JENNIFER "DR. J" THIBEAUX, PHD (ABD)

DAVID WRIGHT (WRIGHT)

Today we're talking with Jennifer Thibeaux. A long-time advocate of education and the empowering effects of personal development, Jennifer has developed a keen expertise for personal, professional, and performance intelligence. She began her growth in development early in life as a U.S. gymnast, most notably medaling three times in a 1988 Junior Olympic Competition. She carried the lessons of dedication, goal attainment, determination, and passion for success to college where she attended Texas A&M University and earned a BBA in Marketing.

Jennifer founded Primary Consulting LLC in 2004. The business focuses on adult education and performance intelligence. She has worked with large clients such as AIG, ConAgra Foods, PepsiCo, and American Airlines. Working as a performance consultant, she has also coached professional athletes in both the NBA and NFL to assist with performance development, career transition, and readiness programs. At this time, Jennifer was currently working on her PhD in Education with a specialization in Training and Performance Improvement at Capella University. Her dissertation research focuses on organizational structure, leadership, and processes that influence diverse employee outcomes. Her mission in life is to affect transformational change in society through education and guided motivation.

Jennifer, welcome to *Success Simplified.*

Jennifer "Dr. J" Thibeaux (Thibeaux)

Thank you very much.

Wright

So let's dive right in. What is your formula for success?

Thibeaux

The first factor is clear vision—clear vision of the outcome, plus an understanding and faith in your own abilities. Adding to clear vision is alignment with resources and a support system that equals successful outcomes. Truthfully, these successful outcomes may offer a slew of unexpected possible pathways if you're really following this formula.

Frankly, I believe most people fail to put the true formula together. Many people know what they want as an outcome, but it's not clearly formed. A lot of people don't understand what their own abilities and strengths are. I often see a lack of faith in their abilities. Without understanding what you're capable of, it's very difficult to apply it.

The other part of that equation is alignment with resources and a support system that you have at your fingertips. Those elements must come into play and be very clear for you to understand. Ask yourself, "Do I have the physical structure and the capability to really make these successful outcomes happen?"

Built into that formula, unknown to you or you don't quite see it (but it's there) is your personal flexibility. These are the personal characteristics for you, your own perseverance, and your commitment. It is critically important that they are also aligned with your faith in your talents and your abilities—a strategic sense, as well as willingness to learn from some of your "mis-targeted outcomes." I don't necessarily call them failures; "failure" implies that there is an endpoint when, in fact, there is just a mis-targeted outcome. When all is said and done, you need to consider your outcomes in the larger sense of what you're trying to accomplish.

Wright

So if success is simple, why don't we have more successful people in the world?

Thibeaux

Success is an interesting concept. Success implies that there is one definition of what success should be. But if people want to define themselves as either successful or unsuccessful, there are obstacles that come into play as we are on this journey to achieve our destined success. Some people just fail to overcome those obstacles, which could be personal or financial. It could be a lack of education—not necessarily formal education, but a lack of the knowledge necessary to be able to tackle that project or that business or that career with the information you need to be successful.

What I find with most models of success is that they guide us to realize these defined outcomes instead of allowing each person to define his or her own meaning of "successful outcomes." Unfortunately, if you're driving to success toward someone else's idea, nine times out of ten you are going to fail. But if you define it for yourself—if you select your own measurements, and determine what makes you happy, and the things you want out of life—then very often you can be successful. The reality is, most people measure their success based on other people's ideas.

Wright

It is just as valuable to understand what something is as to understand what it is not. What examples can you give of false ideas of success?

Thibeaux

I would love to say that I did not have any examples, but the truth is I tend to see what success is not quite often. When people are interested in starting a business, one of the first steps they take is to have business cards made! For many people, the act of saying they are in business at networking events feels like success because it simply sounds like it.

As a consultant to many emerging businesses through the years, the first talk I have is to help clients prioritize their tasks that will lead to their own idea of success. Typically those urges to create the look of a solid business are relegated to secondary tasks as compared to writing the business plan—both the entry and exit strategies. Success means you have done the work to build where you are at that moment. Success is not acting as though you are already there. I have often said that the universe is a giving place if you submit to it exactly who you are, not a façade or who you want people to see. Setting up a success façade is a fast track to achieving the exact opposite of success. Most people who elect to simply act successfully take that fast track with a smile on their face unknowingly participating in their demise.

WRIGHT

I know that you are a storyteller—that's one of the hallmarks of your teaching programs and guidance. What story can you share with me that personifies your journey toward success today?

THIBEAUX

Many years ago, I realized that the best lessons to be learned were from my own experiences. Many people say I have a story for everything! In fact, I do have a lot of stories about my own life in which I am extremely transparent with people. The reason for this is because I knew to achieve breakthrough success in life, I had to understand and be present along the way. My mother and father were two of the most unique people I know. I still learn from their lessons in retrospect today. They were on the same page about the important elements of marriage—faith, family, friends, and business. We ate meals together not because of a "familial formula" but more so because we enjoyed mealtime with each other. Learning about each other's day and listening to each other was an important element in our formula. Simply put, to like something, you must understand it. To love something, you must live it. We groomed our "like" and our "love" for each other through our daily interactions. Our family happiness was rooted in our willingness to understand each other and to be willing to take the journey with each other—we were committed to live.

My father's untimely death at forty-four years old allowed me to understand at nineteen years old that life was short and it should be lived with passion, love, goals, and with no regrets. I look back at the man my father was and I am in awe at how a person who lived for just forty-four years could continue to inspire me today. It is all because I was taught to be present in the moment and live with the thoughts, words, and actions around me—even if they were not my own.

WRIGHT

Most people who meet or work with you agree that you are extremely driven. Where did that come from?

THIBEAUX

Yes, that is probably the top comment I hear from people. All I can do is smile in response because that was purposeful. It was my family who instilled in me genuine faith in myself, faith in humanity, and to see people—all people, not just me—maximize their potential.

I am in a career where my success is defined by other people's ability to meet their success. So I was always in that role. For example, my individual performance in sports always did focus on helping the team. I was raised with a mentality of not having any limits and believing that nothing was impossible. That was an important mentality to establish my strong foundation. Today, I also understand that there were people who came before me who had limits placed on them. I knew how important it was to push ahead and strive for new outcomes—to achieve a great deal for myself, for my family, and for all the people I could touch.

WRIGHT

You've been quoted as saying that, "perfectionism breeds imbalance in one's life." What do you mean by that?

THIBEAUX

That's one of my favorite phrases! It is impossible to be perfect at everything—believe it or not, I've tried. It's truly impossible, it's tiring, and it creates a system where you will certainly stop paying attention to things that are important so you don't have to prioritize. You can only work on one thing at a time. If you try to be perfect in one task or area, something else will most certainly suffer. When we aspire to be perfect in something, we are stealing that time, we're stealing money, and we're stealing mental resources away from other things that are still important to us just to make potentially one perfect outcome happen. When we do that, we thrust ourselves into a state of imbalance.

Wright

So would you explain for our readers the life/work balance concepts that you live by?

Thibeaux

Absolutely, and life/work is really the key. I coach all of my clients in the same concept. Most people hear the term "work/life," they hardly ever hear "life/work." It's important for me to flip those two words because first we were born to live a life—work is simply one aspect of our life, it's not the whole thing. We shouldn't call it a work/life balance; rather, it's a life/work balance. Each person really must treat all other major areas of life as equally important, whether its family or health and exercise or your education—all of those play an equally important part in the balance that is your mental state, your physical state, and your healthy state. Protecting all aspects of that life helps you to achieve a satisfying balance that most people dream about because those people are focusing only on certain areas of their life.

Wright

You know, a wise man once told me that if I were ever walking down a road and saw a turtle sitting up on top of a fencepost that I could bet my last dollar he didn't get up there by himself. So my question is, so who helped you get to where you are—who influenced your life?

Thibeaux

Ah, very good question. I do give credit to many people. I always turn to my family as my strong foundation. Both my mother and my father provided, by both example and guidance, the importance of an education—not just book sense but common sense and sense in community and sense in life. I have a brother who continues to teach me about unconditional love. I have a daughter who inspires me to redefine and clarify the bar for success.

I look at my sports days and even my coach in gymnastics taught me to have the confidence in my own talent that was constantly challenged during competitions, and sometimes during practice. I'm very fortunate as well to feel very close to leaders such as Oprah Winfrey or Earl Graves or Roger Staubach. I'm very fortunate to understand the past experiences of those people who fought for and represent today a zeal for equality of all people. They each stand for a belief in something greater than themselves. Patterning my passion and drive in the same fashion as the people I look up to, I was able to understand that achieving success was not only logical, it was necessary to advance the boundaries of outcomes for my family, friends, and community. I learned that one day I will be called to "put the turtle on the fence post."

WRIGHT

You have a strong sports background; what influence did sports have in your success today?

THIBEAUX

Very early in my athletic career, gymnastics was my prominent sport. My coaches showed me early on how valuable talent can be and how valuable skill can be. I was able to achieve success in gymnastics, but my career was cut short due to an injury. At an early age I was able to understand in a mature way what drive and passion for a goal really meant, and I understood how it energized me. Most people don't get a chance to understand what passion is about at the age of fifteen.

Once I understood that, then I looked for opportunities to apply my passion in other areas of my life. I immediately began to apply that passion for sports and for teamwork and collaboration into the world of education when I was in school and then in the corporate setting.

With my clients, it has been a goal of mine to help each person define his or her passion. This energizes my clients' spirit and becomes their driving force—that intrinsic motivation they need to overcome obstacles or unexpected circumstances.

WRIGHT

Today you have a large number of clients who are professional athletes. What do you tell them about success?

THIBEAUX

I tell them that success is relative to their own definition—it's not defined by others. Very often, particularly professional athletes are placed in a defined role with defined attitudes that people assume about them. It's very tough to break out of that box when so many people came before you. I have them place their own success into context so they won't long for success that can only happen in a short period of time. I want them to understand that the success they have on the court or in the field is the same level of success they can have in a different career setting, and that's important. I talk to them about career transition and how their true success as a person is often defined in the transitional stages of their work and career, not only when they're having success as professional athletes. I tell them that their talent enabled them to be drafted and their passion for success kept their contract renewed.

WRIGHT

So why are personal structures an important element in your coaching program?

THIBEAUX

This is one of the most important elements. The first thing I talk about with my clients is their personal structures. Personal structures are people, resources, and a set of beliefs that create this circle of influence for you. Those are going to be the things that you rely on for information, sometimes for consolation, and for several different circumstances. Most people fail to realize who and what make up their personal structures.

Many athletes are so busy with their athletic careers that they fail to recognize the nuances of their personal structure that are sometimes working against their overall successes. Additionally, many people fail to readjust their personal structure during times of career transition and change. The bottom line is that your personal structure should change as your career changes. Many people fail to transition their personal structures, which is a major red flag when you're seeking success. You must look at each stage of your life and identify those stages. Then ask yourself, "How should I adjust my personal structure? What do I need at this stage to have the greatest amount of success?"

WRIGHT

Why do we see so many athletes fail to achieve success after their sports life as an athlete concludes?

THIBEAUX

I would posture that many athletes achieve success, but unfortunately, that is not nearly as newsworthy as reading about those who have made missteps. The public's perception of success is dramatically skewed by the idea that if the player "never has to work again" he or she is successful. We really don't want to create a career of non-workers. What I hope for most players is that their financial status becomes a non-factor to achieving success, meaning it does not hold them hostage to their possibilities.

What many people never see is the mental transition that the professional athlete must go through as he or she moves into another career. Athletes have been trained to be coached; however, once their career in sports is over, the greatest transition of all for them is oftentimes done without coaching. Changing a career is tough for anyone, however, changing a career that more than likely has a significantly lesser compensation structure and prestige is even more difficult. In fact, current studies suggest that more than 70 percent of professional athletes end up bankrupt within eighteen months of their sports careers ending. Transparently, people who have lost their jobs during a down economy have experienced the same outcomes with similar percentages. Career change with limited options is difficult for most people.

My greatest point as a coach to a professional athlete is to define those successful elements in their actual life—their competitive nature, their strengths, their drive—and apply them to another career so that the options are expanded. Most athletes are never shown this process and therefore many fail to make the transition on their own. Money may buy them a little more time or room for error during their career transition, however, learning about what makes them tick buys them something far greater—it helps put themselves on track for success.

WRIGHT

In your Media & Leadership Academy, you teach principles such as Emotional Intelligence, Personality Type, and Finding Your Strengths. Why are these concepts important in a Media Training curriculum?

THIBEAUX

The Media & Leadership Academy exists because, along with my business partners, I wanted to provide training that gives each graduate of the program a real shot at longevity in his or her media career. The leadership component offers those foundational principles of long-term success in graduates' careers. I have long since abandoned the notion that technically skilled people are good enough. In order to see people achieve true success, we must educate, coach, and guide them by providing the tools they can use to leverage longevity in their lives albeit professionally or personally.

WRIGHT

What skill or talent can athletes and any person borrow from a sports life that would help them achieve success?

THIBEAUX

One of the greatest talents I have developed and top athletes develop is visualization. Their drive and determination is intrinsically driven by their vision of what they can achieve. For many athletes, they had the vision to see greatness when no one else saw it in them. That is because I believe success is born from your ability to have 20/20 vision on the inside. We go to the doctor to check our eyes and what they can see from the outside, but very rarely by practice to we check our internal vision. Imagine what would happen if we got up each morning with a vision of what the successful day would look like for us? What a difference-maker that now becomes for your perspective of the day and your decision-making. Internal vision drives your motivation and your focus. Those elements drive you to your outcomes. The single most important outcome of internal vision is creating a measurement system that offers you a reward consequence model that you set for yourself.

One of my most creative activities I ask my clients to conduct is the mirror-marker exercise. Each morning when they wake up I ask that they write on the mirror with a dry-erase marker what they expect to happen for the day—their purpose. This act makes them recognize the magnitude of what they may encounter and the impact the day will have on their life. Most people wait to see what the day will bring instead of bringing their life to the day.

I tell my clients that once they write their statement, go about their hygiene habits—brushing their teeth, etc. Leave their statement on the mirror and go about their day. When they get home, they should revisit their mirror. Now quickly ask, "Did my day go according to my initial thoughts?" If so, did their statement help them drive to that outcome? If not, they have a chance to reflect on the difference-maker in their day that either supported or derailed their success milestones and/or outcomes. My clients have been amazed at the results of this simple "low-tech" exercise that creates wonderful, forward-thinking and effective reflection at critical moments in the day. It is about being present and addressing their role in each day.

Wright

So if you could have a hand in influencing the success of professional athletes during a career transition, what would you do?

Thibeaux

The world believes I work in a "career transition" environment for my clients. The reality is that I work toward career translation! The first step I would take is to start at the beginning—with the school system. I would turn the clock back a little bit and focus on creating young athletes who understand why they are winners in their sport beyond their pure athleticism. This is usually never explained to them. I would require college athletes to take courses on emotional intelligence. I would love to see professional sports leagues require continuing education for professional athletes that focuses on transitional life skills. Finally, these areas of influence offer opportunities for professional athletes to understand their life, both personally and professionally, while it's happening—being present in the moment and not in retrospect as so many of them tend to do.

WRIGHT

So what would you say to people who desire success but so far it has eluded them?

THIBEAUX

I would tell them to first define what success is to them and, most importantly, to be realistic. I would tell people to understand what energizes them first and then to understand how activities really make them feel. I would have them set goals and priorities based on their own definition of success, and have them set their system of checks and balances. Measurement is crucial—it is how you help yourself stay in a good life/work balance. I want people to include their personal structures and to define them to ensure that they're staying on that path.

Finally, I would tell them to believe in themselves and to protect that belief. Oftentimes others may attempt to attack your own belief system and your belief of success as you climb toward that pinnacle. It's important for each person to understand that success is going to happen and to expect it, but to be prepared to protect his or her own beliefs. That is critically important.

WRIGHT

At the end of the day, how do you know that you have achieved personal success for yourself?

THIBEAUX

Success should be measured incrementally by setting milestones. It is imperative to translate a dream of success to goals for success, tasks that support your goals, and outcomes that satisfy your dreams. People should look at success as evolutionary and be willing to identify and celebrate the milestones.

WRIGHT

Well, what a great conversation. I can see how your clients' success is impacted. I really appreciate the time you've spent with me answering all these questions. This is going to be a great chapter for our book.

THIBEAUX

Thank you very much, I'm excited.

WRIGHT

Today we've been talking with Jennifer Thibeaux, a long-time advocate of education and the empowering affects of personal development. Jennifer is Founder and CEO of Primary Consulting LLC. Her business focuses on adult education and performance intelligence. Her mission in life is to affect transformational change in society through education. Her coaching philosophies and programs teach professional athletes and corporate executives how to achieve breakthrough success during critical life moments.

Jennifer, thank you so much for being with us today on *Success Simplified.*

THIBEAUX

Thank you David; it has been my pleasure.

ABOUT THE AUTHOR

A long-time advocate of education and the empowering affects of personal development, Jennifer Thibeaux has developed a keen expertise for personal, professional, and performance intelligence. Jennifer began her growth and development early in life as a U.S. gymnast, most notably medaling three times in a 1988 U.S. Junior Olympic competition. While pursuing her dream to compete in the 1992 Olympics, Jennifer suffered a career-ending wrist injury at fifteen years old. She carried the lessons of dedication, goal-attainment, determination, and passion for success to college where she attended Texas A&M University and earned a BBA in Marketing.

Leveraging her consulting experience at Deloitte & Touche, Jennifer founded Primary Consulting LLC in 2004. The business focuses on adult education and Performance Intelligence™. Jennifer has worked with large clients such as AIG, ConAgra Foods, Mary Kay, Inc., PepsiCo, and American Airlines to name a few. Working as a Performance Consultant, she has also worked with professional athletes in both the NBA and NFL to assist with Performance Development, Career Transition, and Readiness programs. It was indeed her exposure to a wide variety of organizational issues that influenced Jennifer to gain her Master of Arts degree in Education with a dual specialization in Adult Education and Curriculum and Instruction from the University of Phoenix.

Currently working on her PhD in Education with a specialization in Training & Performance Improvement at Capella University she has become an expert in Adult Performance Improvement and Diversity Intelligence. Her dissertation research focuses on Organizational Structure, Leadership, and Processes that influence Ethnic Minority Recruitment, Retention, and Promotion. Her post-doctoral goal is to offer education that focuses on viable career choices for professional and scholar athletes "beyond their sport."

Jennifer's mission in life is to affect transformational change in society through education. Her success is truly defined in others' triumphs and growth. Managing to uniquely divide her time, she serves a Director on the Board of the Dallas Black Chamber of Commerce, serves as a Diversity Intelligence Consultant to Fortune 100 Executives, and through her virtual training center manages over eighty e-Learning courses, all of which she uniquely authored. When not in the virtual classroom, Jennifer serves as a professional speaker and lecturer on leadership, emotional intelligence, diversity intelligence, and Performance Intelligence™.

Jennifer "Dr. J" Thibeaux, PhD (ABD)

Primary Consulting LLC
6136 Frisco Square Blvd
Suite 400
Frisco, TX 75034
972-980-6442
fearless@jenniferthibeaux.com
www.primaryconsultingllc.com
www.jenniferthibeaux.com

CHAPTER EIGHTEEN

THE LEARNING CENTERED LIFE

BY JILL EATHERLY

DAVID WRIGHT (WRIGHT)

Today we're talking with Jill Eatherly, Founder and Creator of The Learning Centered Life. Jill is a well-known educator, community partnership builder, professional development consultant, mediator, and motivational speaker. Her programs empower individuals within organizational systems to honor, value, and respect others as well as themselves to promote positive communication and improve productivity. Her programs are popular with healthcare organizations and educational systems. Also in demand are her personal growth and development seminars.

Jill, welcome to *Success Simplified.*

JILL EATHERLY (EATHERLY)

Hello, David. It is a pleasure to speak with you today and I am very grateful for the opportunity to share information about The Learning Centered Life.

WRIGHT

I know you've heard many definitions of success, but how do *you* define success?

EATHERLY

Success is totally an inside job. There seem to be so many people ready to judge how others should be that I felt I had to learn to shut them out and go inside. The *appearance* of success is dependent on someone else's perception. When I learned to go within to determine my own criteria of success, I began to actually *feel* successful. I then began to notice the outer demonstrations of that *feeling* began to occur.

It seems I have always been somewhat of an individual who never felt like I fit in and didn't conform easily to someone else's rules. This takes me back to when I was about four years old in vacation Bible school. We had to practice singing the song "This Little Light of Mine" in front of the congregation. I remember so vividly singing the song with great passion.

There came a part in the song about hiding the light under a bushel and I clearly remember screaming, *no!* at the top of my lungs! At four years old I knew I didn't want to "hide." Remembering this early demonstration of personal power helps connect me with a feeling of determination and purpose that the Learning Centered Life was created to bring into focus.

Wright

You describe the direction of your business as the learning centered life. Would you tell our readers what that means and how this approach helps people learn from your success?

Eatherly

Life is full of peaks and valleys. There are always those times when everything is going smoothly and we're just sailing through. Then, all of a sudden, we hit a wall or encounter roadblocks. At that point it's time to *stop!*—stop and ask a very telling question: "What about this am I not getting?"

Life is like a dance. It is always more fun when there are new steps to learn or old ones to remaster. It gets pretty boring doing the same old steps after a while, and dancing with someone who doesn't like new steps can be very boring. The Learning Centered Life is about learning new steps from life's adventures, and living life with enthusiasm, passion, and purpose.

The Learning Centered Life (LCL) programs focus on meeting people where they are and opening up vistas for new potential. The Baldrige Criteria for quality improvement is quite useful here, and I find that the questions it asks work equally well in both business and personal aspects.

- What's working? Review what has been done, what has been accomplished, and how close is my client to accomplishing his or her goal?
- Where are there opportunities for improvement? How could it be better, expanded, or improved?
- Brainstorm suggestions or recommendations; don't discount anything. Keep ideas flowing no matter how strange they may seem.

These are my fallback questions, whether I am coaching or reviewing a project: what's working, what can be improved and what are some suggestions or ideas that can make that happen?

Another means for keeping the door open on learning is to realize there are other points of view. All perspectives are based solely on internally-generated experiences and belief systems. Everyone has different interpretations of experiences even if he or she grew up in the same environment. There is always another perspective and another outlook, and it helps to remember that *different* doesn't mean right or wrong. In our trainings, what gets created is the space to explore new possibilities.

It is very helpful to look outside of our little area of reference and experience to see what might be another point of view. A client of mine, whom I'll call Linda, has two ex-husbands. For years, she held a point of view that if they had done life *her* way, everything would have just been *fine!* The key word in that statement is "ex-husbands." By holding only to internal points of view, there isn't much of an opportunity to learn new ways of accomplishing goals or attaining dreams personally or professionally.

It was relatively easy for Linda to see that her approach wasn't moving her in the direction of attaining her goal of a loving and lasting relationship. Linda took her enrollment in the LCL program seriously and first explored her beliefs about relationships.

She was amazed to discover that a lot of them weren't even hers—they belonged to parents, grandparents, etc. She suspended the majority of those beliefs and gradually installed some others that were much more workable for her personally. She cleared out a lot of expectations for both herself and a potential partner and learned how to stay "in the moment." She was ready and willing to make changes, and I am pleased to report that her latest relationship is working very well for both her and her partner.

Divorce has a major influence on the changes in one's life. Divorce usually means failure to those involved, and it takes a great deal of inner work to turn that around. Counseling is often involved in the beginning of the separation process. During a particularly intense moment in a mediation session between Bob and Sherry, Bob walked out. After several moments of silence I asked Sherry, "What do you see yourself doing if you get a divorce?"

Without hesitation Sherry responded, "I intend to find out why I have done this to myself!" Realizing that no one could continue to do anything to her unless she allowed it was a profound opportunity to begin to take responsibility for her life and choices she had made. She realized she was married to a fantastic man whose belief about marriage did not align with her own. Whose fault was that? Working through these issues definitely helped Sherry and other clients like Linda with the clarity and tools needed to learn another way to be in relationship.

Wright

A very wise man told me one day, "David, if you're ever walking down a road and you see a turtle sitting on top of a fencepost, you can bet he didn't get up there by himself." In your programs, you refer to yourself as a learning coach. Who have been some of the most significant learning coaches in your life?

Eatherly

David, some amazing people have crossed my path. When I need someone the most, that's when he or she shows up. I am also an avid reader. Books fall off the shelf in bookstores with the perfect message for what I am experiencing at the time. There are so many books that have transformed my life that there are too many to mention here so I have posted a bibliography on the Learning Centered Life Web site for review. Of all the authors and coaches who have crossed my path, there are three who especially stand out for me.

First, Danaan Parry of The EARTHSTEWARDS Network was absolutely one of the most important teachers and coaches in my life. He and his wife, Jerilyn Brusseau, gathered men and women together to experience a retreat called "Essential Peacemaking: Women and Men." Danaan also authored *Warriors of the Heart* and held weekend retreats for participants to experience the concepts outlined in the book.

At the core of the gatherings was an interactive model called Collaborative Communication. This model explains how easy it is to go into defensive communication practices, especially when emotions are triggered and vulnerability is experienced. When defensiveness gets triggered, most people only listen to internally stored information so that it can be turned around on the other in order to prevail. Through practice, this model can expand opportunities to know one another with an open heart and remain open to learning different points of view, even when triggered to react instead of learn.

Danaan was an exceptional human being, coach, and mentor to people all over the world prior to and after his passing in 1996. The first training I did with him, he looked at me and said, "You really have the heart for this work; I am glad you are here." That simple statement touched me in a place that I remember often and makes what I do today very heartfelt work for me. I am honored to have Danaan's permission to use the Collaborative Communication model in the LCL programs.

Another important coach in my life is Eleanor Graves, counselor, author, teacher, diversity trainer, and much more. Eleanor introduced me to the National Coalition Building Institute in Washington, D.C., when I was working at the university on the national registry for Historical Black Colleges and Universities as the Director of Minority Affairs.

Eleanor took me by the hand and assisted me to help make a difference for the Caucasian students on campus. This situation was the reverse of what most students experienced as desegregation, with its own set of experiences and challenges. We partnered to provide diversity training to as many departments on campus as possible so the young people involved would have new tools to be successful in the new world they were creating. Today, Eleanor and I do corporate and educational seminars on diversity using the Collaborative

Communication model. Eleanor remains a major part of my life and every time I'm around her I learn more.

Dr. Margaret Wheatley, author of *Leadership in the New Science*, is another learning coach who never stops pushing me to the next level. Her explanation of how chaos in an organization constitutes the natural order of things (much like nature experiences change) has been invaluable to me. I learned how to weather changes through observing the chaos, moving with them and evolving to become even stronger. Margaret is the founder of the Berkana Institute that provides many programs around the globe to help better our world.

One of those programs is the Art of Hosting that brings groups together to explore new ways of working within a community. This program employs tools that promote authentic communication to empower individuals to become leaders in their communities.

WRIGHT

There are many adjectives to describe coaches and of course you've shared the importance of Margaret Wheatley, Danaan Parry, Eleanor Graves, and others as your learning coaches. Will you explain to our readers what you mean by a "learning coach"?

EATHERLY

A learning coach seeks to discover within the client the unconscious hidden treasure that can be coaxed to conscious awareness. Coaches provide encouragement to learn to step out of the box of limitation and support on the path to true self-discovery. They don't plan that path or purport to have the answers. They give opportunities to explore new possibilities in a safe environment and in an encouraging way.

When there is comfort in dysfunction, there is often a need to be encouraged to go beyond self-imposed limitations. Learning coaches see more potential than can their clients and have the ability to assist them to embrace gifts and talents within themselves that open up new ideas and opportunities for success.

WRIGHT

We all have crossroads in our lives, what would you say were some of the most significant times in your life that gave you more courage and determination to be successful?

EATHERLY

When I finished my first year of college, I decided to quit school, move out of my parent's home, and go to work. I was hired by an insurance company to file paperwork at a forty-hour weekly salary of $45.05. Needless to say, that did not begin to cover transportation and housing costs. I made it through the summer and begged to move back home to continue my education. My father agreed on the condition that I would pay tuition for the fall semester, which happened to be $93.40. That was a fortune to me. My last two paychecks didn't quite stretch far enough but my Mom "slipped" me the difference!

It was a good thing I went back to school because during my sophomore year my father passed away, my two older brothers became soldiers in Vietnam, and my mom, my youngest brother, and I were left on our own for the first time in our lives.

My father was very instrumental in encouraging me to be independent and to get the skills I needed to take care of myself, no matter what happened. Years later I looked back and realized Dad might have felt he wasn't going to be there to watch my back—he made sure I had the confidence and self-determination required to follow my dreams.

As soon as I finished college in the early 1970s, I accepted a position in South Carolina to teach during the first year of integration in a black high school. I was one of eight white teachers on a faculty of forty-five educators—and I was very glad to have a job! Little did I know that twenty years later I would become the Director of Minority Affairs at an historically black university. That was most definitely an opportunity to experience firsthand a culture different from my own and, in the process, learn a great deal about life.

There was a particular teacher in South Carolina I credit for getting me into graduate school. He was not my favorite person; and as a role model for good teaching, I could kindly characterize him as quite the opposite. One thing he *did* have was a Master's of Education degree. I looked at him and said to myself, "If he can do it, I can, too!" I applied for and received an assistantship to go back for my master's degree and have been grateful to him ever since! I began to realize that learning opportunities can come from anywhere and anyone! This experience and others taught me how to use resistance productively, like the saying, "when life gives you lemons, make lemonade!"

The fall my son got his driver's license was the same year I first experienced the Essential Peacemaking: Women and Men retreat. The Collaborative Communication model I was learning was changing all my relationships profoundly, especially with my family. I have three brothers and before Essential Peacemaking, I thought I understood what men wanted and how to relate to them—boy, was I wrong! Here is an example:

It was a wet, drizzly morning when my son first began driving his own car. The only thing he was interested in that Saturday morning was visiting his girlfriend without being chauffeured. We agreed he would be back in one hour and he left the security of home in the misting rain. After an hour I began looking for him to return. Two hours later I was furious and went through all the mental control systems I could imagine: no more car for months, grounded until twenty-one years of age, etc. Three hours later I was contemplating calling hospitals. I had the phone in my hand to call the sheriff's department when my sunny young son came strolling in the door.

Luckily I caught myself before tearing into him. I made the decision to practice the collaborative lessons I had just learned. I invited him to sit with me at the kitchen table and began to share the angst I had been through during the previous two hours. My sharing was done with compassion and without accusation or shaming. I just shared my feelings about not being able to protect him on his way to becoming a responsible young man and that the most important thing I needed from him was to know that he was safe. During the next hour we discussed what that looked like for both of us and, believe it or not, we came to an agreement that held up for the next sixteen years! Yes, there were some bumps but nothing so drastic that we couldn't handle it with love and respect for each other.

Another clear example is again in reference to my son, one of my foremost teachers. He arrived home from a seventeen-day Outward Bound adventure the summer after graduating from high school. When asked what the most memorable lesson learned from the experience was, he stated, "If it is going to happen in my life, it is up to me to make it happen." How I would have loved that insight when *I* was eighteen!

Wright

How did you translate these life experiences into the curriculum of the LCL?

Eatherly

Keeping things simple and concise has always served me well. These three phrases in particular have helped to hold things in a perspective that works for me:

Honor the humanness of all people.
Value the gifts everyone brings to the table.
Respect the unique differences we all share.

To honor the humanness of all people is to realize that everyone has a story and experiences that have molded his or her belief systems and behaviors. Everyone has a story—without exception. It is impossible for another to understand that story unless he or she is open to listen and learn.

Value the gifts everyone brings to the table. Sometimes we have gifts that we don't realize, and oftentimes we overlook the gifts of others unless we're open to new points of view or perceptions. Effective learning coaches help to create the space for learning to occur in a way that supports the recognition of their clients' gifts and talents.

Respect the unique differences we all share. Through experience with diversity work, my definition of *respect* has been truly expanded. Not only do differences include race, gender, religion, ethnicity, location, and family backgrounds, the groups to which we belong, even the television programs we choose to watch influence our "stories." Respecting each other's rights and privileges as a human being does not mean we have to agree with another in order to respect his or her choices. It primarily means we are being asked to honor others' paths.

I have found that the judgments I place on others are based on my experience of truth. There is a phrase that can stop me in my tracks when I really get into a point of self-righteousness that blocks my success:

I react to what you say or do as if I had done it.

The best example in my life for learning about honor, value, and respect comes from my stepfather who was dying of emphysema when I began using these concepts in a teaching format. I hadn't always been happy with the relationship he and my mother shared; I somehow felt that she was missing out on something. I think this happens a lot in stepchild/parent situations, and it was easy for me to slip into judgment and make the situation more difficult than necessary.

As they say in Alcoholics Anonymous, I was working my program. So I was working through honoring the human—okay, he *is* a human being. He's got his story. Okay, I could honor that. Next, I had to value the gifts he was bringing into my mother's life, even though I couldn't understand what they were. This opened up the opportunity to accept that it was absolutely perfect for them. My being bitter or angry and thinking it was wrong was doing nothing except putting distance between everybody. I was being asked to just let it go and value the gift. I didn't have to know what it was. When I thought about respecting him, I was reminded of the many definitions of respect. I began to respect him as a human being, different from myself yet worthy of respect.

This process took me about two years to complete, while all the time I was conducting workshops using Honor, Value, and Respect (HVR) as the core teaching. At the same time "Buck" continued to suffer through the effects of sixty years of smoking until his death in January 1998. We had actually come to a place of harmony and mutual respect prior to his passing. I never knew his complete given name since he had gone by the nickname Buck Rogers since I met him. While going through his official papers after his passing, we found Army discharge papers with his full name: Homer Vernon Rogers—HVR! Goose bumps!

Wright

So it is very interesting that you would have that much insight. How does one create the space for learning to occur?

Eatherly

It has been my experience in any situation that if we don't feel safe to be who we are and to bring our doubts and our fears forward, we're going to stay stuck and close ourselves off to new ideas and possibilities. It is human nature to hold on to personality traits, thoughts, belief systems, or ideas that give us comfort because they are what we know. When asking others to explore new possibilities and new perceptions, it's essential—whether it be in a one-on-one relationship or in a large group—that everyone knows and understands each one is honored, valued, and respected for who he or she is and what each person brings to the table.

Creating the space for learning to occur involves the basic principles of honor, value, and respect and having a clear understanding of what is expected of us in that space. This definitely requires new communication tools so that everyone is on the same page. The Collaborative Communication model begins with an understanding that we all have *our* piece of *the* truth that may or may not align to another's and that's *okay!* Learning to listen with an ear for getting to know another better and speak with the intention that I want another to hear me is how a safe space begins to be created.

There are three types of conversation: destructive, non-productive, and productive. These conversations are held internally as well as with others. If a conversation is destructive, there is nothing positive happening. It feels critical, detrimental, and demeaning to both the listener and the one speaking. This is equally true at an internal level. Time spent in this type of discussion often creates barriers that require extensive clean-up. A non-productive conversation is casual with neither productive nor destructive outcomes. A productive interchange creates the space for learning to occur.

Every year I have the privilege to address a group of medical doctors at the beginning of their third year of residency. In their third year, they are responsible for those doctors in their first and second year of training.

I always begin the training with an excerpt from Malcolm Gladwell's book *Blink: The Power of Thinking Without Thinking* (pages 39–43). Gladwell gives several examples of certain doctors being sued, although *other* doctors were guilty of the actual malpractice simply because the doctor being sued did not take the time to connect with his or her patient at a personal level. The physicians being sued may have been better trained but had less expertise at connecting with their patients.

We live in a world of polarities: right/wrong, good/bad, up/down, left/right; it's often difficult to find the center. When we are creating the space for learning to occur, we must find that balance point. It is much like an airplane on autopilot. The plane will veer off course and correct itself constantly. If we have the tools to become aware when we are "off course," in defensive or destructive communication patterns, we can self-correct and come back to the center where we are honored, valued, and respected for who and what we are and the gifts we bring to the table.

Wright

On your journey toward success, what would you say contributed the most to the professional successes that you have experienced?

Eatherly

Perseverance and a willingness to go beyond my comfort zone into the unknown in order to learn a new way or something new about myself; those qualities have contributed to my professional and personal successes. Blessed by a father with a strong belief in humanity and a mother who instilled a core belief in a Higher Power, I am not surprised that my life is filled with opportunities to blend the two. And I'm very grateful to them both.

I think what really contributed the most was my willingness to learn and my willingness to see a different side and a different point of view. I can assure you it didn't come easily. I remember driving to a job where I had a boss I could not stand! On the way I kept saying, "Whatever it is I need to learn from this person, *please* let me learn it today so I can move on!" It wasn't long before I was promoted and moved to a different department, and I did learn a huge lesson from the person in question.

Along my journey I've learned that life doesn't *have* to be done the hard way. Learning to broaden my outlook and to expand how I see others has made life more rewarding. Yes, I still run into roadblocks and hit the wall on occasion. Using the tools I have acquired and always being willing to learn has made my life a journey filled with joyful successes, and I appreciate the simple things along the way. And I am so very grateful that I can share these tools with others in LCL.

Wright

In concluding our time together, is there anything else that you would like to share with our readers on creating a learning centered life?

Eatherly

Often upon entering into an organization, there are complaints from employees about inappropriate comments, racial slurs, people not feeling respected in their jobs, etc. It is important that everyone understand the purpose of a training or seminar for the best possible outcome for the time spent together. Once I attended a speech given by Zig Ziglar. He used a slide that always reminds me of how precious time is in any situation: "The number of people in the room multiplied by clock time = time spent."

When everyone is connected to the purpose for our time together there is more opportunity to communicate on a much deeper level and become more open to different points of view and ideas for change. As new ways of listening and speaking to one another are practiced in the group setting and everyone moves "onto the same page" with communication tools, collaboration around difficult issues gives way for the creation of something beyond what was thought possible when the process began. When we Honor, Value, and Respect one another, we open into a world full of infinite possibilities.

Wright

Well what a great conversation. I've really learned a lot here today and I'm sure that our readers will. I really appreciate all the time you've spent with me, Jill, to discuss this important topic and I'm so happy that you're in our book.

Eatherly

Thank you David; I really enjoyed speaking about it. As you can tell, it touches my heart and it really allows me to live the life that I want to live through sharing with others. It really has been a remarkable journey for me, beginning with the realization that success is an "inside job." I can choose to learn from every step taken.

WRIGHT

Today we've been talking with Jill Eatherly. She is the Founder and Creator of The Learning Centered Life. She is a speaker, trainer, educator, coach, and motivational speaker. Her programs and workshops empower individuals within an organizational system to honor, value, and respect others as well as themselves to promote communication and productivity.

Jill, thank you so much for being with us today on *Success Simplified*.

Jill Eatherly, MEd, founder and creator of *The Learning Centered Life*, is an author, educator, professional development consultant, mediator, and motivational speaker. Jill's philosophy of life is that success is multidimensional and shows up everywhere when we bring an energetic and authentic approach to the work we do as professionals and as people in the world. Jill has dedicated her life to learning and encouraging others to live life to its fullest by creating the space for learning to occur in any setting or relationship with joy and enthusiasm.

Jill Eatherly, MEd

The Learning Centered Life

P.O. Box 12152

Murfreesboro TN 37129

615-308-6923

jill@jilleatherly.com

www.thelearningcenteredlife.com

CHAPTER NINETEEN

CHOICE AND CHANGE

BY KATHY CLEVELAND BULL

DAVID WRIGHT (WRIGHT)

Today we are talking with Kathy Cleveland Bull who is considered to be among the finest professional speakers on change. Her company, N~Compass Consulting, helps clients "Navigate the Art and Science of Change." In her consulting practice, her well-proven methods provide clients the necessary blueprints for successful change strategies, human development, organizational culture change, and personal growth.

Kathy is a Phi Beta Kappa graduate and supportive alumnus of Bowling Green State University where she received two master's degrees. Her powerful change message has been presented to audiences on three continents, sharing the stage with such notable names as Dr. Phil McGraw and Deepak Chopra.

Let's get right to the heart of the matter, Kathy. For you, what is "success simplified"?

KATHY CLEVELAND BULL (CLEVELAND BULL)

Pythagoras said, *"Choices are the hinges of destiny."* From my view, making *good* choices equals success simplified.

WRIGHT

How did you arrive at that conclusion?

CLEVELAND BULL

I was fortunate enough to have an important mentor early in my career in higher education who taught me about what he called "The Power of Choice." Mr. Ronald C. Butler was one of my first supervisors when I was fresh out of graduate school and working at North Carolina State University in Raleigh, North Carolina. He believed in this concept so much that his license plate on his car said, "UChoose"! Countless times he would barge into my office with endless energy and a huge smile and ask, "Are you job satisfied today?" And I knew the correct answer was yes, because he taught me that it was my choice as to whether I was job satisfied or not! Mr. Butler told me the story of how he used the Power of Choice even at home with his wife. He would ask, "Honey, are you choosing to be angry with me right now?" After so many years of living with Ron her response was, "Yes, dear. And you'll be the first to know when I choose to stop!"

While this early exposure to the Power of Choice had a profound and lasting impact on my life, it wasn't until I was much older and had certain key life experiences that I was able to integrate the concept and understand it at a much deeper level.

Wright

What were those experiences that helped you understand the Power of Choice? Would you like to share your story with us?

Cleveland Bull

Yes, absolutely. I call it my "waking up story" and hopefully each of us will have something that causes us to wake up to a more consciously lived existence.

My mother died seven years ago of a rare early onset dementia called Fronto Temporal Dementia or FTD. She showed the first signs of the disease when she was around fifty years old. Her progression was a gradual deterioration of all her mental and physical functions and she passed away in a nursing home at age sixty-four, an empty shell of the vibrant, compassionate, and beautiful woman she had been.

Fourteen months after Mom died, my father, who had retired early from a factory job to be her caregiver, also passed away because of what we all suspect was a broken heart and a broken spirit. The love of his life was gone and he just chose not to live without her.

My two sisters and I were left to face the prospect of inheriting this rare FTD gene mutation that has a 50 percent heredity rate in our family.

The disease comes with a death sentence. There are currently no treatments and no cure.

Could there possibly be a blessing buried in those odds? For me, there was. I knew I had a choice in how to respond. The prospect of getting FTD changed my life completely, as I shifted internally to living as though I would be lucky to still be fully functioning at fifty years old. There was now a sense of urgency, meaning, and purpose. I left my career in higher education to pursue my dream of owning my own firm and becoming an international speaker. My relationships with family and friends became more intimate and deeper. I took more risks professionally and personally, and most importantly, I awakened to my spiritual path.

Duke University had been doing extensive genetic research on FTD in our family and others, and I had always hoped that someday a test could be performed so that my sisters and I (along with many first cousins) could know whether or not we carried the mutated gene or not. Finally, in January of 2006, after successfully isolating the gene responsible for our family's strain of FTD, testing was approved. After increasing the coverage of all my insurance (life, disability, long-term care—I'm an optimist, but also fairly practical!), I decided to be tested. In October of 2006 I got my test results. They were negative. I would never get Fronto Temporal Dementia.

But my celebration was short lived.

The same week that I received my results, my twin sister, Karen, started to undergo a series of diagnostic tests to determine why her speech was slurred and slow. Her words were hard to find and her reading comprehension was rapidly deteriorating. She was often confused, and wasn't functioning at her normal level at work.

Diagnostic tests, including CAT scans, MRIs, EEGs, and even a Spinal Tap were performed ruling out the most obvious causes such as a brain tumor, seizure, stroke, and even encephalitis and poisoning. With each negative test result, the possibility of FTD became more likely.

In January of 2007, neurological tests revealed that Karen did, in fact, have a rapidly progressing form of our family's brand of FTD. And on February first of that year, my older sister, Vivica, and I had the challenging task of helping Karen understand the diagnosis and let her know that based on the advice of two neurologists and her other doctors, it was no longer safe for her to work, drive, or live alone.

In one day, Vivica and I became Karen's full-time caregivers. She would need to be living with one of us for the rest of her life. Her independent existence, which was the hallmark of her life, was no more.

Just three months earlier, at age forty-five, she was leading emergency disaster relief efforts for Health and Human Services for an eight-state region in the Southeast. She was deploying emergency responders to hurricanes, floods, and fires. She was preparing federal agencies to respond to chemical, biological, and natural disasters and creating emergency protocols for our protection.

A year after Karen's diagnosis, we moved her to a nursing home with a high quality dementia care wing just minutes from my home. Her care was simply more than Vivica and I could handle, particularly while managing our own families and professional commitments.

Over time, Karen lost her ability to talk, feed herself, change her clothes, and brush her teeth. She couldn't get into or out of a chair, and she couldn't walk. She showed no signs of recognition and no affect. She was imprisoned in her body just as our mother had been. Recently, Karen was released from that prison. After a two-and-a-half-year battle with FTD, my twin sister, Karen, died on June 20, 2009, at the age of forty-eight.

Wright

It's inspiring that you have been through so much personal loss recently and still seem to have such a positive and upbeat attitude. What lessons have you learned from this that might benefit our readers?

Cleveland Bull

Because of these life experiences, I am better able to recognize the spiritual treasures that exist, even in the most painful circumstances and losses. I have learned to accept the reality of "what is." And every day I remind myself of this beautiful and inspiring quote by Eleanor Roosevelt, "*You have to accept whatever comes your way. And the only important thing is to meet it with courage and the best you have to give.*"

I have found that acceptance of what is, is very different from resignation. I recently came across this quote by Henry Wadsworth Longfellow that says it very well, "*For after all, the best thing one can do when it is raining is to let it rain.*" When you say "no" to changes that come in life—particularly the unwanted, uninvited changes—your energy is directed toward resistance and this creates stress. "No" doesn't stop the rain.

When you say "yes" to whatever comes, your energy is freed to act and consciously respond. So, one of my strategies in dealing with change is to try to get to acceptance. I focused on that when Karen first got sick. My initial response of course was, "No, not again, not to her." But then I tried to see that the sooner I got to "yes," the sooner I could begin focusing on Karen's needs and doing what I needed to do for her as she faced this devastating and terminal illness.

Virginia Satir once said, *"Life is not the way it's supposed to be. It's the way that it is. And how we cope with it is what makes the difference."* To me, this is what Mr. Butler was trying to teach me and others so many years ago. No matter what happens, we are left with that one truly human freedom—our ability to choose what we will do in response.

Wright

Well said. So that leads us into your definition of success—making good choices. How do we do that?

Cleveland Bull

There are really four steps to making good choices. Simply stated, they are:

Recognize your Power of Choice
Access your Power of Choice
Practice making good choices
Focus your choices on what is really important

I think it would be helpful to go through each of these four steps as a way to better understand our Power of Choice.

Wright

Okay. Let's start with the first step. How do we "Recognize" our Power of Choice?

Cleveland Bull

Truly, our greatest untapped resource is our Power of Choice. So recognizing this power is the first step.

When people think about important untapped "resources," they tend to focus on external things: financial resources like cash, credit lines, capital; energy resources like fossil fuels, nuclear power, solar, wind or geothermal; and natural resources like water, forests, soil. And while it is true that these are all very important resources, more important than any of these to our personal success is something internal: our Power of Choice.

One of the main reasons for the success (and challenges) of the human species compared to other animals is that less of our behavior is governed by instinct, and more of our behavior is governed by our power to make different choices and, therefore, successfully adapt to change.

One thing that all successful people have in common is that they have made good choices. But most of us are not fully or effectively utilizing this remarkable ability. We often think, feel, and act as if we have very little choice in our lives. We let others choose for us or we don't take advantage of our opportunities to make our own choices. Thus, our Power of Choice is truly our greatest *untapped* resource.

In order to recognize our Power of Choice, we have to challenge our *thinking* (i.e., our ideas and beliefs that tell us that we have little or no choice). When misunderstood, ideas like fate, karma, tradition, daily structure, rules, laws, schedules, determinism, peer pressure, social expectations, psychological patterns, personality traits, destiny, randomness, astrology, "let go and let God," luck, probability, and other beliefs, can lead us to vastly underestimate our Power of Choice. We have to be willing to be open to the possibility that, just maybe, we have more choice than we "think" we do.

Recognizing our Power of Choice can also be frightening, anxiety-producing, and in other ways *emotionally* uncomfortable—especially at first. There is a kind of sleepy sense of security and complacency that comes with feeling that one has no choice. Having no choice is a great excuse for not taking responsibility for our lives. Just look at the word "responsibility"—it is our ability to respond versus react! We can also become attached to and identify with habits and patterns—even if they are clearly negative and create suffering for ourselves and others. So it actually takes *courage* to recognize and then start tapping into our Power of Choice!

WRIGHT

We all can identify people who have been negatively affected by various habits in their lives. I think it does take courage to see those habits and take steps to break them. So, the next step is access. How do we "Access" our Power of choice?

CLEVELAND BULL

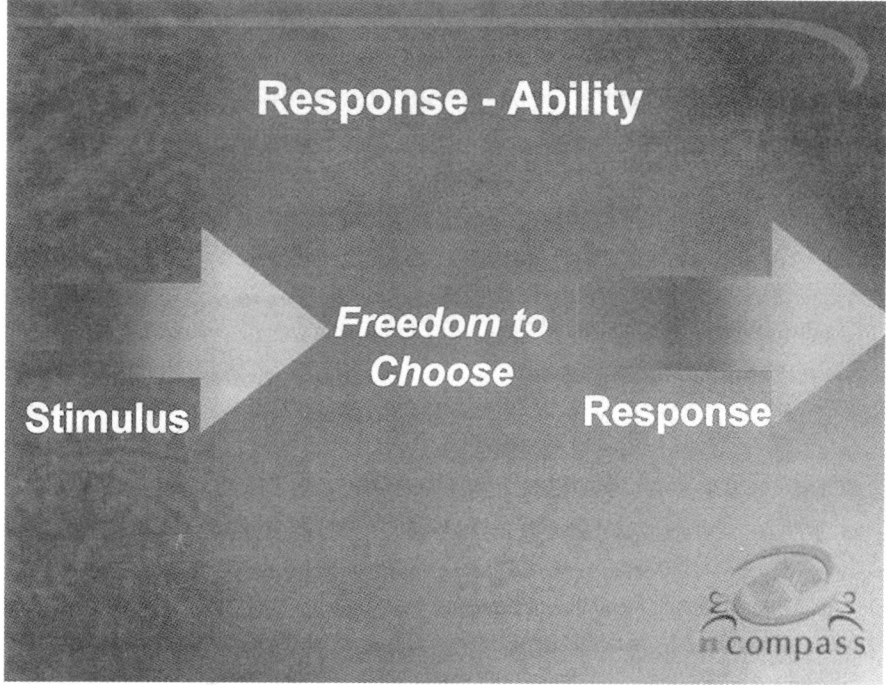

Figure 1.

One helpful way to understand how we access our Power of Choice is by looking at the Stimulus–Response model. *(See Figure 1.)*

This idea gained in popularity when Stephen Covey wrote his international bestseller, *The 7 Habits of Highly Effective People*. Our Stimulus–Response model shows that everything that happens within our awareness is considered a stimulus. Then there is a gap that represents our freedom to choose, followed by some response on our part. All would be wonderful if we actually lived that way. But what happens is the brain likes to find and recognize patterns to make life "easier." And when it perceives a familiar stimulus, it is as if it is saying "Oh, we have been here before. We really don't have to 'think through' the unlimited options of responses. Let's just do *this,* which is what we did when we last faced this stimulus. It seemed to work out okay last time." This is how, over years of "practice," we develop patterns and habits that get wired into our brains. This makes it much harder to actually *choose* a response in that moment after a stimulus when we need to take action. We simply react out of familiarity and habit.

That gap is sometimes called "the magic quarter second" because we only have about a quarter of a second of time to catch ourselves before our habits kick in! That's not a lot of time to stop something that has become wired. But we can do it! The habit has been learned, so it can be unlearned. What we need, as Covey often suggests, is a pause button! We need something that allows us to stop the action between stimulus and response long enough so we can choose a better response, even in the heat of the moment! Personally, I would like a pause button *and* a rewind button! Sometimes I just don't hit pause soon enough!

WRIGHT

I can relate to that too! Okay, your third step is practice. How do you recommend that we "Practice" our Power of Choice?

CLEVELAND BULL

Choice is like a muscle. The more you exercise it, the stronger it gets. We all know people who seem to have great discipline—they make good choices and then follow through with them. We tend to speak of them as though they simply have a stronger moral character. But the reality is that they were not born this way. They have just exercised their choice "muscle" more.

To continue the metaphor, a good way for us to exercise our choice muscle is to start small—make what I call "Subtle Shifts"—and experience success, which will reinforce future good choices.

Quick fixes, miracle drugs, and the "overnight success myth" are pushed on us by the media, cable television, and in our junk mail and e-mail spam. In our culture today, there's a societal value placed on Extreme Makeovers of all types—of our houses, relationships, bodies. We operate under the false assumption that dramatic changes are what really count. But in reality, it is the few small but smart changes and actions that often pay the biggest dividends in work and in life.

The Subtle Shift philosophy can have a real impact, and here's the best part: it's easier and the probability of success is much greater than swinging for the fences or going *all in*.

Wright

So what are some of these Subtle Shifts that can dramatically affect our life experience?

Cleveland Bull

My first examples will relate to lifestyle choices because these are really the easiest to see and do, but there are others in other areas of life of course.

- Fifteen to twenty minutes of exercise when you don't have time versus exercising only when you have one full hour available to hit the gym
- Taking the stairs versus riding the elevator
- Switching from white bread, rice, and pasta to whole grains
- Cutting back on caffeine, alcohol, and sweets versus cutting them out completely
- Consistent base hits versus the grand slam home run

- Steady saving and investing over the long haul thanks to compound interest versus hoping to win the lottery or hit it big in Vegas despite horrible odds

Of course, there are countless other Subtle Shifts we can make that if done regularly will produce big results!

Last year, after I started developing the Subtle Shifts idea, I read an article in the *Wall Street Journal* about how our New Year's resolutions fail for this very same reason. We set unrealistic goals that we can't live up to and only end up being discouraged and giving up.

Two examples I remember from the article:

- Make a resolution to actively play for forty minutes just once a week with your kids and you'll burn off five pounds over the course of the year!
- Downsize (not eliminate) your Starbucks grande latte to a no-fat tall latte and in a year you will save 21,840 calories or six pounds.

And this is one I calculated for myself when I decided a few years ago to stop drinking soda. Give up just one sixteen-ounce regular soda a day and you would save 54,750 calories or 15.6 pounds in a year, *even if you did nothing else!*

Wright

Those really are amazing results from small efforts! Do you help people come up with their own Subtle Shifts in your workshops and seminars?

Cleveland Bull

Yes! It's one of my favorite topics; but again, I always begin with The Power of Choice. I have to make a confession here. My personality leans toward the extremes. I tend to take things on in a big, grand slam, home run kind of way! So, the Subtle Shifts concept was a challenge for me personally. It wasn't easy to shift my perspective. But I can tell you that since I have, the results have been better, and honestly, it is a more manageable process.

WRIGHT

So you were one of your hardest converts!

CLEVELAND BULL

Sad, but true! But that has given me an appreciation for the resistance or skepticism some people might feel about making Subtle Shifts.

WRIGHT

And finally, to your fourth step—how do we "Focus" our Power of Choice?

CLEVELAND BULL

Once we begin to practice proactive choice-making, we begin to realize there are limitless, unending choices that we are presented with every single day. Suddenly the problem isn't one of having no choices, but instead, trying to decide what choices to make. We become aware of how many people and situations are out there trying to influence our choices to serve their own agendas (think the media, advertising, marketing campaigns, promotions, television commercials!). We also start to see more clearly the habits and routines that we enact repeatedly without making a conscious choice. We need a simple way to filter through all the possibilities so that we can make good choices.

As I mentioned, I have been thinking about and working with The Power of Choice since early in my career—about twenty-five years! And over the past year my business partner and clinical psychologist, Dr. Craig Goishi, and I have been working on developing a simple and effective model to help our clients make better choices. I want to give you a brief introduction to this model today and also let you know that we are working on a book with much more detail on how to use this model to create health, wealth, and happiness in your life!

WRIGHT

You're unveiling this new material with us today? Great! Let's hear it!

CLEVELAND BULL

We are calling this model Living The Three Questions. *(See Figure 2.)*

Making good life choices can be based on asking three simple yet fundamental questions. At first glance these questions may either seem obvious or common sense, but upon further reflection we can see how the decisions that can come from running our choices through the three questions can actually transform our lives!

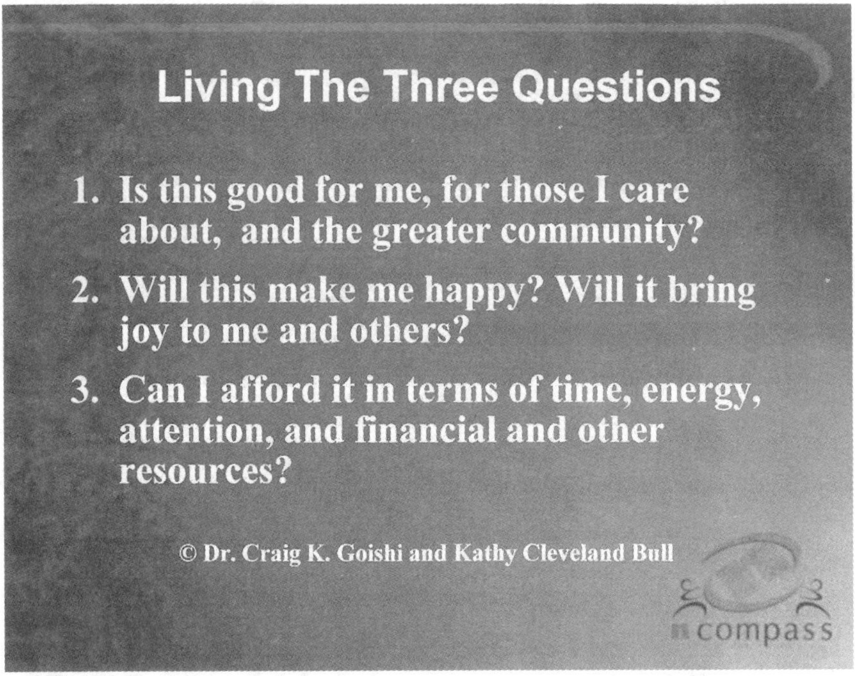

Living The Three Questions

1. Is this good for me, for those I care about, and the greater community?
2. Will this make me happy? Will it bring joy to me and others?
3. Can I afford it in terms of time, energy, attention, and financial and other resources?

© Dr. Craig K. Goishi and Kathy Cleveland Bull

compass

Figure 2.

WRIGHT

So what are the three questions?

CLEVELAND BULL

The first is: Is this good for me? The second question: Does this make me happy? And finally: Can I afford it?

One point about this third question is that when we say "can I afford it?" we really mean that in the broadest sense. Can I afford this choice in terms of time, energy, attention, focus, and financial resources, etc.

Another way to phrase this question would be: *is this a good use of my resources?* again, thinking of resources in a broad way.

It was very important to us to create questions that were so simple that you could remember them after hearing them only once. After all, if you can't remember the concept, you will never be able to apply it to your daily life. So these questions are simple, memorable, and yet, if applied to the choices you have to make throughout your day, can have a profound impact. Again, *success simplified comes from making good choices!*

Also, while the questions begin at the most basic and personal level, as we begin to assume more responsibility for others in work and in life, we naturally need to consider not just what is good for me but others as well. As our influence in the world grows, we extend the questions to wider and wider circles of influence until *ultimately* we consider what is good for all, what brings joy to all, and what is the best use of the planet's resources.

But before we begin to take on roles that impact other people's lives, it's important to master good decision-making in our own lives. Learning to make our own lives work well is our training ground for when we are called upon by position or circumstance to lead and influence others. Wouldn't it be great if our leaders in our communities and organizations learned good decision-making on their own time versus on the job at our expense?

Wright

The three questions do seem so simple and rather obvious. Don't you think that most people intuitively go through this process when they make decisions?

Cleveland Bull

First of all, you're right. They are simple and obvious but I regard this as a strength. Your question reminds me of something I heard Ken Blanchard say, *"It's common sense but not common practice!"* It may be tempting to prejudge these ideas as simplistic, but if we are truly honest with ourselves (and that is probably one of our greatest life challenges!), most of us have to admit that we are not even aware of the multitude of decisions we make throughout the day, much less conscious in real time of the many things that influence our decisions. Moreover, these other influences are almost always of lesser value than those represented by the three questions.

If someone is *really* living his or her life by using the three questions then the person should already be experiencing success, health, wealth, and happiness.

Finally, I would add that no model or philosophy works unless you apply it. You can buy the latest workout DVD but you actually have to put it in your DVD player, turn it on, and do the workout! It isn't going to have any effect sitting in your media cabinet! In our book we will help readers learn how to apply this model in their lives so they can gain the greatest benefit from the three questions model.

Wright

Will you give us a few examples of how these questions might work in everyday life?

Cleveland Bull

Okay, let's start with one of the first choices of the day—what will I eat for breakfast? And one option I'm considering is to stop at the local coffee shop on my drive to work for a cup of coffee and a few donuts. Let's run that option through the three questions.

Is this good for me?—Maybe the coffee is okay, but the donuts are not good for me. The coffee gives me a quick energy spurt, but the donuts give me a sugar high and then make me crash.

Does this make me happy?—Depending on how much I like donuts (and I do!), let's say I answer yes. At least temporarily, it makes me happy.

Can I afford it?—The actual financial cost might not be too great, but when I ask, "Is this a good use of my resources?" I decide that I can spend this money on something more worthwhile.

So, based on the results of this choice as measured against our questions, I make the decision to save a few dollars and eat breakfast at home. I choose oatmeal, juice, and decaf coffee.

Here's another common example: should I exercise this morning?

Is this good for me?—Yes.

Does this make me happy?—Maybe I don't like the idea of exercising or don't really enjoy it while I'm doing it, but I feel good when I'm done.

Can I afford it?—Since my exercise is going for a brisk walk in my neighborhood, there is no real monetary cost—I already own a good pair of walking shoes. I can afford the time and it will actually *boost* my energy resources.

Again, based on the results from running this option through the three questions, I decide that I will exercise this morning before work.

Wright

I can see how this simple model can be helpful in dealing with the countless choices we make every day, from what we eat to whether we exercise and even how many cocktails we order at happy hour. But what about major life decisions? Does it have any applicability there?

Cleveland Bull

That's an interesting question and one way to answer it has to do with our assumption that the big issues and decisions in life have the biggest impact. But think back to the Subtle Shifts model—it is often the small choices made repeatedly throughout the course of our lives that have the greatest impact on our future. Paying attention to our diet on a daily basis can have a significant positive impact on our health twenty or thirty years from now. Or another example has to do with saving or investing versus spending. If you just didn't spend the $3 for a cup of coffee daily at a specialty coffee shop and invested that amount, in twenty years that investment can end up being more than $32,000! On the flipside, if you continue to spend the $3 a day on your morning pick-me-up, you will have spent $1,800 in that twenty-year period! So, it is important to remind ourselves of how much impact the small decisions have throughout the course of our lifetime.

But you asked specifically about our major life decisions and how our three questions model works in that arena. We often think with small decisions that the consequences aren't great, so we don't put much time or energy into thinking about them. With big decisions, however, we generally assume that the consequences are huge and so we can become overwhelmed by the number of options, paralyzed by the possible consequences of the decision, or even impulsive as we throw our hands up in the air out of sheer frustration. Sometimes we don't choose at all and "let things play out as they may," which unfortunately, is still a choice!

The three questions model can be very useful in helping us sort through options, screen out less desirable choices, and ultimately make a good choice. The greatest value of this process, however, is that it can help us consistently consider the fundamentally important things in life as we are faced with choices. Going through the process itself provides much of the value.

Let's look at a few examples. Buying a fancy sports car might be considered a major financial decision. Let's say that two middle aged men are considering this purchase and decide to run it through the three questions.

Middle aged man number one:

Is this good for me?—"I really *want* the car, but honestly, I'm not sure if it would be good for me because I would be tempted to drive above the speed limit and push the car to its performance limits."

Does this make me happy? "Yes, I think this car would really make me happy!"

Can I afford it?—"Realistically, given my current income and the fact that my company is going through some tough times and my security there is uncertain, it probably isn't an investment I can make right now. It probably isn't a good use of my resources."

So, based on the results of this choice, as measured against our questions, middle aged man number one decides to buy a low mileage, used sedan instead. And he makes a commitment to himself that he will start to save every month toward his future sports car purchase.

Middle aged man number two:

Is this good for me?—"I really *want* the car. In fact, buying a sports car has been a dream of mine since I was about sixteen. I have worked hard my entire career and deferred many luxury purchases because I knew this was what I wanted to save for. I think this purchase would be good for me because it would be a symbol of my lifetime of hard work and deferred gratification."

Does this make me happy?" Yes, I think this car would really make me very happy!"

Can I afford it? "Because I have been working and saving with this goal in mind, I have what I need to make this purchase without sacrificing my financial security. It is a good use of my current resources."

So, based on the results of this choice, as measured against our questions, middle aged man number two decides to purchase the sports car.

The point here is that the three questions will be answered uniquely for each person and in each circumstance. Two people can come up with different decisions about the same choice. Only you can determine the outcome based on your own honest reflection and consideration.

I'll share one more example. This is a relationship example and involves a woman already in a fairly long-term relationship with her partner. Certainly this would go in your category of major life decisions:

Is this good for me?—"The relationship started out good for me but now it isn't. I am not getting my emotional needs met and I often feel like I am "parenting" my partner. I'm more than happy to do my share of the work, but while we both work full-time, I seem to get the full-time job of taking care of the home."

Does this make me happy? "Being in a relationship makes me happy, but not this one. Again, it used to, but now I find myself starting to imagine what it might be like to be on my own again."

Can I afford it?—"From a financial standpoint I am better off in the relationship because we share our expenses and only have one residence. In terms of other resources—my time and emotional energy in particular—this has become a real drain."

Based on the results of the three questions analysis, our friend decides that she needs to begin to take steps to end the relationship. She will first be sure to get her financial house in order and establish strong support systems for herself with family and friends. Another woman in a similar situation might find in asking the questions that the relationship is worth the effort it will take to make changes so that it will be good for her, she will be happy again, and she will be able to afford it.

The three questions are not a crystal ball. Since we can never truly predict the outcome of our choices, this process trains us to be more value focused rather than results focused. We develop over time the practice or habit of holding fast to our values (good for self and others, leads to happiness, is a good use of resources) and learn to let go of our control of outcomes. When we don't anchor our choices to our values, we run the risk of slipping into an "ends justify the means" mentality. Utilizing the mirror of the three questions guides us to ponder what is important. Over the long-term, it helps us strengthen the muscle of good decision-making.

WRIGHT

It has been a pleasure talking with you today, Kathy. Thanks for taking the time to share your thoughts with us. I'm sure our readers will benefit from what you have offered today. I know you have given us just a taste of your Three Questions Model, so we will keep our eyes open for your upcoming book!

CLEVELAND BULL

Thank you, David. I've enjoyed our time together.

WRIGHT

Today we have been talking with Kathy Cleveland Bull who is founder and president of N~Compass Consulting, a speaking and consulting firm in Columbus, Ohio, that focuses on helping clients navigate the art and science of change in these turbulent times. Kathy spreads her inspirational message of Choice and Change through keynotes and seminars to audiences around the world.

About the Author

Kathy Cleveland Bull is respected among her peers as one of the finest motivational speakers and consultants in the professional field. Some of Kathy's most notable appearances include: touring with Dr. Phil McGraw and Deepak Chopra at "The Power Within" live event, held in cities across Canada and the United States; presenting a two-day *change management seminar* for African business leaders in Nairobi, Kenya; and keynoting an international medical conference in Rotterdam, The Netherlands, inspiring professionals, caregivers, and family members to successfully adapt to the diagnosis of dementia in a loved one.

Kathy conducts personal and professional development keynotes, seminars, and retreats for Fortune 500 companies, educational institutions, government agencies, and not-for-profit organizations. She has trained more than eighty-five thousand people to successfully manage change in their work and personal life by utilizing her powerful and proven change strategies.

Kathy lives in Columbus, Ohio, with her husband of twenty-five years and their two adopted daughters.

Kathy Cleveland Bull

N~Compass Consulting

919 Old Henderson Road

Columbus, OH 43220

614-324-5944

kcb@ncompass-consulting.com

www.ncompass-consulting.com

CHAPTER TWENTY

INNOVATE YOUR WAY TO THE TOP

BY LISA BODELL

DAVID WRIGHT (WRIGHT)

Today we are talking with Lisa Bodell. When you think about creating success through innovation, naturally you think of Lisa and her firm. Lisa is the Founder and Chief Executive Officer of future**think**, a globally recognized innovation research and training firm. Future**think** helps businesses build the capabilities they need to become world-class innovators. Bodell, a pioneer in the field of innovation and learning, is a seasoned entrepreneur who has built three successful businesses. She sits on numerous boards in an advisory capacity for organizations such as the *Journal of Direct, Data and Digital Marketing Practice,* The Women's Congress, The Association of Professional Futurists, and the prestigious Institute for Triple Helix Innovation, the only innovation initiative of its kind within the United States government.

Bodell has appeared on Fox News, and in publications such as *Business Week, The New York Times, Wired,* and *The Futurist.*

We were fortunate enough to get her views on innovation and its importance. Lisa, why is innovation so critical to business and personal success right now?

LISA BODELL (BODELL)

Innovation is about creating change. It's the drive to improve and the hunger to make things better. In good times and bad times, the ability to continually innovate or improve is what separates leading organizations from the also-rans, and enables individuals to stand out from the crowd.

Being innovative is especially important right now. As technology has become more pervasive, the speed of business has increased exponentially. Ideas can be replicated quickly and competitive advantages can evaporate overnight. People who are able to continually adapt and think differently are the ones who will better manage stress, come up with more creative solutions, and find more fulfilling answers to the challenges they face in their lives and their work.

WRIGHT

Do you believe that everyone can be innovative?

BODELL

Absolutely. Everyone is innovative in their own way. There's no one way to innovate. For example, I'm innovative in identifying new, offbeat business partnerships—my mind thinks in terms of "networks." Another person on my team is excellent at creating new processes; her mind uses logic and mental flowcharts to find solutions. A friend of mine is an inventor, and while new processes certainly aren't his thing, inventing products is something he's great at. His innovative ideas come by using his hands and through continuous experimentation.

One way of innovating isn't better than another. The common theme is the desire to try something new. Innovation requires a passion for creating change and looking at things in new ways. I think everybody is capable of that.

Perhaps the bigger question we need to ask is: "Why don't more people believe that they are innovative?" I think there are a few big mistakes that happen within corporations that prevent people from realizing their "innovation potential."

The first mistake is isolating innovation. Many organizations compartmentalize innovation, establishing a separate group responsible for getting new ideas to market. While setting up an "innovation team" or group can be highly effective in getting new ideas to market, if not managed properly, it sends a message that only these innovation team members are "innovative." Sending such a signal makes others think, "I'm not good at innovation and it's not my job, so I won't even try." The result? Unrealized innovation potential across the organization.

The second mistake is not providing room to innovate. People need time to think differently and time to spend away from the hassles of "business as usual." If we want people to "be innovative," we need to give them a chance to try it. The leaders in innovation with whom I work make innovation part of their routine. They weave it in as an agenda item at the end of each weekly status meeting or they allow their employees to use 10 percent of their time to explore something new that has nothing to do with their jobs. Not only do these types of practices make innovation more of a habit, it signals to people that pursuing offbeat topics or things of interest is a *good* thing and can result in the next big idea.

Finally, many companies fail to give employees permission to innovate. This involves the ability to try new things, to experiment, and—god forbid!—to fail once in awhile. Think about it: leaders are telling their employees to be innovative while at the same time asking them to be cautious, make their numbers, get results, and *not miss a deadline*. So, what are they really saying? The message being sent about innovation is that the penalty for taking a risk is greater than not taking any risk at all, so many people choose not to participate. That's a huge waste of creative talent.

WRIGHT

What makes someone innovative and how will the person know if he or she is successful at it?

BODELL

Innovation is often both a *skill set* and a *mindset*. I say this because innovation often is confused with just "being creative." Innovation is about much more than being creative. Creativity is about coming up with an idea, but innovation requires action—actually making an idea a reality. Innovation is what I call "creativity *plus*." It's about getting comfortable with risk, embracing change, questioning rules and paradigms, and turning ideas into realities.

In terms of measuring innovation success, you have to look at two factors—*results* and *effort*. You're innovating when you come up with a new product, service, process, or idea. You're being innovative when you make positive change happen—no matter how big or small. These are *results*.

But you're also innovating when you recognize that you're more open to ideas and change, and that you're willing to do things in a new way even if it might fail. This change in your innovation *effort* is an important measure of success as well.

WRIGHT

As a futurist and expert in the field of innovation, it's your job to keep on top of the driving forces that are shaping tomorrow. Are there certain trends to follow when it comes to creating your own professional success? In other words, what will make someone successful in business in the next ten years?

BODELL

The skills that will drive professional success through the year 2020 are definitely not the same skills you would have listed back in 2000. This is primarily driven by the changes technology has continued to create for us. Technology makes life and work faster, less predictable, and much more likely to change on a dime. At the same time, technology has introduced incredible opportunities to do far-reaching things that weren't previously possible. Today, success means knowing how to engage and capitalize on these opportunities to improve the work we do and the lives that we live. I think the most valued and successful employees in the future will need to have:

1. **Peripheral Vision**—Tomorrow's winners not only expect change, they are prepared for it because they look beyond the linear path ahead of them. They take comfort knowing there's more than one way to get to where you want to go. The people who will drive success in the future will be the ones who shun tunnel vision and embrace peripheral vision—always driving ahead while looking around to see what else can happen.
2. **Network Connections**—When things change, you need lots of ways to solve problems and get things done. As a result, you'll need to be networked to have a diverse set of brains,

hands, and guts to make things possible. Having a deep pool of resources that can provide perspective, skills, and answers will be critical.

3. **Collaborative Skills**—Lone rangers don't make great innovators. You need the ability to partner with a wide range of people inside and outside your organization and immediate community. You'll see the benefits of leveraging other perspectives and skills to get better solutions faster.
4. **Tech Savvy**—On tomorrow's playing field, you'll need to be significantly tech savvy just to get in the game. You'll have to know how to operate in a technology-driven world and understand how to use a wide range of ever-evolving technologies to do business.
5. **Agility**—In a fast-changing environment, the ability to be resourceful and change directions quickly will be the key to success. Large companies that can't figure out how to be agile will see smaller, more nimble firms start passing them by.
6. **Strategic Imagination**—I call someone with this rare quality a "dreamer with purpose." These dreamers are able to look at the larger changes driving our world, imagine the possibilities, and then actually take action to move their ideas forward. They question rules and existing paradigms, and then come up with offbeat ideas that can take a business to new places. These are the people who push us to try new things, not because it's cool to experiment, but because it's *necessary*.

Wright

Your background includes being an entrepreneur, a teacher, and a coach. Why do you value learning so much?

Bodell

There's no progress if we're not learning.

When we're young, we spend most of our day in school, where we're exposed to a wide range of subjects and experiences. It's a place where asking questions is a good thing, and curiosity is encouraged. But as we get older, we specialize; we focus on the day to day, and often just want to "get the job done."

I believe the role of a teacher or corporate training professional is to show people how to *unlearn* and *rethink*. It's to help us get back some peripheral vision so we can see new things. Beyond providing information, teachers must ignite a sense of possibility and purpose in their students—in us. Giving people access to knowledge is one thing, but it's far more important to give them new ways to think and solve problems.

Wright

So when it comes to learning, "lifelong learning" is the key?

Bodell

Learning is not an event, and we need to stop treating it that way. It's a lifelong process to embrace; it's a habit that we must continually feed.

Take the medical profession for example. A doctor doesn't just go to medical school and then consider his learning done. While doctors are always learning "on the job," they are also required to take continuing education courses that ensure they are aware of the changes that are affecting their profession, such as new treatments, new technologies, and new regulations. Would you want to go to a doctor who went to school thirty years ago and never bothered to learn another thing? We need to treat other professional careers the same way and continuously educate people on the changes that affect their work so they can be better at it.

Wright

So what do you think the role of learning will be in the future? Will it be essential to success?

Bodell

People who embrace lifelong learning can't help but be successful. They're current, they're open, and they have a bigger perspective and understanding of how things are interrelated. The more complex life becomes, the more important the role of learning will be.

Wright

Where do you look to find the future?

Bodell

I have a saying that "the future is here, you just have to know where to look." The key to finding the future is to look in unexpected places, meet unexpected people, and do unexpected things. I stay on top of "tomorrow" in a few ways:

- *I keep my reading list eclectic and offbeat.* Take a minute to think about what you read and where you get your information. How broad or diverse are your sources? If you want to find the future, the answer should be: very broad and diverse.
- I read things from a wide variety of sources on a wide range of topics. I read the mainstream news from places like the *Wall Street Journal* and *The New York Times*. I visit CNN.com, and scan about twenty other Web sites every morning. But the key to finding the future is to go beyond the mainstream. So, I also read financial blogs, scientific publications, style and trend newsletters, medical journals, marketing books, and farming magazines. Doing this gives me a variety of perspectives on important topics like the environment, technology, media, and pop culture. It lets me connect different dots and get a bigger picture. Remember: confirmation comes from reading what you know, but change comes from reading what you don't know.
- *I scan first, then read.* This lets me pick up on themes and commonalities or uncover cast-offs and opposing views quickly. Then I can be selective about what I want to take the time to read in more detail.
- *I meet one new person a week who is different from me.* Conversations are powerful things. And connecting with others is a great way to learn not just new information but new perspectives as well. I've recently learned from progressive education teachers, scientists who study spiders and farm spider silk, chaos theory experts, "green" architects,

and a cop on the Houston police force, just to name a few! An interesting question to ask yourself is: If you had to meet three new people this month, who would you reach out to in order to learn something new?

- *I get out of my comfort zone.* To learn something new, you need to do something new. This can involve big things (start a new job, move to a different country), but even the little things count—take a different route to work, go somewhere new for lunch, or stop by an unexplored museum. Do something on the weekend you don't normally do. For example, last month my family and I went into Manhattan and wandered through neighborhoods we had never been to on the Lower East Side. A few weeks ago, we went to an art store, bought the strangest materials we could find, and then created our own "art." On a recent trip to Dubai, I visited a local grocery store and bought things I had never heard of before.

The idea is to start saying "yes" more. This goes back to my earlier point on continually learning and stretching our minds. You only do that by exploring, taking some chances, and getting comfortable with a different approach.

Wright

How did you come to be a leader in innovation and "futuring"? Was this always your path?

Bodell

When I look back on my life so far, where I am now seems logical. But teaching people to think differently and to find "what's next" was never what I intended to do. My experiences just seemed to lead me here.

My parents were always entrepreneurial, each starting their own businesses. I'm sure I'm very enterprising as a result, and very comfortable with starting something new.

Growing up, I loved games and puzzles, and would often create my own games for fun. In fact, when I was in third grade, our class project was to design a new toy for Christmas. I gave the teacher an entire toy catalog because I just couldn't stop thinking about new ideas. The exploding jack-in-the-box was one of my favorites.

As I grew older, while many people admired the movie stars and designers, I loved the scientists and inventors. To me, these were the people who were doing the cool things. They were taking big, complex problems that seemed impossible to solve and *actually solving them.* I loved their stories about where they found their inspiration, and often it came from unexpected places. I wanted to "learn" how to do that.

When I got out of school, I went into advertising—the stereotypical refuge for creative types. It was there where I learned that everyone can come up with big solutions. Unfortunately, it was also there that I learned only certain people were allowed or expected to do this—the "creative" team. I kept thinking, "Why is only a certain group of people in charge of coming up with new ideas? Why isn't everyone coming up with ideas so we can get bigger solutions?" Something felt wrong.

So I set out to create a business that teaches people that they can all be innovative in their own ways using their own talents. And that's what I do today.

WRIGHT

So what makes your perspective so unique?

BODELL

I believe passionately that everyone can innovate, they just need to know how. They must be shown the tools, be awakened to the possibilities, and often, be *given the permission to think big and take chances.*

I've had the good fortune to work with and study some of the most innovative people in the world during the last twenty years. My goal is to use that learning to show people that they are extremely capable of doing big things, and then teach them how to get started.

WRIGHT

What's your biggest piece of advice to someone who is trying to drive success through innovation?

Bodell

Innovation really comes down to risk and change—taking *smart* risks and getting *comfortable* with change. If you're trying to be innovative in an organization, you need to show people that you are willing to take smart risks and that there's not a penalty for taking a chance. The bad news is that those who can't figure out the rules of innovation are going to be left behind. The good news is that everyone is capable of developing an innovation mindset and learning the necessary skills to help change the world.

About the Author

Lisa Bodell is the founder and CEO of future**think**, an internationally recognized innovation research and training firm that helps businesses embrace change and become world-class innovators.

Ms. Bodell founded future**think** on the premise that *everyone* has the power to innovate–they just need to know *how*. Her company has spent years working with hundreds of leading innovators to create the largest offering of innovation research, tools, and training in the world. Clients such as 3M, GE, and Johnson & Johnson look to future**think** to develop new thinking styles and generate innovative ideas.

Bodell is a leader and pioneer in the field of futuring and innovation, creating a unique approach to an otherwise complicated topic.

She is a seasoned futurist, teacher, and entrepreneur who has built three successful businesses. In addition to running future**think** and lecturing, Lisa currently serves as an advisor on the boards of the *Journal of Direct, Data and Digital Marketing Practice* in London, The Women's Congress, and the prestigious Institute for Triple Helix Innovation think tank, the only innovation initiative of its kind within the U.S. government. She serves as a finalist judge at the annual Idea Crossing Innovation Challenge and FIT's innovation challenge (which future**think** co-created), and has taught marketing and creativity at American University.

A seasoned communicator on innovation, Bodell has appeared on FOX News, and in publications such as *Crain's, Business Week, The New York Times, WIRED, Investor's Business Daily,* and *The Futurist.*

Bodell earned her business degree from the University of Michigan, where she concentrated in business administration and marketing.

Lisa Bodell, CEO

*future***think**

242 W. 30th St.

Suite 402

New York, NY 10001

646-257-5737

lbodell@getfuturethink.com

Innovation tools: www.getfuturethink.com

Innovation training: www.futurethinkinstitute.com

CHAPTER TWENTY ONE

ACHIEVING SUPERIOR PERFORMANCE

BY TED FULLER

DAVID WRIGHT (WRIGHT)

Today we're talking with Ted Fuller, Founder of Fuller Communications. Ted has more than forty years of experience consulting with notable clients including: IBM, Covidien, Price Waterhouse, General Electric, Titleist, Worcester Polytechnic Institute, Bowdoin College, Johnson & Johnson, Bank of America, Lazard Asset Management, and the YPO. He is the author of numerous articles including: "Going Beyond the Transaction" and "Building Relationships: The Key to Successful Selling." He is a frequent speaker at meetings of Fortune 500 companies. He has made numerous national radio and guest appearances. During the 1988, 1992, and 1996 presidential campaigns, he was the commentator on more than thirty radio shows, analyzing presidential debates and evaluating candidates' performances.

In addition to having served as a communications expert for CNBC, he conducts job interview skill workshops for college seniors who are about to enter the workforce. Before founding Fuller Communications, he served as Vice Chairman and Partner of Communispond Inc., and as the company's Chief Operating Officer and Director of Sales and Marketing.

Ted, welcome to *Success Simplified.*

TED FULLER (FULLER)

Thank you; nice to be here, David.

WRIGHT

So what do personal communication skills have to do with success?

FULLER

Everything. Without good personal communication skills you cannot be successful. You cannot make change, add value, and be an effective leader or team contributor. It's as simple as that. Ask any executive, teacher, doctor, attorney, politician, minister, or rabbi, professional athlete, or coach. You simply cannot be successful if you do not master the art of personal communications. The novelist, Harlan Ellison, said it best, "Skill in the art of communication is crucial to a leader's success. One can accomplish nothing unless they can communicate effectively."

Lee Iacocca echoed these feelings when he said: "You can have brilliant ideas, but if you can't get them across [if you can't communicate], your ideas won't get you anywhere"

Charles Kettering said, "A problem well stated is a problem half solved"—a simple statement with profound implications. Think about it. If a person is unable to articulate the importance of the problem his or her solution will not be heard and the battle will be lost. On the other hand, when a person presents a strong, well organized argument and does it with conviction and enthusiasm, the solution will be understood and the battles will be won. The bottom line is it's all about personal communications.

Our mission is to teach people to "achieve superior performance" through personal communications skill training and to use these skills to articulate their messages clearly and precisely so that they can become successful in their chosen profession.

WRIGHT

What research do you have to support your premise that personal communication skills are the core to personal success?

FULLER

In the Army they call it OJT for "On the Job Training." Having spent forty years coaching senior executives, politicians, doctors, attorneys, college presidents, school principals, and others in the art of personal communications, I have been able to consolidate the best research and best practices into a skill-based program.

In 1971, Dr. Albert Mehrabian released the results of his study of non-verbal communications. In this study, Dr. Mehrabian shows that the spoken word only accounts for 7 percent of what a listener perceives, the remaining 93 percent originates from the speaker's body language and tone employed in the delivery of the message.

Dr. Donald Goleman, author of Emotional Intelligence, provides us with an insightful demonstration of how emotions guide our behavior, adding a new dimension to the communications learning process. This research, along with the work done by Bill Bonnsetter, the founder of Target Training International[1], Arnold Daniels the late founder of The Predictive Index, and other experts in the personal assessment field have completely transformed my approach to teaching personal communication skills.

These assessments have given me the tools I need to teach present and future leaders how to recognize individual behavioral styles and use this knowledge to dramatically change how they adapt their personal communications to the individual, team, and organization. Using this new assessment technology, I have developed a "scouting report system" to give participants the ability to prepare for their audiences. Just as coaches scout the competition, we teach professionals how to "scout their audience"

Tony Robbins said it best, "*To effectively communicate, we must realize that we are all different in the way we perceive the world and use this understanding as a guide to our communication with others.*"

With the assessment tools now available to us, we can now teach participants how to recognize differences and guide their communications. These tools give us the guidelines we need to adjust our wording, plan our approach, and select our venue so we can speak in the language that is appropriate to any audience. This is a very big and important breakthrough in personal communication skill training.

1 Arnold Daniels, late founder of Predictive Index, and other experts in the behavioral assessment field.

WRIGHT

Does the behavioral research assessment help you to teach personal communication skills?

FULLER

Absolutely. Throughout the years I have taught professionals how to analyze an audience and deliver their message with enthusiasm and conviction—all very important communication skills.

Now I approach learning from a different perspective. I believe that audiences, small or large, have one prime interest: "What's in it for me?" (commonly called WIIFM). I still believe this and still teach it. The assessment technology just adds a new dimension to this truism.

You can't lead and motivate a team that you don't understand. A leader must learn to distinguish individual differences. Leaders must take the time to listen, appreciate, and respect different opinions and approaches to problems and opportunities. They must learn to identify individual behavior styles and adjust their communications to motivate and build trust. This is where the assessment technology and research come in.

Using the behavioral assessments, we can quickly teach participants how to identify different behavioral styles and plan the correct communications vehicles to bring the audience on board.

WRIGHT

Are personal communication skills learnable or are you born with them?

FULLER

Some individuals have natural people instincts, most do not. Some are naturally shy or conservative, while others are outspoken and confident. Those with natural instincts can always improve their game. Those who do not can learn. The secret is to make communication skills a priority, learn the fundamentals, and work to make them a part of your natural style.

The best way to learn a skill is by doing. You can read about it and learn the fundamentals, but you must practice the techniques if you want to learn how to do it. You need a coach, teacher, or expert to observe your baseline skill level and give you the exercises you need to be an effective communicator.

WRIGHT

What do people need to learn to become good communicators?

FULLER

People need to learn four things: Physical skills, Positioning, Preparation, and Organization

Physical skills: These include voice, eye contact, gestures, posture, and pace. You must learn to be physically committed to your audience and they will be committed to you.

Positioning: Remember that audiences have one common interest—"What's in it for me?" We must learn to position or "book end" our remarks. A bookend is a phrase that tells the audience up front what they might expect to take away from this meeting and is repeated at the end to complete the agreement.

Preparation: Keep it simple, have a theme, have a strong opening, and closing. You must avoid "visual aid overload" (having too many charts with too much information on them) and understand the importance of diagramming. You must understand that your audience is made up of individuals who listen and learn differently.

Organization: Remember your "scouting report," select the correct format or template, check your facts, document your evidence, and personalize your presentation whenever possible.

Having said all that, it must be remembered that the "scouting report" is the most important piece of the organization puzzle. Let me give you an example:

I was working with a customer who was asked to do a presentation on Human Capital (how we select, train, compensate, and motivate employees to achieve superior performance). His "scouting report" noted that the audience was made up of Human Resource executives.

His "bookend" visual aid read: "The Revolution Is On." His remarks spoke to the need for industry to get ready for the new recruiting challenging going forward. His closing statement was, "The Revolution

Is On" followed by a "bookend" stating what was in it for the audience. This bookend was repeated at the end, thus the term "bookend."

Because my client was addressing human resource executives, he prefaced his remarks with the following action verbs: The process must be done in a *logical sequence*, the *support systems* must be in place, the training will be *exercise driven*, and *accountability parameters and measurements* must be in place.

Human resource managers have a low tolerance for risk and accept change only after they are comfortable that the change is best for the organization. The introduction to the presentation (outlined above) includes these elements, so we know we are talking in their language. If our scouting report showed that we were addressing the CEO, COO, and CFO, our "language" (action verbs) would be different.

To answer your question: yes, the skills can be learned.

WRIGHT

Why are people such poor communicators?

FULLER

Some don't realize how poorly they communicate. Some don't care. Others think they are good communicators—even great—when they are not. Some are self-conscious and even embarrassed about "getting help" and they try to learn by doing. Others are just plain afraid of failure and shy away for any kind of training that might help.

Some senior managers feel that they are supposed to know how to communicate so "getting help" might be seen as an admittance of weakness. Junior executives are often reluctant to ask for training and do the best they can.

Several years ago, I was traveling to Chicago to speak to the National Securities Dealers Association (NSDA). Next to me on the plane was the Chief Economist for a major Fortune 500 company. As it turned out, he was speaking at the same conference. He mentioned in passing that he was "delivering a paper" on the state of the economy on Friday (a clue that he came from academia). He went on to say that throughout the years he had spoken to numerous groups like the NSDA and was quite comfortable with the audience. I asked him if he liked to make speeches and he said yes, implying that he was quite good at it.

The phrase "delivering a paper" is a very big red flag to a speech coach and communications skills professional. I decided to give him the benefit of the doubt, as he was obviously a respected economist. Since I had the time, I decided to see how he "delivered his paper." As it turned out, he would have been better off if he had given a copy of his paper to each person. That way people could have studied the information and made their own conclusions.

Here is what I saw and heard. The audience of more than seven hundred was sitting in a large, dark (not good) auditorium. The speaker was barely visible with only the light of the lectern alerting the audience to where he was (not good). One bullet-point chart after another flashed up on the screen, interspersed with graphs that the Hubble Space Telescope scope could not read (not good). The speaker spoke in a monotone as he read his "paper" (not good). He was standing stage left with the slides to his right, again not good. In other words, he broke every rule in the book.

What happened? The speaker assumed too much.

First, he assumed that the audience was as interested in the details as he was. Wrong.

Second, he assumed the audience had the ability to concentrate (i.e., listen and absorb the information). Again, wrong.

Third, he forgot the golden rule: "The audience is only interested in "what's in it for me?"

Remember: It is the responsibility of the speaker to interpret for the audience—to tell them "what it means." Not a bad thought to keep in mind.

In the words of Sydney J. Harris: "Information and communication are often used interchangeably, but they signify quite different things. Information is giving out; communication is getting through." (Dr. Harris was a journalist for the *Chicago Daily News*. For many years he was a member of the Usage Panel of the *American Heritage Dictionary*.)

Wright

So would you tell our readers what person needs to do to become a superior performer?

Fuller

Among the many solutions, I recommend the Behavioral Style Values assessment and the DNA. Together these assessments show you what you need to do to achieve superior personal performance.

The behavioral styles show you "how" you would choose to do your job. The values assessments shows what motivates you and "why." If you understand what makes you tick and what motivates you, you can maximize your talents. As the Chinese philosopher Lao-Tse said, "He who knows others is learned. He who knows himself is wise." These two assessments are key to learning to become wise.

The TTI assessments have nothing to do with intelligence. They merely demonstrate "how" we receive and react to information, how we react to change, what our risk tolerance is, and how we go about solving problems.

The values assessments show "why" we behave as we do. TTI breaks values, or motivators, into six categories: Utilitarian, Aesthetic, Individualistic, Theoretical, Social, and Traditional.

If you score high in the Utilitarian sector you are, by nature, drawn to practical, measurable activities, like safety metrics, balancing budgets, and reducing waste.

If you are Individualistic, you are competitive, motivated by power, and driven to control.

If you score high in the Theoretical sector you are drawn to knowledge, seeking only to observe and reason. You are driven by the knowledge for truth.

If you score high in the Social sector, helping others is your driving force.

The person who scores highest in the Traditional sector works best in structured environments and follows defined rules. Political conservatives or liberals would be examples.

The Aesthetic person favors harmony and form. This person's primary interest is in the artistic episodes of life.

If you define success as being "the best in your field" as I do, you must first know what drives you, what is important to you, and where you can make the greatest contribution. Then you need to take a critical look at what attributes you have mastered and which ones you need to improve. *(The TTI DNA assessment is an excellent tool for discovering what attributes you have mastered and what attributes you need to work on).*

As TTI is quick to point out we are not motivated by any single value, as we operate on all six. However, the research shows that there will be two or three values that will move a person to action.

Wright

Since we are talking about success, do you have any job interviewing secrets for success?

Fuller

I do and they (the secrets) are very much in keeping with the title of this book, *Success Simplified*:

Secret 1. Nonhuman resource people are not very good interviewers. This gives you the opportunity to lead the conversation.

For example: A good interviewer will do his or her homework and ask questions that relate to the skills needed to do the job, like: leadership, flexibility, strong personal communication skills, time management, goal orientation, and so on.

The job posting or ad will list these attributes. It might say: "We need people who learn quickly, are flexible, and have good personal communication skills *(everyone is looking for good personal communication skills, it is on every list of attributes for a job, guaranteed).* Knowing the criteria for the job, you prepare stories from your life demonstrating that you have these skills.

If the interviewer is trained, he or she will ask about your experiences in these categories. If not, you must take the initiative and bring them up yourself. How? You might say something like, "I know that you are looking for people who are leaders, quick learners who can communicate well, and are flexible." Now see where the conversation goes and notice how comfortable the conversation becomes.

Secret 2. If your resume shows your interests in art, literature, sports, and entertainment, and you have achieved any awards or recognition for your success, drive the interviewer to this section.

Good interviews are comfortable conversations. If you can find a common interest like schools, colleges, sports literature, sailing, golf, theater, or whatever, bring it up or point it out. Usually, this will turn the rest of the conversation into a dialogue where your real personality can shine.

Secret 3. People hire people to solve problems, no matter what the occupation or the job. For example, a company is hiring a new customer relations consultant. Three candidates have qualified for the job. The one picked talked about several problems he personally solved. One involved handling a difficult customer, the second involved a computer glitch, and the third involved stepping in to help an associate who was having trouble.

Most candidates talk about their different jobs, their different employers, and the job they held but then they do not elaborate. Most responses are factual. They do not know how to elaborate on questions to show how they personally took charge, how they contributed to the team effort, or went about solving problems.

The secret to storytelling is to present your story using the first person pronoun, "I was—" I saw—" I moved in—" "I analyzed the situation and my solution worked." It is you they are interviewing, not your associates. Take credit for your contributions.

All the information you need is out there; all you need to do is tell your story. Just be sure you know how to communicate your story

Wright

So how important are personal communication skills to achieving superior performance?

Fuller

Of course it depends on how you define "superior success." If you define it as excelling in your chosen field, then personal communications skills are paramount. You can't lead if you can't build trust and you can't build trust if you can't communicate. You can't motivate others to succeed if they lack confidence in your ideas. You can't initiate change without articulating a clear explanation of the need, and you can't maintain lasting respect without projecting confidence and optimism.

Superior performance is a function of personal communications

WRIGHT

What would be an example of how poor personal communication skills have affected history?

FULLER

All failures are the result of poor or missed communications—business, politics, war, society, human catastrophes, etc.

Companies fail because someone was not listening to or was refusing to hear the warning signs.

Armies fail because those in command ignore the warnings, do not trust the intelligence, or just ignore the intelligence.

Administrations are voted out of office because they don't listen to the people. They think that they know best when the reality is they do not have the trust of the electorate and are consequently voted out of office.

Dynasties fail because dictators refuse to recognize that their constituents are so frustrated that they are compelled to revolt.

Most human catastrophes could be minimized if the proper precautions are taken. Somehow we want to believe that it "won't happen here." We want to believe dikes will hold, even though reputable engineers have indicated (not proven) that the dikes are too weak to hold if we get a severe storm. If the experts were skilled in the art of communication, perhaps the dams might have been shored up and the flood averted.

It's all about communications. Listen, speak clearly, build a logical argument with real facts, and speak the truth.

WRIGHT

Ted, what do you offer people that can measure their personal communication skills? What instruments do you use?

FULLER

I use several. These three: The Behavior Factor Analysis, The PIAV Managing for Success assessment, and the DNA Managing Your Career report are among the best in my experience.

The Behavior Factor Analysis, commonly referred to as the DISC, measures four dimensions of normal behavior:

- How you respond to challenges
- How you influence others
- How you respond to your environment
- How you respond to rules

As the research shows, the most effective people are those who understand themselves. This assessment helps you to do just that.

The PIAV Managing for Success Assessment measures the relative prominence of six basic interests or attitudes (value of life). The rankings give the person a clear idea of what drives him or her.

The TTI DNA assessment, lists twenty-three attributes for success in business. Eight of the twenty-three relate to personal communications. Respondents who are considered good communicators score well on three or four of the eight communications attributes. This may be enough since their job may not require them to master skills like negotiating or writing. If, however, they rank low on presentation skills, they should take steps to improve in this area.

Wright

So what does confidence have to do with personal communication skills?

Fuller

Personal communication skills have everything to do confidence. If you do not believe in yourself and your principles, you cannot build credibility and/or trust. Without these two attributes, you cannot be successful and you cannot achieve superior performance. As stated, success breeds success and confidence is the result. If you want to be successful, you will be. But you must commit yourself to the task. Do your homework, learn the skills, commit to a program of continuous improvement, ask for honest feedback, and accept criticism gracefully.

WRIGHT

What a great conversation this has been today. It's been fascinating for me and of course this is a subject that we all need to understand. I really appreciate your giving us this much insight based on your training and experience. I really appreciate all the time you've taken with me today to answer these questions.

FULLER

I've enjoyed every minute of it; I hate to hang up.

WRIGHT

Well, I got a lot out of it already and I know that our readers will.

FULLER

Great, that's good to hear.

WRIGHT

Today we've been talking with Ted Fuller who is Founder of Fuller Communications. He is also an author of numerous articles including: "Communicating at a Higher Levels," "Going Beyond the Transaction," and "Building Relationships: The Key to Successful Selling." He is a frequent speaker at meetings of Fortune 500 companies and trade groups. A graduate of Bowdoin College, he received his Bachelor of Arts Degree in Economics and Political Science.

Ted, thank you so much for being with us today on *Success Simplified*.

FULLER

David, thank you; I've enjoyed every minute of it.

About the Author

Ted Fuller, the Founder of Fuller Communications, has more than forty years of experience consulting with notable clients including: IBM, Covidien, Price Waterhouse, General Electric, Titleist, Worcester Polytechnic Institute, Bowdoin College, Johnson & Johnson, Bank of America, Lazard Asset Management, and the YPO. He is the author of numerous articles including: "Going Beyond the Transaction," "Building Relationships," and "The Key to Successful Selling." He is the personal communication columnist for the Portsmouth Herald, in Portsmouth, New Hampshire. He is a frequent speaker at meetings of Fortune 500 companies. During the 1988, 1992, and 1996 presidential campaigns, he was the commentator on more than thirty radio shows in which he analyzed presidential debates and evaluated candidates' performances.

In addition to having served as a communications expert for CNBC, Ted conducts personal communications skill workshops for small and large companies across all industries.

As Stephen Sondheim said, "Everything depends on execution; having just a vision is no solution." At Fuller Communications, we teach individuals and companies how to execute their business plan. This we believe is the key to the "success simplified" philosophy included in this book.

Ted Fuller

Fuller Communications
579 Sagamore Ave., Suite 95
Portsmouth, NH 03801
603-433-6866
603-490-2287 (C)
tfuller@fullercommunications.com

CHAPTER TWENTY TWO

SALES SIMPLIFIED

BY STEPHEN FACELLA

DAVID WRIGHT (WRIGHT)

Today we're talking with Stephen Facella. Stephen is a principle consultant for The Body Language Institute, a Washington, D.C. based professional consulting firm with exclusive certification programs that provide companies the fastest ways to save time and make money. Stephen started his professional career at Planet Hollywood–Times Square, as a sales intern where he developed his Create–Relate–Initiate success method and is credited with increasing net earnings by more than $58,000 during a five- day implementation of his method. His experiences in New York changed the direction of his life. He went on to implement Create–Relate–Initiate at other Fortune 500 companies including the Walt Disney Company and Wyndham Worldwide.

Before joining the Body Language Institute, Stephen held the position of Director of Sales Training for Wyndham Vacation Ownership in the Washington, D.C. area. In less than one year, Stephen's students increased sales by 7.9 percent, contributing more than 19 million dollars in net revenue.

Stephen, welcome to *Success Simplified.*

STEPHEN FACELLA (FACELLA)

Thanks for having me David, I appreciate being here today.

WRIGHT

From Planet Hollywood to Disney to Wyndham to The Body Language Institute-Do tell.

Facella

Alright, I will admit, it's a pretty unique background. I started my professional career when I was a student at Elon University in Elon, North Carolina, where I was an Isabella Cannon Leadership Fellow and received one of two leadership scholarships to attend Elon University that year.

Toward the end of my freshman year I began looking for summer work. I applied for an internship at Planet Hollywood–Times Square in New York City. Now, this opportunity had me moving up to a big city for my first "real job," taking the subway into work and punching a time clock nine to five every single day, but what I learned there was immeasurable.

I learned so much about myself but also about how big business operates. I was a fast learner—so fast that the general manager of Planet Hollywood offered to pay for my education if I would go to New York University and continue to work for them. However, one of the things that I learned was that I didn't want to be a restaurant manager! I say that because the hours were so long and the pay was inequitable.

That summer experience changed the course of my life. Every day we had two and half million people walk by our front door; going back to a university of only three thousand people was going to be rough. So I relocated myself to Orlando, Florida, where I received my Bachelor of Science degree in Hospitality Management at the University of Central Florida Rosen College of Hospitality Management. To give you a timeline, this was the year following 9/11, probably the worst season in the hospitality industry's recent history and it was hard to find employment.

The last place I applied was the Walt Disney Company and was offered a position as an Event Guide. Now, from what I understood an event guide to be and what it actually was were two different things. I was told it was more in line with what I was doing at Planet Hollywood; instead, I was a human stanchion. I would literally stand there and tell people, "Can't go past this line." It was ridiculously boring and mindless and I knew that I wasn't increasing my intellect or my understanding of the industry, so something needed to change fast.

After two shifts of standing around (literally) my manager, Brook Edwards, came to me and said; "Tomorrow I need to you dress like me." Event Managers at Walt Disney World wore business professional dress, the same as I was familiar with wearing at Planet Hollywood. The "dress like me" comment was all that she said to me and I wasn't sure exactly what she meant by it; but I came dressed the next day in a suit and tie. For the next two weeks, I shadowed Brook, doing everything that she did. She then promoted me to the role of Event Guide Coordinator. In this position I was responsible for all the other Event Guides. I spent the next three years working at Disney being promoted seven times.

After I graduated from the University of Central Florida, I knew that I wanted to continue my path in the hospitality industry and more specifically in some sort of sales position. During my studies, I learned about a company named Fairfield Resorts. Fairfield invited me to come see their newest resort that was being built on more than four hundred acres of land at Walt Disney World, right behind Epcot.

During my first visit I immediately fell in love! The leadership at Fairfield took me under their wings and increased my knowledge of the sales world even more than what I learned with Planet Hollywood and Disney.

At the time, I was a full-time Guest Service Manager with Walt Disney World and didn't need a second job, but the respect that I was shown while visiting Fairfield that day made me want to get a second job just to learn.

Shortly after this visit I started working for Fairfield at the front desk, checking people in who already owned Fairfield's vacation ownership product. Almost instantly I knew that I wanted to sell for Fairfield in Las Vegas. I had never lived in or had any ties to the West, but as a new college graduate I had too much fun in Las Vegas as a tourist so, I thought it'd be a nice place to live! I packed my bags, moved out to Las Vegas— where I didn't know a soul—to buckle down, study sales, and be committed to my success.

In my first year of sales in Las Vegas I sold 1.3 million dollars of vacation ownership interests. Of course, 1.3 million dollars could be a lot or it could be a little depending on what kind of sales you're doing. The average transaction was about $18,000 and the average sale took two hours from meeting your cold lead client to closing paperwork. It took a lot of $18,000 transactions to get to 1.3 million dollars! Today, Fairfield Resorts is known as Wyndham Vacation Ownership and is still the world's leader in the Vacation Ownership Industry.

Fast-forwarding to the summer of 2009, I was on a 5:45 AM flight from D.C. to California. I was exhausted as I boarded the plane and I do not get worked up in crowds or lines because I'm a pretty laid back guy. As I walked into the aircraft, I noticed a woman leaning over my seat talking to the passengers behind her. I didn't say anything or get worked up, and when she finished using my seat she apologized and went back to her correct seat. Initially I wanted to sleep on that early flight, but I ended up talking to the woman for the entire trip to California. That woman is Janine Driver, President and CEO of The Body

Language Institute. Janine and I spoke about her career as a federal law enforcement officer, corporate speaker, sales trainer, and "lyin' tamer." We also spoke about my history in corporate America, which impressed Janine very much

Janine and I stayed in touch and one evening I went to The Body Language Institute and spoke to her staff. I did a very brief training for them and impressed Janine and her partners. They offered me a position that night, and as they say, the rest is history!

WRIGHT

So, who were your early influences that shaped you into the person you are today?

FACELLA

Well, without sounding too cliché, it would be my mother. My mother raised me right and I attribute both my success and my moral foundation that I still live by today to her example during my formative years.

In the professional world, one of my early influences would have to be my manager at Planet Hollywood, Cara Oates. Cara is the one who encouraged me to not only to step out and do things that I thought would be beneficial for myself but to also to take risks within the company. It was Cara's guidance and daily inspiration that would lead me to realize that I needed to switch the course of my studies to Hospitality Management.

When I moved to Orlando, the person who shaped me into who I am today would be Carl Gatti. Carl is the Vice President of Sales for Wyndham. When I went on that tour of the Bonnet Creek resort while it was under construction, Carl's words really spoke to me and to my heart; he showed me that I could be successful. Carl wanted to hire me right there but I was still a full-time student and my class schedule wouldn't work with the sales schedule. If I hadn't listened to Cara and Carl's words I would not be where I am today.

WRIGHT

I understand there are three rookie mistakes that even seasoned sales people can fall into; what are they?

Facella

People assume that there is some magical way to get sales without trying—if they would just do this, or that, they would get a sale. The three rookie mistakes that I'm going to share with you would be the ones that I come across most often.

The first rookie mistake is in order to get sales you need to be someone or something you're not. What I mean by that is when people get out there, they think they're going to be able to take someone else's message, someone else's success, and just copy it and follow it like a parrot. When they do this they fail to allow their own personality to shine through and create that human connection with another individual. You cannot buy a sales pitch. It's not possible to be successful by regurgitating someone else's style, pitch, and success because there is an emotional connection into sales that needs to come from your heart and this cannot be found in a book or on a tape.

The second rookie mistake is when salespeople underestimate their clients' ability to understand what exactly they're doing. Whether this is at the sales table, over the phone, in person at an office or at their home, both the client and salesperson know that a sale is going to be made. Trying to make a sale is a good thing, not something you should try to hide or be ashamed of. Think of all of the things in your life that you purchased from a salesperson: Your car? Your pool? Your landscaping? Whatever it may be, a salesperson helped you do that. When I deal with a salesperson and I hear the phrase, "I'm not going to make any money on this deal" or "I don't do this for the commission," I always ask, "Then why are you doing it at all?" Be proud of the fact that you're selling something, but only if you're proud of what you're selling. There is no need to hide and act like there is not a financial benefit to your company, yourself, or your family.

Finally, the third rookie mistake is your presentation. I don't mean your sales presentation, but rather the way that you present yourself. I tell my students that if they're going to be asking people for $60,000 after just meeting them, they'd better look like $60,000 and they'd better look like they've got $60,000 of disposable income themselves to hand over.

Let me share a story with you about what I mean. I was at a Nordstrom with a friend who was telling me that I don't spend enough money on my jeans—my jeans of all things! I'm standing there saying, "I don't understand what you're telling me. I need to spend more money on my jeans? Jeans are jeans, this one is made in China, and that one is made in China. They're probably all from the same sweatshop, but you're telling me to choose that one because its $300 and it's better than the other? That's incorrect, I do not agree with you."

I left my friend and I started walking away when a table full of sweaters caught my eye. I walked over to a simple, cotton sweater with a big sticker saying it was on sale for $89. A sale at Nordstrom! I had to be getting a deal, right? I was getting a sweater in return for $89. So I picked up the sweater, I looked at it, thought about it, and I finally put it down. And I said to myself, "What am I doing? What am I thinking? Eighty-nine dollars for a sweater when I can go right next door to Macy's and get one for $30! What is wrong with me?" Nothing. Nordstrom just looked the part; I knew exactly what I was getting into when I walked into Nordstrom. Nordstrom's appearance demands a higher price point for the same product.

Dress the part. Don't look out of place. When I sold in Vegas, I wore Hawaiian shirts. People were on vacation and I was selling vacations. Here in Washington, D.C., we wear suits and ties as though we belong on Capitol Hill. So remember, your appearance is part of the merchandising.

Wright

You say the sale begins at the close; what does that mean? When do top producers think the sale ends?

Facella

People think that the sale begins when they make their first contact with their clients. I teach my students that the sale begins at the close.

I'm going to tell you a story about a woman named Debbie Kennon. Debbie is a sales associate at Furnitureland South in Jamestown, North Carolina. Now, the reason I know about Debbie is because when I purchased my home I took a trip down to North Carolina for furniture. Furnitureland South is the world's largest home furnishing store. Before I even arrived I called and I said "I'm coming into your store. I have a home that needs to be furnished. What do I need to bring you?" I was put through to Debbie. Debbie was so polite and told me everything that I needed to bring—blueprints, measurements, carpet, tile, paint and wood samples—everything. So I brought everything I needed down there and met with Debbie over the course of two days. Once I selected my furniture and gave Debbie my money, you'd think that it was over. There was our transaction, my furniture will arrive in four to six weeks, and that's it, right?

Wrong. What I didn't know was that Debbie not only was going to keep in touch with me almost every two weeks, until that furniture arrived six weeks later, but Debbie also sent me a thank you card in the mail and an e-mail to ensure that I got home safely after I left North Carolina and headed back to Washington, D.C. Most importantly, do you know what Debbie did the day that my furniture arrived? Debbie called me and was on the phone with me the entire time the delivery men were at my house. She was reminding me where everything needed to be placed, asking me if everything looked the way that it should, and if not to give it right back to the delivery driver. Debbie wanted to make sure that my house looked like a million dollars. Debbie was there for me. Not only that but after my furniture was delivered, Debbie let me know, "Hey remember what we were talking about, well guess what? I think you should come down in February and go ahead and pick that up because we will have a fantastic sale going on then."

Now, let's say that I turned one of those pieces of furniture down. That would have been money out of Debbie's pocket, but Debbie was more concerned that I was happy and that I would be a customer for life, more so than just getting the one-time sale. To this day, I keep in touch with Debbie and I ask her things about designing, not only for all of my home furnishings, but if I've got a question about color for my walls, Debbie doesn't make a cent on the paint but she's going to tell me what color a wall needs to be.

So what I mean by "the sale begins at the close" is that it's the service after the sale that's crucial. Unfortunately, some salespeople are so commission hungry that they forget about their clients or anything that the customer has told them the moment that they've got their clients money.

Wright

I recently came across an article on PsychologyToday.com called "Three Body Language Secrets Your Competition Prays You'll Never Find Out About." I noticed that you were the sales expert quoted. Would you share with our readers some of these secrets?

Facella

Sure, that's fantastic that you saw that. Well, the article was a body language blog on PsychologyToday.com by Janine Driver, President and CEO of the Body Language Institute. Janine and I were talking about how to bring body language into the sales world. The first secret is how to leverage your body by standing, kneeling, or sitting. When are you going to stand, when are you going to sit, and when are you going to kneel? Well, it depends on the sales scenario. Are you doing the sale in your office, or are you doing a sale in someone's home or are you selling to a group of people? It will all depend on the location of the sale. When do we stand higher than someone? When we need power we need to leverage our body and our body language to ensure that we have the upper hand. Now, we can do this when we're talking about something with conviction or we can do this when we are trying to convey the fact that we're proud of what we're selling.

The other strategy that Janine and I mentioned was getting lower. You want to get lower than people when you want to make them think that they're in charge or powerful. This can be in your office when you're showing your clients something. Instead of towering over their shoulder, you bend down on one knee and you do your presentation and talk about their needs, their wants, and their desires. So we're going to get lower than they are.

Janine is the New York Times bestselling author of "*You Say More Than You Think*" and she has developed something she calls the "belly button rule" or "naval intelligence." What you always want to do is ensure that your belly button is facing toward the person you admire and trust. You want this person to feel that they're in charge and, the alpha in the relationship. Your belly button is very important; you can see this when people are not paying attention to you. People who don't trust you or who are not listening to what you're saying stand with their belly button not facing toward you. I guarantee you, the next time you have a conversation with someone, pay attention to where their belly button is facing. That person is going to be the most dominant person in the room.

The third strategy is touch tips. This is essential for salespeople when dealing with the opposite sex. While you want to avoid sending the message of a romantic interest, you also want to be sure that you touch people and show them that there is an emotional connection with what you're doing right there. You want to make sure that you touch people with the back of your hand only, so your palm is facing up. Unless you're shaking someone's hand you want your palm facing up when you're talking to them or touching them.

You also want to make sure that when you're speaking with people you're not showing someone the backside of your hand. You want to speak with your hands at your waist, palms open, showing that you're open and receptive to what your client has to say. Janine goes into a lot more of this in her book, and I teach this in the courses offered at The Body Language Institute.

Wright

In your workshop you talk about Create–Relate–Initiate. What is this formula when it comes to uncovering hidden income?

Facella

Create–Relate–Initiate is something I came up with when I was at Planet Hollywood. It led to $58,000 toward the bottom line when we implemented it. Create–Relate–Initiate is for people who need to break out of what they're doing right now.

For example, you've been in your position for a couple of years, and you are doing everything that your boss tells you to do. You want that next step—that next promotion, that next pay raise, that next commission bump. You want that, but you don't know why you're not getting it. What you need to do is create *something*—something that shows your talent, something that drives you and is a compliment to what you are doing.

At Planet Hollywood I created a method to make more money not only for the company, but also for me and all of the waiters, waitresses, busboys, bartenders, and kitchen staff. That summer the World Cup was going on in South Korea and Japan. There is a very large time difference between New York City and South Korea and Japan. ESPN's restaurant was a block away from us and can you believe that they were not showing the World Cup at a sports restaurant? This was an obvious void that needed to be filled.

New York City is an international destination; it's the capital of the world with tourists from everywhere. I told you earlier how two and a half million people walked by my front door every day at Planet Hollywood and a lot of those people were stopping and they were asking, "Are you showing the World Cup? Is the World Cup going to be on here?" Well, as a sales intern I decided to *create* a program that would put more money in everybody's pockets by showing the World Cup Games on giant movie screens around the entire restaurant. Because of the time difference, the games were playing anywhere from 11 PM until 4 AM.

What I had to do is *relate* this to my role. I brought my idea to my supervisors and said, "You've been telling me to take risks. Well, I want to go out there and take a risk and I need your support. I want to take the ball and I want to run with it. It's all after-hours, it's not going to affect our overhead, and we're going to make money. I want to show the World Cup events on the big screens outside of our regular business hours. We'll serve eggs, potatoes, or things with extremely low food costs and extremely high profit margins."

So we created a breakfast buffet that had never been on our menu. We charged a $15 cover charge for anyone to walk in the door who wanted to see the game. The cover charge was for the breakfast; whether or not they ate it was up to them. We had our bar open. We had our full kitchen open in addition to the breakfast, and we related the World Cup into our daily operations. So everyone was able to continue to make additional income from what they already expected to make during the course of our daily operations.

I was given the go-ahead to *initiate* this for five days. During those five days we brought in more than $58,000 in net revenue. To drive the success, I went out and I spoke to every concierge from Times Square to Central Park to Penn Station and told them to send their clients over to Planet Hollywood to see the World Cup. After I did all that, and $58,000 later, everyone was happy. This is when they asked me to go to NYU.

Wright

What can someone do to be loved, adored, and admired by customers and people in their daily lives?

Facella

That's a great question. It's also a very important question that goes back to the soul of the person. Are you an honest person in your dealings with your fellow man? That's number one. There are good salespeople, there are bad salespeople, there are good cops, there are bad cops—there are good and bad of everything.

You have to respect yourself, your morals, and your own foundations in order for that to permeate through your body and your soul.

Let's talk about Debbie again. Do you think that I love, admire, and adore not only her as a person but also as a salesperson? Absolutely! Debbie showed me who she was as a person. So did Cara at Planet Hollywood, Brook, my manager at Walt Disney World, and Carl at Wyndham Vacation Ownership. All of these people have done what we all need to do in order to be loved, adored, and admired by people in their lives.

Wright

Earlier you mentioned the three things that you do immediately when you feel like you're losing a sale. Do these really work?

Facella

They do. When you feel you made that emotional connection with someone, you feel that you are listening to his or her wants, desires and needs, but you feel that you're not getting somewhere, you've got to change the environment. Get the person up, and move somewhere else. Go outside, go somewhere else in the room, go get a drink—do something!

The second thing you want to do is change your body language. Do you have "commission breath"? Are you dominating your clients during your sales presentation? I always say "check yourself before you wreck yourself!" You've got to be cognizant of what you're saying when you're lips aren't moving.

Finally, the third thing to do when you feel like you are losing the sale is to just ask your client if you're losing the sale. People will tell you anything you want to know if you just ask! They'll tell you yes or no. If they tell you no, you can go ahead and correct whatever it is. But if you never ask, you'll never know and you'll lose your sale.

Wright

You mentioned that the biggest career-killer is a bad attitude. What can we all do to ensure we never catch one and what can we do to maintain an edge in the game of life?

Facella

The great thing about attitude is that you get to choose your own attitude every day. Our attitudes are one of the few things in life that we have complete control over. When you wake up and you've been given another day on this earth, you get to choose what kind of day it is going to be. When salespeople choose to have bad attitudes, I don't understand how they expect to make any money. If you have a horrible attitude, you're not going to get anywhere, not only with your career, but with your life.

As I say, "A bad attitude is a cancer that has no chemotherapy—there is no cure for a bad attitude once you catch one." Avoid people with bad attitudes. In the sales world there is always the naysayer; there is always that salesperson who doesn't want to do it, can't do it, won't do it, and just isn't going to be successful. Stay away from those people. This is particularly critical for new salespeople.

I tell my new students to fill their iPod with positive music or audio books and listen to it when negative people are around. That way the negative people don't want to come and talk to you because they think that they're going to be interrupting you. If they do try to interrupt you, just point to your ear—you've, got an earphone in there, and you can't talk right now. Misery loves company and you've got to ensure that you keep yourself and keep your mind in check or it's over.

Wright

I listened to you on a popular sales training podcast about how job applicants trick you into thinking they can sell. Would you share some of the things that you said in that interview?

Facella

Sure, gladly. I was a sales recruiter before I became a sales trainer, so I've seen both sides of the coin. I've been the one who advanced salespeople from being applicants to being employees. As you may already know, it is very expensive to hire someone. So if someone is in your office looking for a job, it's obvious they're going to show you their best side all of the time because they want the job. It's your duty to find out what they are telling you, what are they trying to do, and what they're trying to convince you of right then.

One of the things that I do is remarkably straightforward, and I'm sure people out there have had this done to them. Before an interview with a prospective salesperson I make sure my desk is clear before he or she comes into my office. There is nothing on my desk except for the keyboard—not a single piece of paper on the desk. All I have is a Bic pen in my suit pocket.

At the end of the interview I just look that person in the eye and say, "Hey, do you think you're a closer?"

The person always says, "Of course." Why? Because the person wants the job.

I then say, "Can you sell anything?"

"Absolutely!" the person will reply.

So I'd hand over my Bic pen and say, "Sell me this pen."

Some people would freeze; they wouldn't know what to do. They had read Web sites out there telling them how to interview, how to get the job, and how to win over an interviewer. I've seen these Web sites, too. Some people I interviewed froze because they weren't expecting this. Some people went straight into a sales pitch. "This is a Bic pen. It writes in blue—" They would just continue on and tell me everything I might want to hear about the Bic pen. That person is someone I don't want to hire because he or she hasn't done anything we've been talking about today.

People who launch into a sales pitch haven't gotten to know me; they haven't gotten to show me that they care about my wants, my needs, my desires for this product, or for the this Bic pen. They haven't asked me any questions about my needs for the pen or what I'm going to do with the pen.

Some people would get thrown off when I would tell them, "No, I don't want your pen." They wouldn't know what to do. The people that I did hire were the ones that did exactly what we've been talking about, which is get to know me, show me a little bit of themselves, and show me how I need this pen. I would throw curveballs at them, David—I would tell them "nobody uses pens anymore. We live in an electronic age. I've got my phone here or I can send email from or my computer. Handwriting is a lost art. Who uses pens?" The people who got the job were the ones who reiterated what was beneficial to me. When they asked me questions like who, "Who is the most important person in your life?" Then followed up with, "Well don't you want to write a Valentine's Day card to her or don't you want to write her a poem?" You can't type or e-mail a poem. You don't type or e-mail a Valentine's Day card." Those are the people that I gave jobs to. Those are the people who are today making plenty of money out there in the sales world.

That's, what we talked about on that podcast. I'm glad you heard that.

Wright

What a great conversation. I can see that you're really into personal service and getting to know people. I've really learned a lot here today and I'm sure our readers will, too.

Facella

Well, thanks a lot, David, I appreciate that.

Wright

I really value the time you've spent with me today. I'm so glad that we could do this for the book and I appreciate your answering these questions for me.

Facella

Likewise, David I appreciate your time and I've appreciated the conversation that we've had today; it's been fantastic.

Wright

Today we've been talking with Stephen Facella. He is a principle consultant for The Body Language Institute, which is a Washington, D.C. based consulting firm with exclusive certification programs that provide companies the fastest ways to save time and money. I think he knows a whole lot about selling; at least I'm listening to him.

Stephen, thank you so much for being with us today on *Success Simplified.*

Facella

Thanks David, have a great day!

About the Author

As a Washington, D.C.-based sales trainer and corporate speaker, Stephen Facella is a principle consultant for The Body Language Institute. Stephen loves traveling the world and learning about cultures through firsthand experiences.

Stephen Facella

is represented by: Traci Allen

Traci Allen, Inc.

1220 L Street NW, Suite #100-558

Washington, DC 20004

202-216-0660

888-216-9915

TAllen@TraciAllen.com

www.BodyLanguageInstitute.com

CHAPTER TWENTY THREE

THE CRY THAT CONQUERED

"To become, you must believe; to succeed, you must strive; to perform, you must never procrastinate; and to achieve, you must act"—Lourdes Valdes.

BY LOURDES VALDES

DAVID WRIGHT (WRIGHT)

Today we're talking with Lourdes Valdes. Born in New York, a daughter of Cuban immigrants, Lourdes was raised in New Orleans, Louisiana, during her early teens and Barcelona, Spain. Later, her family resided in Miami, Florida, where she attended high school and earned a bachelor's degree in Communications with a minor in Political Science from the University of Miami. She has now been a resident of Georgia for two years. Most of her life was spent as an on-air radio personality for five major radio stations in South Florida, one of them being her own radio talk show, *Woman Talk*. The show focused on close-knit women related issues.

While working in radio, television also opened doors for her and she became an entertainment reporter for Telemundo. Later, she became a stunt actress for many of the Univision and Telemundo soap operas. Her passion for writing and adventure also brought her an opportunity to write for *The Car Connection* in Spanish, test-driving cars and writing about the experience from a female perspective. Her curiosity for another venture intensified, and she entered the field of law enforcement. She became a law enforcement officer for the Hallandale Beach Police Department, but shortly after working in the field, she had to resign because of health-related issues.

In the midst of career changes, she's also owned several home-based businesses. She has been a strong advocate for fitness throughout her life, a long-time runner, a spinning instructor, and kickboxing instructor. She's taken flying lessons and owns a motorcycle license. Lourdes has bungee-jumped and skydived and is looking forward to being certified in the only fear she has—scuba diving. Aside from her personal adventures, she is a motivational speaker, a passionate voice for teens, and is in the process of finishing her first book.

Lourdes Valdes, welcome to *Success Simplified.*

Lourdes Valdes (Valdes)

Thank you, David; it's great to be here.

Wright

So tell me about yourself and a little bit about your background.

Valdes

My parents were born in Havana, Cuba. They came to the United States as Cuban immigrants back in the early '60s before Castro took power. They met in New York City, and they had me. When I was a toddler, we moved to South Florida, and we lived in Miami for a couple of years. When I was ten years old my dad's job transferred us to Barcelona, Spain. I attended an all-girl Catholic school and was the only American girl in the entire school—an interesting experience!

After living in Spain for a year, my father was transferred again, this time to New Orleans, Louisiana. We lived in the outskirts of New Orleans in a city called Kenner for about three and a half years. When I was fifteen, my dad was transferred one last time back to South Florida where I attended high school and college. I graduated from the University of Miami with a degree in Communications and a minor in Political Science.

Wright

You've had several careers in your lifetime. Would you tell our readers a little bit about what you've done?

Valdes

Yes! Wow! What *haven't* I done? And there is still more to do! Pretty much my first "passion" for what I wanted to achieve, as far as a career was concerned, was evident very early on. I can remember being eight or nine years of age and listening to the radio for hours on end at my grandparents' house where most of my time was spent during school breaks and summers. I vividly remember the rocking chair in their outdoor patio area where I would spend hours rocking. Close to me was an old piece of furniture that had a radio built into it where I heard the voices of the familiar jocks I knew so well. (I don't know if those are even built anymore!). There was very limited conversation between this set of grandparents and myself, so most of my time was spent visualizing and listening to those radio personalities I had come to know as friends.

My "dream job" became a reality when I landed my first radio job six months after I graduated college. That enormous drive and eagerness to be in radio early on in life lingered on into adulthood, so during my last semester in college I began searching for opportunities in the field. Although I had done my internship with television, something pulled me instead toward radio. The childlike voice inside of me reminded me to pursue what I longed to have. Radio was my first love and therefore I listened to the passion from within me and pursued it.

While working in radio, other opportunities came to me like a magnet. I believe that when you're actually living out what you wholeheartedly love doing, everybody and everything you are passionate about are automatically drawn to you. It all works in such an alignment. I am a firm believer that we are not limited to just "one" talent or "one" dream. Opportunities come in your direction like waves when you are literally executing the "purpose" you were destined to fulfill. I believe God wants and longs to give us the desires of our heart. He doesn't state "desire," he states "desires" meaning there is always more than one gift you are intended to have. That's why he gave each of us talents. It's what we do with those talents that will eventually dictate the true joy we will experience in our lifetime.

While working in radio and happy as pie, doors began opening with television as well. I was given the opportunity to work as an entertainment reporter for one of the shows that aired with Telemundo, a

Spanish Television Network in Miami. I was also asked to do stunt work for a company that had a contract with Telemundo and Univision that filmed their soap operas. I was thrilled once again because now I had the opportunity to really explore the adventurous side that I knew definitely existed within me! It was great! I jumped off a couple of two-story buildings, landing on cushioned mattresses! I was allowed to race cars on Miami's freeways at two in the morning because I was part of a film crew! I was literally a stunt actress as well! In the midst of stunt work, I was also given the opportunity to train in self-defense classes, which brought to me an even higher level of learning about "self" that was so refreshing and empowering!

In the midst of all these opportunities, the journalist/writer side of me was also brought to life when I was asked to write for *The Car Connection* En Espanol. This was a Web site that featured reviews of new cars coming out into the buyers' market. The company needed a female journalist who could write about the experience of test-driving cars from a female perspective. I vividly remember testing the Ford GT when it first came out. Its performance and agility around the race track at a speed of 180 miles per hour will forever be "unforgettable"!

Although much excitement and adrenalin did come through for me for many years, there also came a time when things slowed down. I refer to these moments as the "inevitable rollercoaster pinnacles of life." The radio and television industry began changing drastically, taking an unexpected turn in all sorts of directions. A lot of the major corporations and radio stations were bought out by other corporations, causing instability to all those in the field. It was time for me to take a different approach, to shift gears so to speak, and begin searching from within as to what other area of work I wanted to explore. It was time to reinvent and to take action with something new, and I knew the time had come.

Although I never let go of the passion I had for radio and television, I knew that these industries were not bringing me the financial security I needed at the time. Letting go of them for awhile did not mean I could never return. The industry had changed without my control in the matter, but I did have control to determine what I could do in the meantime. I could always return to them and that belief allowed me to see beyond the disappointment I could have felt otherwise.

I began exploring other ideas and passions that I had inside, eventually tapping my curiosity for the field of law enforcement. I felt a need to begin something totally unknown to me. I feared guns, but I thought of how I had feared so many other things in my life and had conquered those fears! Why not this tiny fear? The irony was that a greater fear lurked in me that was much more important to conquer than guns. I feared I lacked mental strength. I began to think that if I got into law enforcement, it would shape me into the person I believed I needed to become.

As I will speak about shortly, by no means did I ever need to be trained to become mentally stronger. I was already mentally capable of surviving anything. My childhood experiences had already given me the ammunition I needed to survive. What I needed was "restoration," which has been life-changing for me ever since.

Right now, I am living my ultimate passion for life. I am a motivational speaker and author. I have realized that I've been a motivator all my life, first to myself, and then to countless others through my radio talk shows or my news reports. Motivation has been the actual "core" of what I've done subconsciously; it has been both effortless and self-fulfilling for me. Everything I did in my life, all the titles I obtained, came from that one word "motivation." I grabbed hold of the finite principles needed to attain success. While learning, I also began "sharing" my knowledge with others, allowing them to see what they, too, may have been missing out on. If I had accomplished this—if I survived and if I had succeeded—anyone could! There's no specified "blueprint" for life other than the one you choose to draft for yourself.

Wright

So what is your philosophy of success?

Valdes

My philosophy stems from the belief that you need to "break" before you "make." In other words, you need to understand that there are things in life you might have felt "broken" with. Most of the time those feelings of inadequacy are emotional ones. In my case, I experienced mental breakage. I had to understand that my brokenness was due to the "false belief" about myself that I was holding onto for so many years.

Once I learned and accepted the truth that what had happened to me was not my fault, the insecurities I had held onto for so long finally began to decrease in significance until they ultimately disintegrated. I no longer placed emphasis on the "what" had happened to me but began focusing on the will that lay within me to keep it moving. No more was I going to sabotage every wonderful experience that was waiting to surface in my life. God had granted me the power to overcome, by the faith I had in Him. It was up to me to choose 1) "*survival*" in order to achieve my destiny or 2) to "*submit*" to the belief that the calling intended for my life was overcome by my unfortunate circumstances.

As I speak about this, I remember listening to Dr. Laura Schlesinger one afternoon. I remember how she totally broke it down for me in the simplest of terms. She said to visualize a slab of concrete and understand that most people are born in an upright position from this solid block. Others, however, aren't as fortunate. These people are born underneath this slab of concrete. They first have to break through it before they can begin to start living the life that the majority of people take for granted. I was one of those who were born underneath this "imaginary fortified block." So when I say to "break before you make," I believe that people need to know in which category they are currently in their lives in order to reach their ultimate God-given potential. Ask yourself where you are right now—above the slab or under it? Once you know the answer to that, you can begin changing your circumstances by controlling them. Allow what comes into your life to be what you want *in it*—period. This involves understanding the place you once had in life and the place where you are *now*. No one can give the meaning of what success really means but *you.*

Wright

In this chapter of our book, you want to convey to the reader the steps you used as a survivor to bring about success in your life. What did you survive?

Valdes

I am a survivor of my mom's mental handicap. Since the time I was born until just recently, I was treated quite harshly by my mother. No matter what I did, I was told continuously that I was not the daughter she had hoped to have. At birth I was a colicky baby, as a child I was too playful and energetic, in my teens I wanted to engage in sports and school activities. It seemed that everything pertaining to the person I was created to be was just plain wrong in my mother's eyes.

Childhood memories were very painful to me for the longest time. I had no foundation to build self-esteem from. I had no fortress I could run to for protection. I had no comforting arms to hold me when the world tried to drown the best out of me.

My mother had suffered a severe trauma as a teen when her mom committed suicide. She was only sixteen. When I was born, I became a victim of my mom's inner pain. I was the one she took out her frustrations on—she had no one else. Never had she truly released all the suffering she felt inside. Through me, her oldest and only daughter, she felt free to do so. I suffered physical as well as mental abuse on a daily basis until I left home at the age of twenty-seven and got married. In my book, *Silent Screams—A Woman's Outcry* (to be released soon), I explain in more detail the storms I wrestled with and the triumphs I achieved simply by understanding the very thing that everyone should know. Everyone should know that the life that is given to you is yours to protect, yours to live out, and yours to enjoy. One of my favorite quotes is by Eleanor Roosevelt who said, "No one can make you feel inferior without your consent."

Through it all it was God's amazing love that healed me. I accepted him as Lord and Savior at the age of thirteen. It was through this acceptance of faith first that clarity began to manifest itself in my life, allowing me to see another picture other than the darkness I had lived in for so many years.

After the spiritual awakening that came to me that Friday night as a teen, it wasn't long before I learned that there were steps I could take to survive the emotional beatings I had already endured in my life. Before I had confirmed my faith in Christ, I had learned at the age of six or seven that if I would choose to see life as nothing more than a "play" whereby characters played their temporary role, I would be alright! It so clear to me now that God, in His infinite wisdom, was literally setting the stage for how my life would eventually turn out! This play had scenes. Each episode, through my experiences, was playing itself out. Sure, a theatrical play is, for the most part, fictional, but this story was real. The good news is that I chose to focus on the fact that all of this was a play, whether it was fictional or not! We all watch scenes change and characters come and go. The actors go through a change in wardrobe. They laugh, they cry, and there's always an ending that, for the most part, is quite different than the beginning.

I saw life and the experiences I was dealing with in that exact same way. I knew I wasn't going to be playing my current character all my life. I knew my scenes—my surroundings—would one day change. I was going to have my own house, my own family, and have the opportunity to live and experience the gifts of life the way I wanted to experience them. One day there would be options, opportunities, and on-going happiness intended just for me, if I truly desired to have them.

It was that *belief system* that I so wholeheartedly held onto that kept me sane and kept me alive, even though I felt dead inside. I knew I would one day experience love through others. I knew I would be given the opportunity to love others. I knew that although everything that was happening around me was real, my life was not going to stay in that same state forever. One day, Lourdes was going to audition and be given another character to live out—one that she was going to be delighted in playing and one that was positive, loving, giving, adventurous, and nurturing, not only to myself but also to others.

My steps in achieving success were rewarded when I allowed my mind to clear itself of past misfortunes. It's when I allowed new thoughts of revival to emerge from within me. A play, for the most part, is fictional, but if you take its content and create within you an alternative thought process whereby you realize that the opportunity to live out your dream life does exist, then and only then will you become the maker of your intended happiness! Simply stated, by having faith in your Creator first, you will become the Michelangelo of your personalized sculpture. Success, happiness, and your desired life will all begin to unfold piece by piece right before your eyes, miraculously, with or without your awareness.

WRIGHT

Statistics show that the average person changes careers about seven times in his or her lifetime. You've reached that percentage and done even more. What were the factors that persuaded you to take the leaps that you did?

VALDES

Well a cat has nine lives, right? Can't we as humans have more? What actually persuaded me was the fact that I get bored so easily! I get bored at looking in the mirror every day and seeing the same hairstyle! I love variety and the ability to feel comfortable with change. Self-gratification for me is huge! Feeling happy, enthusiastic, and fulfilled on a daily basis is what I call my "mandatory daily dosage." It's the happy pill I take every day that assures me that blessings are just waiting to be poured upon me if I allow it.

Success is a personal decision. That determination is sought first from within you. It's your inner spirit that gives you the green light in order for the blessings to emerge. If you do not believe in the spirit that connects you to the highest power you could ever be linked to, then the electrifying experiences you want so badly will never happen.

Whatever experiences, good or bad, that I lived through I gave them the meaning I wanted to give them. Anthony Robbins explains this best when he says that a word is defined by the meaning you choose to give it. Webster has no authority on this—*you* do.

My mother's ailment was not her fault, neither was it mine. Therefore, I chose to define the experiences I had with my mother to be ones that would empower me. I knew that if I survived what I had gone through with her, I could survive anything. With this mindset, I allowed countless experiences to come my way. Were they all great and dandy? Of course not! There were more negative and disempowering ones than empowering ones!

The inner strength I gained from all this was what I ultimately gained. I realized I didn't fear failure because failure had been prominent in my surroundings for most of my life. I had already been put down, broken, abused, neglected, and scorned. Whatever else came my way, I knew I had the one thing that no one could take away from me—personal power. I had the ability to block or allow the comments and experiences I wanted to receive. Only I could grant that power to myself.

I encourage anyone to take chances in life! Those chances you take become an empowering tool for you to have, if you wish to pick it up. Think about it—all the experiences you encounter in your life, you either place in memory lane or you become repulsed at the thought of reliving it forever.

For me, careers were what I considered to be the "fortified tools" I loved being able to own. What rule is there that states that in life you are only allowed or expected to carry out only one profession in order to be labeled as a successful human being? That is why I do not believe in the statement that emphasizes the importance of judging the phrase that states whether you are a jack of all trades and the master of none. Why?

If we were to believe that we cannot successfully master several skills in our lives, then how do we explain Benjamin Franklin's success? If it wasn't for the multiple hats he wore, we wouldn't have ever experienced most of the businesses we depend upon today. In today's world, we see Donald Trump, Wayne Huizenga, Robert Kiyosaki, and countless others who learned their strengths early on and applied them to not only one area of their lives but several. What did they encounter? They obviously encountered an enormous amount of success and, most importantly, an incredible sense of personal fulfillment, which is of utmost importance for all human life! The sky is the limit, so why would you close the doors to an everlasting floor plan like the one that lies right above you?

WRIGHT

Would you tell our readers about a suggestion you have made to others to guarantee success?

VALDES

I told many in my lifetime to never rely on anyone to fulfill any of their dreams! I don't care who it is! Allowing anyone to do this would only limit the capabilities and the God-given talents you have inherently received from your Creator.

Another point I wish to make is to never allow yourself to believe that you "need" anyone to reach success. I struggled with this for quite some time. There are so many people who have succumbed to the belief that without a boss giving them a promotion or without the help of a coworker or business partner working a deal with them or without this or without that, they could never receive the blessing of obtaining what they truly desire. Sure, having contacts, connections with executives, and attending meaningful functions pertaining to your area of expertise helps tremendously. What I am saying is that while having the right contacts undoubtedly helps, it doesn't mean it is the only way to get to the level of success you desire to reach.

I've met countless individuals who could have helped me attain a position that matched my credentials and didn't do so. They were so powerful that all they had to do was make a call to their personnel department and I would have been given a job that met my credentials. It wasn't just doing me a favor because of a friendship, but rather it was their knowing that I fit the job description. However, for whatever reasons, the fact is that they simply did not want or ever offer to help.

The important thing I learned from this was that I never allowed it to get me down. On the contrary, it drove me to conquer things even greater than the job I longed to have. I would then set higher goals for myself and reach them without knowing absolutely anyone in the departments or company I was hoping to work for. I simply stayed focused and never quit trying! Through perseverance, I was able to achieve every single position I ever longed for and wholeheartedly desired to have! The formula is that simple.

Every successful person will tell you that he or she has failed in life many more times than he or she has succeeded. People will also tell you that they were put down an enormous amount of times by others who chose not to believe in them or help them out in any way. What enabled these successful individuals to reach their highest God-given potential was simply the fact that they believed in themselves regardless of what others thought. I look back now and realize that this mindset was definitely engraved in my subconscious very early on. I had already experienced and had survived the greatest emotional letdowns any person could have ever experienced. The lack of receiving love and the unconditional motivation that only a mother could give to a child was never received in my case. I still learned to live, get by, and eventually survive life without it. If I did that, I knew I could survive anything.

For years my struggle was in learning to accept what I did not have with my mother and still find gratitude within me, knowing that regardless of the enormous amount of lack I felt inside, I could still make it through life. My happiness, my accomplishments, and my dreams could only be lived out by me. My mother could have been the coach, the cheerleader, the mentor we all yearn to have and believe we need. But the reality of it all is that when you are faced with that job interview, when you have that test you must pass in order to graduate, when you have the deadline you need to adhere to, neither your mom nor anyone else is going to be there for you to get the job done. *You* are the one who must do it. It's *you* who either "breaks" or "makes." It's ultimately you who ends up at the finish line of your own race. No one, I mean, *absolutely no one,* can ever fill those shoes but *you.*

I'd like to share an example of how I once motivated someone very close to me to challenge his entrepreneurial skills. It ended up being one of his greatest accomplishments. One day my husband came home and told me about an opportunity that had come up for him to invest in. It was an eight-unit apartment building in Hollywood, Florida, just a couple of blocks away from the beach. It was a prime location for anyone who loved living close to the water without having to pay the astronomical prices that come with South Florida real estate.

He shared with me how he wished to be able to partner up with his business partners in this deal because he didn't think he would be able to make this investment on his own. He was a prominent chiropractor and had done very well in the business world, but all his investments and business ventures had been previously done with partners. He had never done anything solo. I asked him if he had thought about just signing the deal on his own. I noticed right away in him the fear that creeps in all of us when we think we're all alone in a big picture.

He looked at me for a moment and stated that he didn't think the bank would give him the loan he needed. I asked him if he had tried to find out. Of course his answer was no. And the moment I knew he dreaded would come arrived. He knew me so well and he knew I loved challenge! I asked him why he had not given it a try to go solo on this. Perhaps it was time to cut the "umbilical cord" he believed he had with the men he had been doing every single business proposition with.

After looking at me with the deepest stare I had ever seen from him, he vowed he would speak to the bank the next day and find out if he would qualify on his own. Much to his surprise (and mine to be quite frank) he qualified! All by himself, he qualified! I'll never forget the smile on his face when we signed the papers as proud owners of an eight-unit apartment building that resembled the ones in the show *Beverly Hills, 90210.*

Hubby had reached an enormous sense of self-gratification that day, and I learned the valuable lesson that whatever you don't take action to achieve, you will *never* achieve! The excuses that had engulfed him because he was the youngest in the group of well-established doctors were gone. He achieved an income he thought he would never have, and had the amount of credit he felt he wasn't capable of having. What I refer to as "umbilical lies" were no longer a part of his life! Perceiving failure is nonsense!

You are the one who once planted an idea for success in that mind of yours. It's in your destiny for you to obtain all the fruits that amount to accomplishments one day. You did this in your subconscious mind whether you realized it or not. When you become aware that the only way to bring it to life is through the actions you take to attain it, is when you succeed with absolutely anything! The Bible states, you reap that which you sow. You planted your seeds a long time ago and you watered them unconsciously along the way. Now, my friend, is the time to reap! It's time to blossom! It's time for *you to do you!* So *let's get it!*

Wright

So what motivates you?

Valdes

What motivates me? Good question! Challenge, challenge, challenge—give me challenge! "No challenge, no conquer" is my motto! You've got to feel a disturbing eagerness to excel from within you in order to arrive at the next level in your life.

Being truly passionate about something is the fuel you need to reach the things you long to have. No one likes to feel pushed or dragged into things that are boring.

All my life I saw my parents unhappy and miserable with the jobs they had. They viewed life as difficult because they were so bored with what they did all day. I remember my mother working as a data entry operator all her life and hating it! She was an excellent typist, but the reality of sitting in front of a computer all day long inputting information was not what she truly wanted to do. She stayed as a data entry operator all her life, never reaching out or even trying to do things she truly wanted to do. Her favorite saying was, "The bills had to be paid and in life, whatever job comes one's way needs to be taken, whether you like it or not."

I agree with the fact that sometimes in life our choices are limited and we should take what comes our way. But it doesn't mean we have to stay there and hate what we do for a living for the rest of our lives! I mean, it's not winter for twelve months out of the year right? Even Alaska warms up at some point! If we set our minds to think that there is no hope, then no hope will arrive. That very thought will keep us enslaved for years. One day we'll realize that we never even tried to take other steps that could have gotten us to where we wanted to go. Then what?

Everyone told me how difficult getting into radio was. To be an on-air personality is a very low-paying job and one of the most difficult to attain! Any radio jock will tell you that! Unless you're syndicated and have your own show, you are getting paid far less than what the public imagines. The passion I had for the field and the talent I also had propelled me to do the very thing that made me happy. Sure, money was important, so what I did was hold another job to make ends meet. So I had two jobs? Who really cared? As long as I walked into both of them with a smile on my face every day, that is what really mattered to me.

There's no human rule that exists out there stating we have to limit ourselves to just doing one thing in our lives. At this moment, I'm actually taking yoga, something I've never done in my life! Some people tell me that maybe this exercise will calm me down a bit because I'm so hyper. I hope it does!

New stuff coming at me constantly is surely what motivates me!

Wright

It's obvious that you have had a painful past, one that you finally feel open and willing to talk about now. Will you tell our readers a little bit about one of your toughest struggles to overcome?

Valdes

The toughest challenge that ever came my way was to break free from the belief my mother had about me. That had to be the most challenging. I also had to understand that another person's heartache is not intended for me to take responsibility of. The cross another carries, does not have to be the one that you have to endure as well. It's obvious my mother had something very unfortunate happen to her. I truly believe that she did the best she could under the circumstances she had to live with. She had an enormous amount of emotional pain that surrounded her. Understanding that my childhood experiences were not my fault was the greatest eye-opening experience I had. Once I accepted that, all other heartaches became less intensified.

Someone else's issues do not have to be yours. Their mishaps are not your mishaps. You just happen to be at the place where they feel comfortable enough to dump their load on you. It's not your fault! I can't stress this enough! I had to not only tell myself and convince myself of this, but I also had to *believe* it! How could I have been the culprit and the problematic child I was told I was when I didn't believe it to be true? Think about it! You know your flaws, your virtues, your desires, your wants, and your dreams more than anyone else does. God built inside of you the gift of knowledge. It's tapping into the box that lies inside your soul that will determine whether you find all the treasures that are intended exclusively for you!

Wright

The meaning of the word "success" is quite different for you; how do you define it?

Valdes

Success in my book is defined as emotional survival. It amazes me how the word "success" is defined so differently by so many people. To some it means the big house they live in or the title they hold in the corporate world or even the popularity they have in school, work, or in their personal life. Although all these things can be definitely viewed as accomplishments, in my world they are not the core beliefs I hold to see myself as a successful person.

Success to me has come packaged a little differently. To me, success has been defined as attaining mental stability, mental strength, and mental assessment. It's in knowing that I had enough self-control within me to never allow any kind of verbal or physical abuse destroy the innocent soul living within me.

Most of my early life, I practically lived on an emotional roller coaster ride with no "exit" sign that would allow me to get off when needed. When I would wake up every Saturday morning, which was the day I saw my mom the most, I did not know what kind of day I was going to have. I didn't know if I was going to wake up to yelling and screaming, or if I was going to do something to disturb her so drastically that I would receive a physical beating. Was I going to be verbally abused throughout the day so much so that I would eventually break down in tears? I didn't know what a Saturday would hold for me when I was growing up. What I did know was that it was my worst day of the week. Now it's my favorite!

Here's the point I want to emphasize: I knew that if I could survive what I was experiencing with my mother, which I knew few were able to do, I would be able to survive *anything* and I mean *anything* later on in life. I made a *decision* that allowed me to become the person I am today. The question I asked myself early on was this: Was I going to end up in mental ward or was I was going to create the picturesque perfect haven I envisioned in my dreams?

That answer had to come from me and no one else. Where I ended up depended solely on me. I chose the picturesque perfect haven. I chose freedom. I chose a life filled with unbelievable dreams that would come true. But most importantly, I chose acceptance of self. I am a child of the almighty and everlasting God who had created me just as I was. His love is unconditional!

If you were to ask yourself if you think you are successful, what would you say? Be sure that before you answer the question, recognize the *definition* you are placing on the word. Don't define it the way the world defines it, but in the way *you* define it and how you understand it. I promise you, you will acknowledge a new perspective and a clearer picture will surely be evident.

Wright

Has all the negative input that you have had down through the years affected your relationships?

Valdes

Of course it has! It was very difficult for me to believe that there was a reason for me to be loved. I had great amounts of insecurities and uncertainties inside of me, but at the same time I had an enormous amount of self-love, which is difficult for me to explain. I truly believe it was my faith in God that allowed me to see past what was happening to me. I felt His love from inside of me. I felt a sense of warmth, a sense of connection to something greater than me, and I knew I was going to be alright. I was going to make it.

The insecurity I used to deal with did indeed cause me a lot of heartache because as we all know, all human connection stems from inner emotions. I had defined love the only way I knew existed and that was through what I defined as "tough love." The kind of love my mom expressed to me was the only one she knew. As a result, my personal relationships and my romantic relationships all suffered great turmoil. An introduction of a mother's love in a person's life is obviously huge!

But here's the same point I wish to make that I stated earlier: how I defined what was happening to me, and how I defined the love I wanted in my life, even though I wasn't getting it at the time, determined my ability to withstand the pain I was experiencing. Amazingly, I did not hate women or feel as though I lacked their trust or wish to disconnect from them altogether. Instead, I longed to get closer to women by connecting with them through the *Woman Talk* radio show I created and hosted. It pertained to women-related issues and through topics and discussions with several professional women in all sorts of fields, many women were healed and connected to a deeper sense of self-actualization.

It was a wonderful experience. I learned that no matter who may have brought you some form of pain doesn't mean that everyone from the same sex, race, or culture will do the same. *Learn* to *Learn* from each experience—good or bad. Grab on to what strengthened you from that experience and release the threads that had no importance in the bonding that occurred. Just like every wave in the ocean is different and every hair follicle on your head is not the same, the relationships you will encounter throughout your life are also not the same. Learn and embrace each and every one of them, for through the good, the bad, and the ugly, you will be fortified and mature to withstand the unthinkable.

Wright

There was a time your health took a blow. Would you tell us about that? How did you cope with all the hard times and pull yourself up to continue pursuing your dreams?

Valdes

I had been very healthy all of my life until I had my first child. I had my son at the age of thirty. Several reports from pap smears showed precancerous cells in my uterus. In a period of two and a half years after my son's birth, I underwent two major surgeries and a miscarriage. My body took an unexpected blow to say the least! Here, I was, a fitness instructor, spinning instructor, and true advocate runner, and all of a sudden I am diagnosed as a potential cancer patient!

What I was being told, and what I chose to believe were two different things. I chose to think survival. With faith and God's healing grace, no more signs of precancerous cells were found until nine years later. Two years after the birth of my daughter, and after enduring one of the most traumatizing bullying experiences I faced at the police academy I attended in South Florida, I was diagnosed once again with precancerous cells. This time, they weren't in the mild or moderate category—they were in the "severe" stages and a hysterectomy was highly advised by my doctor.

During those six months at the police academy, I was harassed extensively by another female cadet who was in the same class. This experience affected me so much that four years later I still have nightmares and flashbacks. The experience I underwent is in its writing stages now and I hope to convert it into a major motion picture someday.

The enormous amount of stress inevitably took a huge toll on my body, during the training at the academy, which lasted six full months. As I look back now, I'm amazed how our bodies react to any form of trauma.

As soon as I graduated and was assigned to a department, a huge surprise came to me during one of my yearly routine check-ups. After nine years of good health, my pap smear returned showing some serious issues once again. This time it was much more serious than years before. The problem needed to be addressed right away. A hysterectomy was advised as soon as possible. I was totally shocked.

Something inside of me; however, told me to hold off and simply resign. This was dreadful to bear because I had endured so much during my training at the academy to make it to this point. I had pulled an Achilles tendon during one of my runs, and I had failed two fitness profiles due to the injury. However, through it all, I ended up receiving "The Rookie Award" at graduation! I had endured so much, both mentally and physically, and now, to have to make a decision that would negate all the hard work was devastating.

Because of my loyalty to the field, however, I chose to resign. I realized I didn't have a clear mind to work in a profession where my life was not the only one that would be at stake. Although the chief of my department encouraged me to stay and gave me all the time necessary I needed to recuperate, something inside told me I needed to leave the field altogether. Not only did I leave the field of Law Enforcement, but I also chose to leave the city we were living in and move to a completely new environment.

We moved to Atlanta, Georgia, and shortly after being in our new surroundings, I decided to get another pap test and see what was going on. Much to my surprise, and to the surprise of all the doctors involved, I was completely cancer free! Nothing abnormal showed—no signs of cancerous cells! Absolutely nothing was evident! Removing myself from the ties that were associated with an enormous amount of stress and trauma had actually allowed me to heal completely! I had listened to the voice inside that was guiding me to make a change. A change—a mental and physical change—was all that I needed.

It was God's amazing love and faithfulness that encouraged me to make a decision that changed the course of my life—forever. Will life's tribulations force you to make decisions? You bet they will! But it's through those trials that our inner structure is fortified.

Wright

The title of this book is *Success Simplified*. How simple do you think success is?

Valdes

Success is as simple as knowing that God gave each of us a talent. What we choose to do with that gift determines whether or not we feel successful. Basically it boils down to that. It's your definition of how you want to see your life defined. You don't have to be in *The Guinness Book of World Records* as the *best* jelly bean juggler to feel successful. You don't have to be in the front cover of *Fortune* magazine either. You don't even have to hold a title in anything for that matter. Titles are usually given to you by others. The definition of that title is solely given by you.

Being the hopeless romantic that I am, I view success very much like defining love because it could be interpreted in so many ways by so many different personality types. I loved reading Gary Chapman's book, *The Five Love Languages,* because he clearly identified five different ways whereby people feel loved. Success, in my opinion, is very much the same way. It's really quite simple to define because its definition strictly lies in the place whereby you wish to give it its allegiance.

Wright

From your story, it seems that you had a double whammy in obtaining success. You first had to survive what the average person simply takes for granted in order reach the next level of learning. What was the most difficult time in your life?

Valdes

My childhood was undoubtedly the most challenging time of my life. It's where our foundation for everything begins. It's where the mold, the concrete, the actual structure is first built. If these components are missing, then, of course, it's quite challenging to get a solid infrastructure. Notice I said "challenging" and not "difficult." If we choose to refrain from thinking something is difficult, we'll somehow see it as possible.

For years, I labeled my life as one that was difficult to deal with. It was not easy dealing with a mentally ill mother; however, I chose to begin labeling everything I saw as difficult in my life as challenging. I gave "difficult" a new name—challenging!

Here's a funny story. My six-year-old daughter came to me the other day complaining about how first grade was so difficult! I looked at her and told her that "difficult" was really a bad word. First grade wasn't difficult, it was "challenging"! The next day this avid, little first-grader went up to her teacher and declared that she no longer saw first grade difficult, but, rather, challenging and she was going to get through this! Wow! That's what it's all about! It's taking one aspect of your life that you feel has a hold on you in a destructive way and turning it around by simply giving it another meaning.

Sure, my greatest challenge was my childhood! But, hey, seasons change, barometric pressure changes, and even we as humans change constantly. Nothing in life is stagnant. My childhood was a part of my life, but it never encompassed *all* of my life. Today, I'm in my own episode, living the moments to the fullest!

Wright

I know this book is about the subject of success. But we all know that success is not usually achieved without failure. What was your "failure rate" and how do you define it?

Valdes

Oh my goodness, I've failed so many times! I've failed more times than I've succeeded. But like a boxer, you get punched and you get back up in order to conquer and win. Failure is simply quitting. I had every opportunity to quit while I was in the police academy. I was miserable. The harassment I received daily in that class from one particular female might have been enough to get me to quit. I chose to fight through it—mentally. Nothing was going to get me to quit unless I wanted to quit. Fear was not going to conquer me.

I am a firm believer that you finish what you start. You don't go through only one year of college and say, "Well, I got enough of what I needed to get," and then decide not to graduate. You always seem to regret those things you never finish. In my book, life is all about leaving this world with the fewest amounts of regrets. Success is in knowing that you did all you wanted to do. You touched as many lives as you possibly could. And you gave as much love as you wanted to give. You made a difference, somehow, in some way.

The bumps we endure we actually grow from. Sure I failed! Who doesn't? If I were to analyze every failure in my life, I could go back to my very first breath I took and think I failed throughout my entire life because of my mom's reaction toward me. If I had chosen to see the reflection of "failure" coming from her eyes when she looked at me, then my life would have taken a completely different turn. I chose instead to see "an instrument for success" when she looked at me. Her belief was not my belief. Failure lies in the false belief that one is incapable of being capable. *Failure is the antonym for success.*

Wright

Regarding the people who negatively influenced your life, have you made your peace with them?

Valdes

With my mom there is now a level of understanding between us. There are no more put-downs, no more negative comments, and no verbal abuse is tolerated. I stopped talking to her for about a year while I was writing my book. Just recently we've reconnected. She understands now that there is no need for condescending words or any other form of disrespect. God has truly united us now more than ever.

As far as other people in my life, I've made peace with them as well, if I have felt that they would bring more joy to my life than sorrow. I realize now more than ever the importance in selecting the right individuals to be a part of my life who will be deserving of what I am willing to give. *Reciprocation is golden if it's given and received with the utmost respect.*

Wright

Well, what a great conversation. I really appreciate all the time you've taken with me today to answer these questions. I know how hard it must be for you to talk about the difficult times in your life, but I think you have given some real insight to our readers. I know you have given me a lot to think about. We all make our way through life and relationships.

VALDES

Thank you so much, David. Thank you for having me. I always believe that we go through things in life in order to lift others. If we were once down and were lifted or lifted ourselves up, then it's time to do the same for someone who's hurting. In the act of giving, healing is received.

WRIGHT

Today we've been talking with Lourdes Valdes. She has been a strong advocate in the fitness arena all her life. She is a long-time runner, a spinning instructor, kickboxing instructor, and much more. Aside from her personal ventures, she is a motivational speaker, a passionate voice for teens, and is in the process of finishing her first book. I know she'll finish it and I wish her well.

Lourdes, thank you so much for being with us today on *Success Simplified.*

VALDES

Thank you. And God bless you.

About the Author

Born in New York, a daughter of Cuban immigrants, Lourdes was raised in New Orleans, Louisiana, during her early teens and Barcelona Spain. Later her family resided in Miami, Florida, where she attended high school and achieved a bachelor's degree in Communications with a minor in Political Science from the University of Miami. Lourdes has now been a resident of Georgia for almost two years.

Most of her life was spent as an on-air radio personality for five major radio stations in South Florida. She had her own radio talk show, *Woman Talk,* that focused on close-knit women related issues. While working in radio, television also opened doors for her and she became an entertainment reporter for Telemundo. Later, she became a stunt actress for many of the Univision and Telemundo soap operas. Her passion for writing and adventure also brought her an opportunity to write for the *Car Connection En Espanol* by test-driving cars and writing about the experience from a female perspective. Her adventure for life then intensified, giving her the curiosity and determination to enter the world of law enforcement. She became a law enforcement officer for Hallandale Beach Police Department. Shortly after working in the field, however, she had to resign because of health-related issues. In the midst of career changes, she's also owned several home-based businesses.

She has been a strong advocate in the fitness arena all her life—a long time runner, a spinning instructor, pilates instructor, and kickboxing instructor. She's taken flying lessons and owns a motorcycle license. She has bungy-jumped and skydived and is looking forward to getting certified in her next adventure quest, scuba diving. Aside from her personal adventures, she is a motivational speaker, a passionate voice for teens, and is in the process of finishing her first book.

Who Lourdes says she is: "I am the unthinkable outcome in a conscious state. I am a fireball of excitement waiting to burst. I am a rhetorical being, never conforming to repetition. I am a believer that truth lies inside those who believe in themselves—a living proof that inner passion prevails through perseverance!"

Lourdes Valdes
www.Jubilouslife@gmail.com

CHAPTER TWENTY FOUR

BOUNCING BACK FROM LIFE'S SETBACKS

BY SUSAN STERN, CPCC

DAVID WRIGHT (WRIGHT)

Susan Stern, CPCC is a Personal Success Coach who works with individuals and organizations in times of change and transition. She travels nationally speaking and leads workshops and retreats on Work/Life Balance, Transition, Relationships, and Resiliency. Whether it's developing business ideas or life transformation, Susan challenges her clients to shift perspectives, break old patterns, gain clarity, and open up to new possibilities. From this new place, she helps clients redesign professional and personal visions while being true to their core values.

Susan has a BA from Goucher College and is a Professional Certified Life Coach, entrepreneur, and an active member of ICF (International Coaches Federation). She is a devoted wife, mom, and stepmom. Susan's strong belief in "giving back" and living her values helped her spearhead the U.S. division of African Promise, Kids4Kenya. Kids4Kenya is a kids' charity that raises money to build schools in rural Kenya while empowering children in the United States to make a difference!

I'd like to welcome you, Susan, to our program.

SUSAN STERN (STERN)

Thank you, it's great to be here.

WRIGHT

Susan, why do you believe resiliency is the main ingredient to happiness?

STERN

I believe this because of my own life experiences and from what I have seen with clients throughout the years. Life is always changing. It's changing in good ways and changing in challenging ways. It's easy to be happy and feel good when life is changing in good ways, so if we can master how to deal with the unexpected, tough times, disappointments, and failures, we could be happy and feel successful all the time.

We rationally know this concept that "life is always changing," but do we really understand the enormity of this phrase? It might be impossible to completely grasp what this means in full. Life is constantly changing. The Earth is constantly rotating, the weather is different every day, and flowers are either in the process of blooming or dying. But what about all the dynamics that are going on well beneath what we can see or know about our planet that are in a constant state of change at every moment?

Take for example, the earthquake in Haiti in January of 2010 at 4:43 PM. Children were in the middle of playing, people were working, it was an ordinary sunny day. But underneath the Earth's crust, things were changing in massive ways that we could not have predicted. This is a great example of the enormity of the phrase "life is always changing."

Here's an example in my professional life. When I started my new career in coaching back in 2005, I had to beg for clients because people in my hometown had never heard of anything but an athletic or fitness coach. As I worked hard educating my market on life coaching, I also spent many hours networking, giving away free coaching, and marketing my business. The first three years were slow and I questioned whether or not I was going to be able to make it in my own coaching business. Then, into the fourth year, the momentum really started picking up and I had steady growth. By the fifth year, during the worst economic downturn in modern history, I had clients on a wait list after tripling my prices. I'm constantly trying to nail down exactly what "changed" or shifted in my business, but there were so many dynamics that I will never really know. That is another great example that "life is constantly changing" and how resiliency is key to success and happiness.

What I do know about change is that it is critical for personal and professional growth. When I find myself getting anxious about change, I let go of the desire to "what if" every scenario. I immediately to go to the most extreme, negative possibility and find a way to be okay, even if that happens. I know that God and the universe have an amazing life for me, and more is going on below the surface than I will ever know. I choose to let go and let life happen. As I have watched doors close, I have seen many new doors open.

WRIGHT

That's a great statement of life for us there.

How do you define resiliency?

STERN

My definition is very simple—it's the ability to bounce back. Resilience is actually a scientific term that has been adopted by psychology over the years. Resiliency has to do with energy. An object's resiliency is the ability of the object to reshape itself. As human beings, made up of energy, how quickly can we reshape or rebalance after a setback? That is resiliency!

WRIGHT

So I think it's safe to say that you're an advocate of getting back on that proverbial horse?

STERN

Yes.

WRIGHT

What are the keys to building resiliency?

STERN

I like to keep things simple, so I've boiled it down to three keys for building resiliency—adapt, improvise, and overcome.

This phrase was used in a Clint Eastwood movie called *Heartbreak Ridge* and it's also the unofficial mantra of the Marine Corps. It's easy to remember and easy to use. I use adapt, improvise, and overcome with my children and clients all the time.

WRIGHT

Will you expand on each one of those points?

Stern

Sure. To adapt to setbacks, you need to first understand that there are many emotions around them.

Adapting = Emotions and Perspectives. First, acknowledge your emotions. What emotions are you feeling—anger, sadness, disappointment, resentment, rejection, or loss? With any setback, there is a sense of loss. Whether you lost your biggest client, didn't get the promotion you wanted, your spouse wants out of the marriage, a death, or you are diagnosed with an illness, you've experienced a loss of what you had and you need to grieve. There are five classic stages of grief that you must complete—denial, anger, bargaining, depression, and acceptance.

Denial is "this can't be happening to me"—there is no acceptance or acknowledging the loss. Anger is "why me?" You want to fight back and blame others. Bargaining is trying to make deals for the person, client, or health to come back. Depression is overwhelming feelings of frustration, hopelessness, and self pity. It makes one feel numb or out of control. Acceptance is not just resignation. There is a difference between quietly dealing with the setback or truly accepting the loss. This is a time of personal growth and finding the positive in the setback.

You must complete the process of grieving or you will get stuck in one stage and will not completely heal. If you do not heal, you will not move on and you will not have personal growth. A person must go through *all* five stages and the process is different for each person. Some people go two steps forward and then three steps back. The process cannot be forced and it is unique to each person. But to adapt, you have to find a way to acceptance.

The other piece of adapting that is very important is a willingness to find a new normal—a rebalancing. You need to let go of what you thought was going to happen or what it was going to look like. When life changes, we have to be willing to change, too. We must be willing to shift our goals and shift our perspectives to find a new paradigm.

The third piece to adapting is persevering. That is digging in and finding your inner strength, which is a lot deeper than people think. Believe in yourself and believe that everything happens for a reason. Don't let a setback identify you. Have the determination to live the life you want regardless of the clouds on the horizon. If you cannot find your way to this mindset, get some help from a professional.

Wright

So I guess it's safe to say that the improvising section of this, as you expand on it, will be part of an adaptive stance itself?

Stern

Yes, they feed into each other. As you start to adapt, you automatically start improvising. Improvising is focusing on looking forward and discovering new paths. You start asking visionary questions like: What do I want now? What am I willing to do to get that? Where do I need to refocus? In the improvising phase, you start regaining control again.

Improvise = Learning and Choices. This key to resiliency is about personal growth and knowledge. This is where you become thirsty for knowledge, you are the most creative, and it becomes a pivotal time in our lives. The first part of improvising is to focus on what you have learned about yourself and life, thanks to the setback.

You start to take ownership of your strengths and weaknesses; you become aware of your pitfalls, challenges, and fears. The learning part is about becoming more mindful of yourself and the world around you. Too many people start distracting themselves and just jump back into the game without learning anything from setbacks. In my opinion, that is an adolescent way of thinking. I remember reaching an age in my young adult life, where I thought I had it all figured out. As I continue to get older and hopefully wiser, the one thing I know for sure is that I do *not* know. Staying curious is important in the learning process.

To build your learning muscles, I recommend working on mindfulness. Look at any sage, wise, or spiritual person. Wise people have all developed mindfulness. Mindfulness is considered the "gift" of becoming more awake. We stop regretting the past or fearing the future. We learn to be an observer without judgments. This gives you a deepened inner strength and peace. From this place of inner strength and peace, you make the best choices. You can choose integrity over ego.

Overcoming = Action. This key should only come into play after you have gone through the first two keys. How do you know the best course of action if you haven't learned anything from the setback? How will you make better decisions?

The overcoming phase is the culmination of everything you have experienced and learned from the setback. This is the time for goal-setting and strategizing and setting out a new road map for success in your personal and/or professional life. This is where you become proactive and really grow in your journey. This is where you start implementing the change you have chosen, not the change that has been handed to you. This is where the pendulum of change shifts from fear to excitement. You made the choice, you are being proactive, you are moving forward—this is where all of us feel empowered!

Wright

Why celebrate life's setbacks?

Stern

It seems like a dichotomy to hear "celebrate life's setbacks." But truly, our setbacks are some of the greatest gifts we will receive in life. When you can emotionally and mentally see your setbacks as gifts, it shifts your energy and perspectives. All things happen for a reason and usually you have no idea what the reason is until years after the setback.

Setbacks are such a big part of our lives, just like our successes. It's easy to look at our successes and say "This is fantastic—it is exactly what I wanted! What a gift!" With success, we can see an immediate, perceived benefit. But how many times have we received something we thought we wanted and it turned out to be a lot of heartache and drama? I had a client who was ecstatic after getting the promotion he desired and two years later, he regretted the new position when his wife left him because his career always came before their relationship and family.

Setbacks create the opposite emotions than successes; they do not give us the "temporary feel-good" that successes do. Setbacks are very challenging for people who like to feel in control. People who want to control life are attached to certain outcomes. When the outcomes don't meet their expectations, they have a difficult time handling it. Setbacks tap into fears of "not being good enough" and they hit us right in our self-worth. There is no immediate perceived benefit with a setback, just work and disappointment.

Setbacks are your red flares; they are the moments when life is telling you, "Whoa, things need to change!" The first question I ask myself after a setback is, "What needs to change?" Setbacks are natural, free gifts to all of us; the universe is giving us an opportunity to know that we need to do things a bit differently.

Celebrating setbacks help us start making better decisions and better choices to move us in new directions. Setbacks are one of the only ways we will take a step back from our daily habits and beliefs to question ourselves or learn something new.

WRIGHT

So learning from both the good and the bad are essential?

STERN

Absolutely. How else do you learn or grow as a human being? Because of our human intellect, the only way we make changes or grow is through experience.

WRIGHT

Why is it so hard to celebrate setbacks?

STERN

Well, it's because they're unexpected—nobody expects or wants to fail. Human beings do not set themselves up for failure and disappointments. Setbacks are surprises. Many times, the setbacks are out of our control, which throws us off balance. When we don't plan for a setback and we don't want the setback, we get frustrated and angry. It's not fair, why me?

It's also hard to celebrate setbacks because we become aware of our fears. Usually our greatest fears come to the surface and cause tremendous waves of emotions to swirl around internally. We are faced with deep emotions, like sadness, shame, anger. These strong emotions create feelings inside of us that are uncomfortable like anxiety, depression, insecurity, and feeling paralyzed.

Setbacks are also hard because they usually have us question ourselves—we start questioning our choices, we question who we are, and what we're capable of doing. So setbacks feed into our ego and insecurities. They confuse us about which direction to go and who we really are. Be careful not to let your ego win—don't let your successes or failures define you.

WRIGHT

So you would agree that we individually need to somewhat alter our perspectives to embrace these setbacks?

STERN

Yes!

WRIGHT

What needs to happen before you can fully celebrate setbacks? Are there several steps necessary and are there key points?

STERN

Yes, I have four steps that I use with clients to be able to celebrate setbacks. The first one is awareness that there are many emotions around setbacks, and these emotions need to be acknowledged and worked through. Moving through five classic stages of grief is critical so that you can get to acceptance.

That tags into that second step—before you can celebrate the setback, you have to accept the setback. Acceptance has to happen before you can move forward and make changes. If you do not move through the grief stages, you will get stuck in a toxic way of thinking—denial and hope. The longer you stay in denial and hope, the worse the situation or circumstance becomes.

The third step is letting go. For some people, this is very hard. Typically, the more of a motivated type-A personality you are, the harder it is to let go of expectations and outcomes. You think, "What could I have done differently and would that have mattered?" If you could have done something differently and it would have mattered, then you have learned something. If you couldn't have done anything differently to change the outcome, then let it go. This can be challenging if you have a manager or spouse who does not want you to "let go"!

It is vain and omnipotent thinking, that we have control of our lives. We only have control of our actions, behaviors, speech, and choices we make—and everything else is *not* in our control. That leaves most situations in our lives beyond our control.

The fourth step is finding a way to indifference. You will know that you have fully "let go" and moved through the third key when you feel indifferent. My barometer of this feeling is being able to shrug my shoulders and say "whatever." Being able to let go is the difference between someone who is resilient and someone who is not.

WRIGHT

Well, this should be probably one of the most important questions we ask you today: what are some of the ways people can celebrate life's setbacks?

Stern

One of my favorite ways to celebrate setbacks is through humor. I try and find some humor in every setback. It's always there—I'm usually laughing at myself! I don't put myself down in a self-deprecating way, but I don't take the things that happen in life too seriously.

My dear friend, who happened to be a client at the time, found her breast cancer recurring after seven dormant years. She was forty-three, married with a young daughter and she was shocked by this setback. That year, every three months when she would get an MRI, they would find cancer in a new place—her ribs, her brain, her pelvis, her kidney. It was a very challenging year for her. It was so important for her to use humor to lighten up her situation and make others feel comfortable. She didn't want to be treated like a victim.

I will never forget after one meeting, she had returned from a girls' weekend at a fancy hotel in Washington, D.C., to celebrate one of the ladies' fortieth birthday. They had gone to a fancy dinner, come back to the suite, and the ladies were hanging out catching up like old school friends. A few ladies had fallen asleep and suddenly she and a few other ladies thought it would be a good idea to get one more glass of wine down at the fancy, hotel lounge in the lobby. Well, she put on her bright pink wig with her pink tiara and fuzzy bedroom slippers to go to the lounge (it was about 11:30 PM)! She has an innate way of using humor to celebrate her life, regardless of the situation.

Another way to celebrate setbacks is by using gratitude. This will force you to refocus on the things you are grateful for in your life right now. Your focus will start to shift on positives even when you are feeling low, frustrated, and negative. Gratitude is the base of most religions, so this one is easier for people of different faiths.

Having gone through my divorce with young children, moving, and trying to build a business at the same time, I began a quest for inner peace and strength. I believe in God and draw strength from my faith. I also discovered one way to have inner strength and peace was to practice non-attachment—to act like a Buddhist and practice the Zen teaching of nonattachment. I have found the Zen teaching of non-attachment is extremely helpful to live a happy life. My client with cancer would go everywhere without a wig, she did not want to be attached to her hair and how she looked.

You can also use curiosity. Get curious about the experience that you are going through. My client with cancer was wonderful about encouraging my three boys to come touch her bald head and ask questions. She would make it a learning experience for herself and those around her.

Another tip is using indifference. As I said earlier, the sooner I can achieve indifference, the sooner I can celebrate my setbacks. Practice reporting about life and not judging life. Drop your ego and try being neutral about the situations that happen in your life. Instead of being high when you experience success, just be grateful that life is good. Instead of being low during setbacks, find reasons to be grateful and happy. Remember, life is always changing and the lows and highs will come and go. Nothing is static. This too shall pass!

WRIGHT

What happens if your clients don't celebrate setbacks? As business owners, we all have missed deadlines or have experienced employee issues that can have a resounding effect on missing opportunities to celebrate with our clients.

STERN

This is difficult. Even though we know the normal cycle of life includes successes and the disappointments, it's still hard to celebrate the disappointments. But if we don't celebrate them, we will get trapped in that same kind of decision-making that brings the same outcomes—Einstein's definition of insanity! Doing the same thing over and over again expecting different outcomes will have you stuck and paralyzed. You will live small because you will fear failure. Your fears will have you making reactive decisions instead of proactive decisions. If you're not willing to celebrate setbacks, your progress is painful.

There is a great quote by Alexander Graham Bell: "When one door closes another opens but we often look so long and so regretfully upon the closed door that we did not see the one that is open for us." Learn from the past, don't live in it!

WRIGHT

That's a great quote. I'm reminded of Ron White who used to say, "If life gives you lemons, you should make lemonade. And try to find somebody whose life has given them vodka, and have a party." I believe that is similar to what you're saying.

We found that in those celebrations when your clients are not so adverse to the hardships you might be dealing with, the honest approach is the best because it allows so much clarification during the setbacks. This enables everyone to have a realistic view of the expectation at that point.

Stern

Recently, one of my clients knew he needed to let four to six people go within four months because of the recession. He was struggling with doing the "right thing" for his business or doing the perceived "right thing" for the four or six people. Two months later, he knew he had made the right choice. He said it was the best thing that had ever happened. That action completely changed the attitude in the office. With those people gone, his company was thriving again and the office morale was much better.

This is a perfect example of a perceived setback. He was really struggling with letting some employees go, but as he looks back today, it was a big positive for his business.

Wright

What did you mean by adapt?

Stern

Adapting means letting go of what you thought something was supposed to look like or what you thought was supposed to happen. It is figuring out how to shift your perspectives so you can be optimistic and see some positives in the setback. How can you take ownership of your emotions and fears to get to a new paradigm? Adapting is persevering, courage, and inner strength. It is the time to step up to the plate and show the world what you are made of.

Wright

Again, going back to your keys of building resiliency, what did you mean by improvise?

Stern

Improvise is a time of creativity. When you look at authors, song writers, or artists, so many incredible pieces have been written, drawn, or created when someone is experiencing loss. So it's a huge opportunity to be creative. It is also about visioning. You need to answer these visioning questions: What do I want? What do I want this to look like? How am I going to get that? Refocus on new goals, new perspectives, and moving forward.

I think learning is key to improvising, "What are you learning?" Not only what are you learning about yourself, but what are you learning about your business, what are you learning about relationships and/or the world around you? This is also a good time to educate yourself in other areas of your business or other areas of your life. It's a very proactive place. You chose what to learn. You also need to be willing to fail.

When you think back in your life, childhood and adolescent years are filled with learning and creativity through successes and disappointments. It is interesting that our failures usually turn into our success and vice versa. For example, we practice and practice to learn to ride a bike. We fail many times before it clicks and then it becomes a huge success for us. So why is it so hard to accept this as an adult?

Wright

Well, without giving away trade secrets do you have specific keys to unleashing creativity for those who are not great improvisers?

Stern

Yes. People who struggle with improvising struggle with "thinking out of the box," struggle and being open to new possibilities. Some people are stubborn and resistant to learning something new. Unfortunately, this results in being stuck—stuck in old habits and stuck in old thinking.

In the improvising phase (learning phase), I use the four keys of learning. It works every time, but you must be honest with yourself and follow the process through all four steps.

First, reflect on the setback. Second, acquire new awareness of yourself and the situation. Third, throw out multiple choices/options for moving forward. And fourth, take action. Until you go through the process of the first three steps, you are not ready to make the best decision on which action you are going to take to move forward.

This learning phase is the most important in our personal and professional lives, in my opinion. For businesses, this is the time to be creative, look forward, and come up with new visions. It is a time to go slow and take a step back. It's a time to ask questions and reflect on past experience. Become aware of what is and isn't working and throw all the possibilities on the table. Hmm, what is it we want now? What's the environment that we want? Do we want to head in a different direction? Unfortunately, many businesses today are so caught up in the hamster wheel of making money that they do not take the time to follow this process. When you do not follow this process, you are constantly making choices and taking action based on being reactive instead of proactive.

We should also follow this process in our personal lives. We are so busy in today's world; life has sped up so quickly thanks to the explosion of technology. It allows us to do so many things throughout the day. We tend to get on that hamster wheel and run on it all day, every day. While we are busy doing, doing, doing, we should be simultaneously asking ourselves, "Who am I being while I'm doing all these things?"

The learning process will help you take that step back to reflect on your "doing." We are human beings, not human do-ers. Ask yourself if the doing serves a fulfilling purpose or if the "doing" is really solving your customers problems. Become aware of the doing and see the true benefits of the energy being expended. This will guide you in making conscious choices.

Wright

What are some success stories you have seen from people who have built their resiliency by celebrating their setbacks?

Stern

The stories of resiliency are the best part and the most fulfilling piece for me. I get juiced up working with clients who take adversity and "make lemonade"—ordinary people who start living extraordinarily. Who doesn't cheer for the underdog? I love watching clients become crystal clear on what success and happiness is for them, and then making the changes necessary to get what they really want out of life! It's amazing to be able to help people step out of their comfort zone and reach for something bigger than they thought was possible.

There are famous names of people whose lives mirror success stories of resiliency. Some examples are: Lance Armstrong, Jackie Robinson, Oprah Winfrey, Bill Gates, and Helen Keller. But I have the pleasure of working with clients who overcome setbacks and adversity every day.

One client who came to me had been fired after twenty years and his wife left him. He was a single father and was struggling to get back on his feet. It was inspiring to watch him take a step back, learn from the setbacks, persevere, and creatively set new goals. He changed careers, got remarried to a wonderful woman, and was much happier than before. That's a success story of resiliency.

Another success story is a client who owns a multimillion-dollar company and had his CFO steal money from his business. He was turning fifty and the recession hit. He was looking at his life and thinking, "This is not where I thought I would be!" He questioned everything in his life, mostly the passion and happiness factor. It was incredible to watch this person take the time to reflect and make conscious choices for changes that created a life that he fell back in love with. In fact, it is hard to get the smile off his face now.

Instead of trying to blame other people for his unhappiness or maybe not being who he thought he should be, he turned his focus on himself. He decided to go back and pursue his passion of car racing. Within a year, he went on to win two regional races and acquire his national driving status. He had multiple offers to buy into his business and he is looking into a possible car racing team.

He took the time to reflect and be aware that he was lacking passion and zest for life. He did the work and realized he needed to find more passion and competitive juices, so all of pieces in the puzzle are now thriving. He had the motivation and courage to look at himself honestly without judgment. He became aware of habits and patterns he was willing to break that were no longer serving him well. In fact, he realized those habits were causing him angst.

Wright

Well, today we've been talking with Susan Stern, who is a personal success coach. Susan has worked with hundreds of individual clients and organizations throughout the years.

Thank you, Susan, for being a participant in *Success Simplified.* It's been wonderful talking with you.

Stern

Thank you, this has been wonderful. I appreciate your time and the opportunity to share my insights.

Wright

Thank you.

About the Author

Susan Stern, CPCC is a Personal Success Coach who works with individuals and organizations in times of change and transition. She travels nationally speaking, leading workshops and retreats on Work/Life Balance, Transition, Relationships and Resiliency. Whether it's developing business ideas or life transformation, Susan challenges her clients to shift perspectives, bust old patterns, gain clarity and open up to new possibilities. From this new place, she helps clients redesign professional and personal visions while being true to their core values.

She has her BA from Goucher College; a Professional Certified Life Coach, entrepreneur and an active member of ICF (International Coaches Federation). She is a devoted wife, mom and stepmom. Susan's strong belief in "giving back" and living her values, helped her spearhead the US division of African Promise, Kids4Kenya. Kids4Kenya is kids' charity that raises money to build schools in rural Kenya while empowering children in the US to make a difference!

Susan Stern, CPCC

Live Now

Towson, MD

(410) 960-4446

susancwg@comcast.net

www.livenow.bz